PREACHING, WORD AND SACRAMENT

PREACHING, WORD AND SACRAMENT
Scottish Church Interiors
1560–1860

Nigel Yates

t&t clark

Published by T&T Clark
A Continuum imprint
The Tower Building   80 Maiden Lane
11 York Road   Suite 704, New York
London SE1 7NX   NY 10038

www.continuumbooks.com

All rights reserved. No part of this publication may be reproduced or transmitted in any form or by any means, electronic or mechanical, including photocopying, recording or any information storage or retrieval system, without permission in writing from the publishers.

Copyright © Nigel Yates, 2009

Nigel Yates has asserted his right under the Copyright, Designs and Patents Act, 1988, to be identified as the Author of this work.

British Library Cataloguing-in-Publication Data
A catalogue record for this book is available from the British Library.

ISBN-10: HB: 0–567–03141–1
ISBN-13: HB: 978–0–567–03141–9

Library of Congress Cataloging-in-Publication Data
A catalog record for this book is available from the Library of Congress

Typeset by RefineCatch Limited, Bungay, Suffolk
Printed and bound in the UK by the MPG Books Group

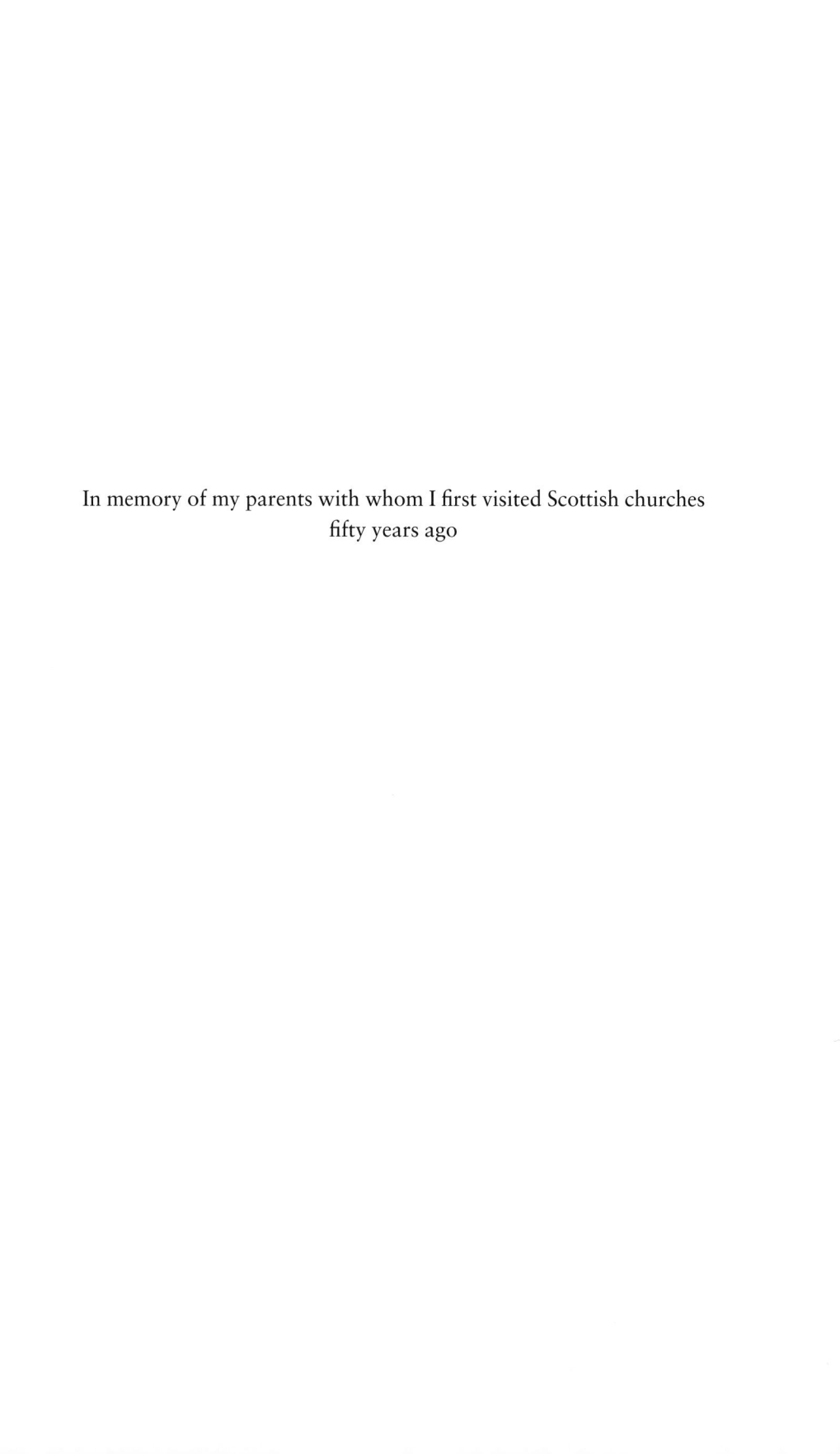

In memory of my parents with whom I first visited Scottish churches fifty years ago

CONTENTS

List of Abbreviations ix
List of Tables x
List of Figures xi
List of Plates xii

Introduction 1

1 The Scottish Reformation and its Aftermath 5
2 Scottish Church Interiors 1560–1690 28
3 Presbyterian Church Interiors 1690–1860:
  Worship and the Care of Buildings 44
4 Presbyterian Church Interiors 1690–1860:
  Furnishings and Liturgical Arrangement 65
5 Roman Catholic and Scottish Episcopalian Church
  Interiors 1690–1860 92
6 Liturgical and Architectural Developments since 1860 111

Appendices

  A. Extracts from the First Statistical Account of Scotland
     (1791–1799) relating to the condition of churches 139

  B. Churches with substantially complete pre-1843
     furnishings listed by George Hay: An update 155

  C. Examples of substantially unaltered interiors of
     Scottish churches built before 1860 159

  D. Selected list of Scottish churches with traditional
     Presbyterian interiors of a date later than 1860 175

CONTENTS

E. Selected list of Scoto-Catholic Protestant church
    interiors in Scotland   179

Bibliography   184
Index   191

LIST OF ABBREVIATIONS

BFW	Nigel Yates, *Buildings, Faith and Worship*, 2nd edn, Oxford 2000
BS	*Buildings of Scotland* series, followed by relevant volume title
DGA	Dumfries and Galloway Archives
MLGA	Mitchell Library, Glasgow Archives
NAS	National Archives of Scotland
NSA	New Statistical Account of Scotland
OA	Orkney Archives
RSCHS	*Records of the Scottish Church History Society*
SA	Stirling Archives
SAS	*Statistical Account of Scotland, 1791–1799*, East Ardsley 1973–1983
SPC	George Hay, *The Architecture of Scottish Post-Reformation Churches*, Oxford 1957

LIST OF TABLES

1	Comparison of the Eucharistic rites of the *Book of Common Prayer* (1552) and the *Book of Common Order* (1564)	10
2	Provision for festivals in the calendar of the *Book of Common Order* 1564–1635	12
3	Comparison of attenders and communicants in selected highland and island parishes in 1837	50
4	Churches recorded as new built and in good or poor repair in the *First Statistical Account of Scotland*, 1791–1799	53
5	Comparison of condition of churches in selected Scottish counties in 1791–1799 and 1845	54
6	Descriptions of churches in Wales in the early nineteenth century	56
7	Relative popularity of different liturgical arrangements for Presbyterian Churches in Scotland	66
8	Provision of box pews or open benches in Scottish Presbyterian Churches before 1860	81
9	Scottish counties, cities and towns recording high levels of inhabitants born in Ireland in the census of 1841	96
10	Building of new Presbyterian Churches in Scotland, 1850–1899	122

LIST OF FIGURES

1 Seating plan of St Peter's, Thurso, before 1833 — 72
2 Seating plan of St Mary's, Lauder, refitted in 1820–1821 — 73
3 Seating plan of Ceres Parish Church, built in 1806 — 74
4 Seating plan of Lochbroom Parish Church, built in 1844–1845 — 75
5 Seating plan of St Stephen's, Edinburgh, built in 1828 — 78
6 Seating plan of Queen's Cross Church, Glasgow, built in 1896–1899 — 130

LIST OF PLATES

1	Magistrates' pew of 1606 at St Columba's, Burntisland	33
2	Engraving of the interior of the Choir of Glasgow Cathedral in 1822 (Glasgow University Library, Special Collections)	60
3	Engraving of the interior of Coldingham Priory Church as restored in 1855 (Glasgow University Library, Special Collections)	61
4	Seating plans of the ground floor and galleries at the Barony Church, Paisley, 1789 (Stirling Archives)	67
5	Watercolour drawing of a service at St Giles's, Elgin, c.1770 (Elgin Museum)	67
6	The interior of St Nicholas West Church, Aberdeen, rebuilt and refurnished in 1755	68
7	Seating plan of Hamilton Parish Church, 1732	77
8	Pulpit and precentor's desk at St Modan's Church, Ardchattan, built in 1838–1839 (Royal Commission on the Ancient and Historical Monuments of Scotland)	80
9	Sutherland Loft of 1739 at St Andrew's, Golspie	85
10	Long communion table and benches at St Modan's Church, Ardchattan, built in 1838–1839 (Royal Commission on the Ancient and Historical Monuments of Scotland)	86
11	The late-eighteenth-century interior of St Ninian's Roman Catholic Chapel, Tynet, as refurbished by Ian Lindsay in 1951	95
12	The furnishings of St Mary's Roman Catholic Chapel, Edinburgh, as designed by James Gillespie Graham in 1814	98
13	View of the interior of St John's Episcopal Church, Edinburgh, as built in 1816–1818 (Glasgow University Library, Special Collections)	103
14	The Episcopal Cathedral of the Isles at Millport, designed by William Butterfield in 1851	108
15	Photograph of the interior of St John's Episcopal Church, Edinburgh, after extension in 1881–1882	113

LIST OF PLATES

16 The interior of St Nicholas East Church, Aberdeen, refurnished in 1882 and 1937   117
17 Photograph of the interior of the Choir of Glasgow Cathedral in the 1890s (Glasgow University Library, Special Collections)   126
18 The sanctuary of St Cuthbert's, Edinburgh, showing the marble pulpit, font and communion table, 1892–1895   128
19 The Choir of Dunblane Cathedral as refurnished by Sir Robert Lorimer in 1914   129
20 The font in the form of an angel supporting a Breton fishing boat at St Conan's Church, Loch Awe, completed in 1930   131
21 The Medieval Church of St Moluag at Eoropie, Lewis, restored to ecclesiastical use in 1912   132
22 The reordered sanctuary at St Mary's, Haddington, 1977   135

Introduction

SCOTTISH CHURCH INTERIORS 1560–1860

The primary intention of this book is to update what has been, until now, the standard and authoritative work on Scottish post-Reformation churches, George Hay's *Architecture of Scottish Post-Reformation Churches, 1560–1843*, published by Oxford University Press in 1957. Hay's work has long been out of print and second-hand copies are notoriously difficult, and expensive, to get hold of. However, in many respects it requires modification, particularly in respect of contextualization and the important work done on Protestant churches in other parts of the British Isles and in mainland Europe in recent years. In revising Hay's work I made a conscious decision not to model my book on his. Hay was a practicing architect, whereas I am an ecclesiastical historian with particular interests in worship and the architectural setting of worship. There is, therefore, much less architectural detail in my book than there was in Hay's and much more on the historical and liturgical developments in the Scottish churches which impacted on the design and liturgical arrangement of church buildings. However, in two important respects I have followed Hay's model. In the first place, like Hay, I have considered the buildings of the Roman Catholic and Episcopal churches and not just those of the established Church of Scotland. In the second, I have included lists of significant buildings. They are much shorter than those of Hay and focus particularly on two groups of buildings: those listed in Hay as 'substantially unaltered' which have been either altered or ceased to be used for worship in the period since Hay compiled his lists; and those which still retain 'substantially unaltered' interiors, many of which were not recorded by Hay, or recorded in far less detail than they are here.

The major departure from Hay's text in this book is to extend the period of coverage. Hay stopped at the Disruption of 1843, which, although a dramatic watershed in Scottish religious history, is architecturally insignificant. The decision that then had to be made was when to terminate the detailed study of surviving buildings and, after much consideration, it was decided that 1860 was a sensible terminal date. This is shortly before major changes began in Scottish church architecture, when the Presbyterian churches began to be strongly influenced by both the English Free Churches and the ecclesiological movement in terms of church design and liturgical arrangement. However, although the lists of 'substantially unaltered' buildings terminate in 1860, I have included a substantial final chapter which endeavours to give a comprehensive overview of developments in worship and church building in Scotland from 1860 to the present time.

In writing this book, I have to make three very substantial acknowledgements. The first is to Thomas Kraft of T&T Clark, who commissioned it in the first place. The second is to my own University of Wales, Lampeter, which generously granted me study leave in the Easter term of 2007 in order to conduct the research for this book. The third is to the University of Glasgow which, equally generously, elected me to a Visiting Senior Research Fellowship for the same period, and provided a most congenial base from which to carry out my research in Scottish libraries and record offices and to visit those Scottish churches which I had not already visited over the previous 15 years. The descriptions of buildings in Appendices B and C are based largely on those visits and represent the condition and arrangement of those buildings at the time I visited them. It may well be that in some cases alterations may have been made subsequent to my visit which have not been recorded. Some of the earlier visits were financed by a grant from the Cromarty Trust and the Marc Fitch Fund, for which I am extremely grateful. I am also grateful to the many ministers, session clerks and other individuals who have made the necessary arrangements for me to visit buildings listed in the appendices. I am also grateful to the staffs of the following institutions for use of their collections: the university libraries at Glasgow and Lampeter, the National Library of Wales, the Mitchell Library in Glasgow, the National Archives of Scotland and local archives in Dumfries, Kirkwall and Stirling. Useful advice was also received from the Revd Nigel Robb, the Associate Secretary of the Church of Scotland's Committee on Church Art and Architecture, and Ian Riches, Secretary of the Buildings of Scotland Trust. In my early years of visiting Scottish churches, I was also much helped by John Hume, then of Historic Scotland and now Convenor of the Committee on Church Art and Architecture. I have also benefited greatly from discussions with my former colleagues at Glasgow – Professors Ian Hazlett, David Jasper and George Newlands – and with Professors Stewart J. Brown and Duncan Forrester at Edinburgh.

In determining which buildings needed to be visited for the purposes of inclusion in Appendix C, I have relied very heavily on the descriptions of churches published in the volumes of *The Buildings of Scotland* series, originally produced by Penguin Books and now being produced by Yale University Press with support from the Buildings of Scotland Trust. To

INTRODUCTION

date 9 of the projected 14 volumes in the series have been published covering all of the north, north-west and south-east, and much of the south-west of Scotland. The remaining gaps are now the whole of the north-east and much of western Scotland except for the city of Glasgow. Some use has also been made of other recent publications, such as John Hume's splendid *Scotland's Best Churches* and *Churches to Visit in Scotland*, published on behalf of Scotland's Churches Scheme, but the lack of the relevant *Buildings of Scotland* volume for certain parts of the country inevitably means that the list of churches included in Appendix C will not be quite as comprehensive as I should have liked.

Nevertheless it will be the most accurate and up-to-date list of 'substantially unaltered' pre-1860 church interiors available and, in this respect, will I hope be some use to church, heritage and planning bodies in identifying those buildings which need to be preserved as the relatively few remaining examples of a particular tradition of church furnishing and liturgical arrangement. The criteria that have been used in identifying an interior as 'substantially unaltered' are that it retains the majority of its core furnishings, and all the essential elements of its original liturgical arrangement (i.e., pulpit, seating and, where they existed, galleries or lofts) intact. Minor alterations, such as the removal of the precentor's desk or the insertion of a modern communion table, have not been considered sufficiently damaging to prevent inclusion. On the other hand churches, such as those at Canonbie (Dumfries and Galloway) or Dunnett (Highland), which retain pre-1860 box pews but have a post-1860 pulpit, have been excluded, as have churches, such as Duirinish (Highland) or Livingston (West Lothian), where pre-1860 pulpits and galleries or lofts have been retained, but the body of the church has been re-seated. An important example of the working of the criteria has been the decision taken in respect of the former East Church at Cromarty (Highland), now vested in the Scottish Historic Churches Trust. In many respects, this is one of the most significant post-Reformation churches in Scotland. The date of both its fabric and many of its furnishings, especially the lofts and their seating is much earlier than that of many of the churches listed in Appendix C. Most of the seating in the body of the church also pre-dates 1860, but the authenticity of the interior has been seriously compromised by the installation of a new and unsympathetic pulpit and communion table in 1901. By contrast, the interior of the church at Golspie (Highland) was not regarded as being compromised, despite some alterations, as the pulpit of 1738 remained intact and *in situ*, and the seating, though replaced, was an exact replica of the seating removed in 1953–1954, when the existing pews were found to be rotten. The descriptions of all the churches included in Appendix C were accurate at the date that I visited them, and in every case this has been since 1990. However, there will inevitably be some in which some, possibly quite major, changes have taken place in the intervening period, so total accuracy at the date of publication cannot be guaranteed.

I have been conscious that in writing this book I am doing so for both a Scottish and an international readership and this has meant the making of difficult choices in respect of some terminology. I have not attempted to replace specific Scottish terminology where to do so would have been perverse: thus terms such as charge, heritor, precentor, teinds (or tithe) and so on are used, where necessary with an explanation of their meaning. However, where the Scottish terminology replaces a well-known international terminology I have chosen the latter. Thus I have, except in cases of direct quotation from primary sources, used the term 'church' rather than the Scottish 'kirk' and saints have been referred to in their international rather than Scottish form, as, for example, Brigid rather than Bride and Kentigern rather than Mungo, except where the latter has international recognition, as in the case of St Mungo's Cathedral, Glasgow. I apologize if this practice irritates some Scottish readers but it will be less confusing for readers who are not Scottish.

The illustrations in the book have been taken largely from my own collections. I am, however, grateful to Stirling Archives for the seating plan of the Barony Church at Paisley [Plate 4] and the elevation of the proposed pulpit in Stirling East Church illustrated on the front cover, Elgin Museum for the watercolour drawing of a service at St Giles's, Elgin [Plate 5], and the Royal Commission on the Ancient and Historical Monuments of Scotland for the photographs of furnishings at St Modan's, Ardchattan [Plates 8 and 10]. Four other illustrations [Plates 2, 3, 13 and 17] have been reproduced, with permission, from volumes held by Glasgow University Library. The church seating plans reproduced as figures in the text have been kindly drawn by Abi Hyde. The typing of the text was undertaken by my son David, who also provided useful comments on it. I am also grateful to the Revds Drs Doug Gay and Paul Middleton for kindly reading and commenting on the core chapters of the book. Neither should be held responsible for the imperfections that remain. Finally, as always, I am grateful to my wife Paula for her continued support throughout this project and, especially for driving me to most of the churches described in this book

†Nigel Yates
University of Wales, Lampeter, June 2008.

1

THE SCOTTISH REFORMATION AND ITS AFTERMATH

1. The Scottish reformation

Unlike the Reformation in many countries of northern Europe, notably England, Ireland, the Scandinavian monarchies and some of the German states, the Reformation in Scotland was not one imposed by government on a, sometimes reluctant, populace. The Reformation in Scotland was essentially a religious *coup d'etat* in which a vigorous reform lobby, with a good deal of popular support, forced a reluctant, even hostile, monarchy to accept that Scotland could not, as a corporate nation, remain part of the western Catholic church. Although this *coup d'etat* did not take place until 1560, its origins were a good deal older than that. An earlier attempt to make Scotland Protestant, following the example of England, had been defeated in 1543 and five Protestants executed as an example to other would-be reformers. The eventual Protestant victory of 1559–1560 was, in Alec Ryrie's view, largely the result of apathy from the anti-Protestant side. It was essentially a victory of a Protestant parliament over a Catholic monarchy. Once a Protestant victory looked settled 'Reformist Catholics of undoubted sincerity converted – some enthusiastically, some reluctantly – to the Protestant cause.'[1] However, because the Scottish Reformation was a 'bottom up' rather than a 'top down' affair the success of its implementation across the country varied and has been the subject of much debate between Scottish historians in recent years.

At one end of the spectrum Ian Cowan has attempted to suggest that the Reformation was only successful in parts of Scotland, chiefly the Lowlands, before the end of the sixteenth century. It was most successful in those areas

---

[1] Alec Ryrie, *The Origins of the Scottish Reformation*, Manchester 2006, especially pp. 53–68, 196–9; quotation on p. 197.

where the bishops themselves – Robert Stewart of Caithness, Alexander Gordon of Galloway and Adam Bothwell of Orkney – were early supporters of the Reformation. In other areas, where Catholic bishops remained in office, the Reformation was long delayed. This was the case at Aberdeen until 1577, Argyll until 1580, Dunkeld until 1585 and Ross until 1592. Catholic bishops effectively prevented the setting up of reformed ministries in their dioceses until after their deaths and Cowan notes that no appointments of reformed ministers were made to Hebridean parishes before 1609, and that Islay was still predominately Roman Catholic in 1615.[2] His views have been reinforced by others.

> The Scottish reform movement, although ratified late by the standards of most other Protestant countries, was a gradual, evolutionary, at times deceptively low-key, process.[3]

No permanent kirk session was established at Aberdeen, a bastion of pre-Reformation Catholicism, until 1573 and even then 5 of the 13 elders had previously been opponents of the Reformation, and some of their wives were still Roman Catholics in 1574.

Cowan's views have, however, been strongly challenged by James Kirk, particularly in relation to the Highlands. Whereas Cowan considered the impact of the Reformation to have been minimal in this area before the late sixteenth century, Kirk suggests that this was not the case. Kirk notes reformed ministers at Dingwall, Dunkeld, Fortrose and Kiltearn, as well as Thurso in the diocese of Caithness, by 1561. He also suggests that the publication of a Gaelic version of Knox's *Book of Common Order* in 1567 assisted the spread of the Reformation in the Highland areas. By 1574 every parish in central Argyll, Cowal and Lorne had a resident minister or reader. In the same year, 215 parishes in the Highland dioceses of Caithness, Moray and Ross, and parts of the dioceses of Dunblane and Dunkeld were served by 65 ministers and 158 readers. The figures in Scotland as a whole, excluding the dioceses of Dunkeld and Dunblane, were 289 ministers and 715 readers for 988 parishes.[4] By the early seventeenth century there were 32 ministers to serve the 44 parishes in the diocese of Argyll.[5] To some extent the way that one interprets these figures depends on whether one follows

---

[2] I.B. Cowan, *The Scottish Reformation: Church and Society in Sixteenth Century Scotland*, London 1982, pp. 159–81.

[3] M.H.B. Sanderson, *Ayrshire and the Reformation: People and Change 1490–1600*, East Linton 1997, p. 141.

[4] M.F. Graham, *The Uses of Reform: 'Godly Discipline' and Popular Behaviour in Scotland and Beyond, 1560–1610*, Leiden 1996, pp. 114–15.

[5] James Kirk, *Patterns of Reform: Continuity and Change in the Reformation Kirk*, Edinburgh 1989, pp. 449, 457, 459, 470.

Kirk's view that a reader was equivalent to a minister, bearing in mind that the former could not preach, celebrate Holy Communion, baptize or solemnize marriages, but could conduct the first part of Sunday worship, read the daily services and catechize.[6] Certainly in the Lowlands the impact of the Reformation had been speedily felt. 97 out of 101 parishes in Lothian and Tweeddale acquired reformed ministries in the 1560s, as did 31 out of 42 parishes in Ayrshire, all but ten out of 92 parishes in Clackmannanshire, Perthshire and Stirlingshire, all 63 parishes in Fife, 87 out of 90 parishes in Angus and Mearns and, by 1570, every parish in the diocese of Galloway. Even some of the Highland figures were impressive, with reformed ministers by 1570 in 85 out of 91 parishes in Aberdeenshire (despite the continuation in office of a Catholic bishop) and 52 out of 72 parishes in Moray.[7] By 1606 there were no fewer than 20 presbyteries operating in the north and west of Scotland.[8] Again one has to be careful about what is meant by a 'reformed' minister since some were clearly ex-Catholic ones. In Argyll, Gilbert Macolchallum was parson of Craignish 1544–1571, Cornelius Orney parson of Kilkenny and dean of Kintyre from before 1550 until about 1577 and Patrick Graham parson of Kilmore 1553–1576.[9]

One messy element to the Scottish Reformation was the quasi-survival of bishops in what was supposed to be a church designed by John Knox on the Geneva model with kirk sessions, presbyteries, synods and a General Assembly as the final arbiter of doctrine and practice. The office of bishop, however, continued. Some bishops used their influence to either support or hinder the Reformation. As they were replaced the office-holders were not consecrated, lost any administrative functions and simply enjoyed the revenues of their estates. The fact that episcopacy had not been formally abolished meant that it was easy enough for the office to be given a proper place in the Church of Scotland and the decision of James VI to upgrade the office was eventually to prove extremely controversial. We must, however, be wary not to read subsequent opinions about bishops back into the late sixteenth century. Margo Todd suggests that at that time the office of bishop was generally accepted and not considered that important, even when James VI restored episcopal jurisdiction in 1584. This was balanced by the legal recognition of presbyteries in 1592 and thereafter there was '*de facto* a system of presbytery within prelacy admirable to moderate Puritans in England'. Todd thinks that most clergy and laity identified primarily with the kirk session and, provided that its discipline remained paramount, were fairly neutral about higher administrative arrangements:

---

[6] W.R. Foster, *The Church before the Covenants: The Church of Scotland 1596–1638*, Edinburgh 1975, pp. 193–4. Readers often acted as session clerks and schoolmasters.
[7] Kirk, *Patterns of Reform*, pp. 152–3.
[8] Ibid., p. 483.
[9] Ibid., pp. 285–6.

rulings by 'bishops and presbytery' or 'bishop and synod' recur in minute books with no hint of controversy or local objection. A few contemporary radicals, more obsessed with Presbyterianism and episcopacy than any of the laity and surely most of the clergy, have for centuries led historians a merry chase, distracting us from what religion may have meant to its ordinary practitioners with their inordinate, often well-nigh exclusive, focus on polity.[10]

This may be to push the argument a little too far but it is still a useful reminder not to believe everything that the opponents of episcopacy were later to allege.

In economic terms the Scottish Reformation took place at the same time as significant changes in land tenure. During the late fifteenth and early sixteenth centuries the two major landowners in Scotland, the crown and the church, were both suffering from something of a cash-flow crisis which they attempted to resolve by introducing a new form of hereditary land tenure known as feu ferme. The feuar made the landowner a down-payment known as the grassum and paid an annual rent known as the feu duty. These rents were fixed in perpetuity so that in the course of time their actual value was eroded by inflation. As a result a significant number of the larger feuars were able to increase their economic and social status to become the lairds or heritors, who were the most conspicuous figures in Scottish rural society between the seventeenth and the nineteenth centuries. It was the lairds who were the most vociferous in their demands for the abolition of episcopacy in the late 1630s. Between two and three hundred signed the supplication for the removal of bishops in October 1637. At the General Assembly of 1638 they outnumbered the burgh representatives by seven to one. From the last quarter of the sixteenth century they became the principal voice in most kirk sessions. During the course of the seventeenth century some of the richer feuars bought up land feued by their neighbours, thus reducing the number, and increasing the power, of the remaining heritors in many parishes. It is estimated that by the late seventeenth and early eighteenth centuries there were some 5,000 heritors in Scotland of which about a fifth were by then substantial landowners. In Aberdeenshire, the average number of heritors per parish fell from 9.7 in 1667 to 6.5 in 1741, and the total number of heritors in the county from 621 in 1667 to 250 in 1771.[11]

---

[10] Margo Todd, *The Culture of Protestantism in Early Modern Scotland*, New Haven and London 2002, pp. 405–6.

[11] T.C. Smout, *A History of the Scottish People 1560–1830*, London 1969, pp. 136–7; Michael Lynch, *Scotland: A New History*, London 1992, pp. 181–3, 252–3; Ian Whyte, *Scotland before the Industrial Revolution: An Economic and Social History*, London 1995, pp. 88–91, 155–9.

An interesting snapshot of the state of the Reformed Church of Scotland in what might be seen, certainly on Cowan's analysis, as unpromising territory, is revealed by events in the diocese of the Isles after Thomas Knox, minister of Tiree, succeeded his father as bishop in 1619. In 1622, the leading landowners in the diocese – the McDonalds of Sleat, the Macleods of Harris and the Macleans of Coll and Lochbrine – promised to repair their churches. When Knox carried out a formal visitation of his diocese in 1626 he found the island of Bute served by three ministers and that of Arran by two. There were two ministers each in Islay and Mull and one each in Coll and Tiree. Colonsay was, however, only served by a reader. There were three ministers in Skye, one of which also served the Small Isles (Canna, Eigg, Muck and Rhum), two ministers in Lewis and one to serve the Uists and Barra. In Kirk's view,

> the provision of ministers for the Isles, then, was less than ideal, but it was far from being wholly inadequate. Indeed the very existence of 19 ministers and two readers[12] for the Isles is an indication of the Kirk's resolution to discharge its responsibilities in this area and to fulfil its mission as a national church.[13]

It also made every attempt to ensure that its ministers and readers in western highland and island parishes were competent to conduct services, catechize and preach in Gaelic.

2. *The worship of the reformed church*

The Scottish reformers took an extreme position on the worship of the pre-Reformation Catholic church. They were disciples of Zwingli and Calvin, rather than Luther, and desired not just to purge the pre-Reformation mass of its most obvious corruptions, but to replace it altogether with a service that was built around the sermon as its chief element. Although they had not yet got to the stage, adopted by some of the sixteenth-century radical reformers and later assumed by the English Puritans, of denigrating any form of set worship, they were keen to keep set prayers to a minimum and quite prepared to radically reform the structure of both eucharistic and non-eucharistic worship. Initially the Scottish reformers used the *Book of Common Prayer* that had been briefly authorized for use in England and Wales from 1552, and had been reissued, with a few minor amendments, by Elizabeth I in

---

[12] The second reader was in Skye.
[13] Kirk, *Patterns of Reform*, pp. 486–7.

1559. It was a liturgy on the Reformed rather than the Lutheran model and, therefore, basically acceptable to the Scottish reformers.[14] However, in 1564, John Knox produced his own *Book of Common Order*, based more firmly on the Geneva model, and this quickly replaced the use of the 1552 *Book of Common Prayer*. The differences between the two rites are illustrated in Table 1.

Table 1 Comparison of the Eucharistic rites of the *Book of Common Prayer* (1552) and the *Book of Common Order* (1564)

BCP 1552	BCO 1564
	Ante-Communion
Lord's Prayer	Confession
Collect for Purity	Prayer for Pardon
Ten Commandments	Psalm
Collect for the Day	Prayer for Illumination
Collects for the King	
Epistle	Lesson
Gospel	
Creed	
Sermon	Sermon
Offertory Sentences	
Prayer for the Church	Intercession
	Lord's Prayer
	Apostles' Creed
	Communion
Exhortation	
Invitation	
Confession	
Absolution	
Comfortable Words	
Preface	
Sanctus	
Prayer of Humble Access	
	Preparation of Elements
Prayer of Consecration	Words of Institution
	Exhortation
	Fencing of Tables
	Prayer of Thanksgiving
Communion	Fraction and Distribution
Lord's Prayer	
Prayer of Thanksgiving	Hymn of Thanksgiving
Gloria in Excelsis	
Blessing	Benediction

[14] G.B. Burnet, *The Holy Communion in the Reformed Church of Scotland*, Edinburgh and London 1960, p. 9.

One of the enormous advantages of the *Book of Common Order* over the *Book of Common Prayer* was that only the Ante-Communion was meant to be used on Sundays when the Holy Communion was not celebrated. In the *Book of Common Prayer*, the Ante-Communion had been preceded by Morning Prayer and the Litany, a service of considerable length and repetition, which left little room for preaching. In the Church of Scotland, on non-sacrament Sundays, the sermon was the chief element in the service.

What distinguished the Church of Scotland from many other Reformed churches was not so much the texts of its services as the manner in which they were conducted and the extreme iconoclasm with which the Reformation was implemented. According to Knox, saint's days were 'utterly to be abolished from this realm'. It was decreed that at Holy Communion 'sitting at table [was] most convenient to that holy action'. Organs were considered unacceptable so those at Aberdeen and Edinburgh were dismantled and sold. According to Bishop Jewel, who would have liked England to have moved in the same direction, in Scotland

> the theatrical dresses, the sacrilegious chalices, the idols, the altars are consigned to the flames; not a vestige of the ancient superstition and idolatry is left.[15]

In fact that was not entirely true. The *Book of Common Order* had in fact retained some festivals in the calendar and, with one or two variations, these were included in subsequent editions, as shown in Table 2. What is even more remarkable about these calendars is that some of the festivals listed here were not included in the calendar of the *Book of Common Prayer*. However, the inclusion of these festivals in the calendar does not mean that these festivals were observed. The General Assembly was keen to repress all festivals but in 1570 agreed to permit communion at Easter (Pasch) 'where superstition was removed'. At St Andrews ten people were disciplined by the kirk session in 1573 for observing Christmas (Yule), and complaints about its continued observation were made at Aberdeen in 1574 and Glasgow in 1583. The popular hankering after the festivities of the pre-Reformation church were illustrated at Perth in 1577 when several inhabitants were disciplined by the kirk session for taking part in a Corpus Christi procession.[16]

The normal Sunday morning service in Scotland in the late sixteenth century comprised confession of sins, psalms, lections, a sermon, intercession,

---

[15] Kirk, *Patterns of Reform*, pp. 338–9.
[16] Cowan, *Scottish Reformation*, pp. 156–7.

Table 2 Provision for festivals in the Calendar of the *Book of Common Order* 1564–1635[17]

Festival	1564	1594	1615	1625	1635
Circumcision		✓	✓	✓	✓	✓
St Edward Confessor				✓		
Epiphany			✓	✓	✓	✓
Conversion of St Paul		✓	✓	✓	✓	✓
Purification of BVM		✓	✓	✓	✓	✓
St Matthias			✓	✓	✓	✓	✓
Annunciation of BVM	✓	✓	✓	✓	✓	
St George						✓
St Mark					✓	✓
SS Philip & James		✓	✓	✓	✓	
St Barnabas			✓	✓	✓	✓
Nativity of St John the Baptist	✓	✓	✓	✓	✓	
St Mary Magdalene			✓			✓
St James			✓	✓	✓	✓	✓
St Peter in Chains		✓	✓	✓	✓	✓
St Lawrence			✓	✓	✓	✓	✓
Assumption of BVM		✓	✓	✓	✓	✓
St Bartholomew		✓	✓	✓	✓	✓
Beheading of St John the Baptist		✓		✓		
Nativity of BVM	✓		✓	✓	✓	
St Matthew			✓			
St Michael		✓	✓	✓	✓	✓
St Luke		✓	✓	✓	✓	✓
SS Simon & Jude		✓	✓	✓	✓	✓
All Saints			✓			✓
St Martin		✓	✓	✓	✓	✓
St Andrew		✓	✓	✓		✓
Conception of BVM			✓		✓	
St Lucy		✓	✓	✓	✓	✓
St Thomas		✓	✓	✓	✓	✓
Nativity of Our Lord		✓	✓	✓	✓	✓
St Stephen			✓		✓	
St John Evangelist		✓		✓		
Holy Innocents		✓		✓		

Lord's Prayer and Apostles' Creed.[18] It generally lasted about 2 hours. Sunday afternoon services were shorter and the sermon was generally replaced with catechizing.[19] Although the range of music was more limited than that in some other Reformed churches, it was less so in the late sixteenth and early seventeenth centuries than it was to become after 1640:

---

[17] J.A. Lamb, 'The Kalendar of the *Book of Common Order*: 1564–1644', *RSCHS*, xii (1958) pp. 15–28.

[18] Gordon Donaldson, *The Scottish Reformation*, Cambridge 1960, p. 83.

[19] Foster, *Church Before the Covenants*, p. 179.

instead of every one of the hundred and fifty psalms being associated with its own tune and no other, a group of tunes known as Common Tunes became popular because you could sing any psalm to them. . . . People everywhere relied on the precentor to set them off on the right tune at the right pitch and with the right words . . . so if the precentor was poor the repertoire was bound to narrow down.[20]

In addition to common psalm tunes, some of the early Scottish psalters included settings for other material to be sung in church. Edward Miller's psalter of 1635 contained 31 common psalm tunes and settings for the Ten Commandments, *Magnificat*, *Nunc Dimittis*, Lord's Prayer, Creed and *Veni Creator*.[21] At this date the sort of music being sung in Scottish churches, and the manner in which it was sung, with the precentor leading the congregation, was not that different from that sung in most English parish churches, where the parish clerk fulfilled the same function as the Scottish precentor.

In addition to Sunday services, most Scottish churches in the late sixteenth century, not just in the towns but in the country areas as well, had daily, or at least some weekday, services. In the larger towns, daily services were the norm. In the smaller towns and rural parishes, at least one weekday service, usually on a Wednesday or Friday, was the established practice.[22] At Elgin there was a daily service at 4 p.m. with a sermon on either a Tuesday or a Wednesday. Service was held at Culross on Wednesdays and Fridays between 8 a.m. and 9 a.m. There was a daily service at Tarves (Aberdeenshire), only a small village, at 6 a.m., and weekday sermons and prayers between 8 a.m. and 9 a.m. at St Andrews.[23] In the larger towns, churches were generally kept open all day for private prayer. In 1619, the Glasgow kirk session resolved that the door of the New Kirk of St Andrew be opened from 5 in the morning and closed at 9 at night for the summer half-year, and for the winter from 7 in the morning till 5 in the evening.[24]

The most distinctive aspect of Scottish reformed worship was the communion service. Practice in relation to the reception of communion varied a good deal in the Reformed churches. The English church, which was quasi-Reformed, was unique in insisting that the Catholic and Lutheran practice of receiving communion kneeling should be continued, though the Black Rubric in the 1552 prayer book, removed in 1559, had explained that reception of communion kneeling did not imply any veneration for

---

[20] John Purser, *Scotland's Music: A History of the Traditional and Classical Music of Scotland from Earliest Times to the Present Day*, Edinburgh 1992, p. 145.
[21] Millar Patrick, *Four Centuries of Scottish Psalmody*, London 1949, p. 209.
[22] Cowan, *Scottish Reformation*, pp. 139–40.
[23] Foster, *Church Before the Covenants*, p. 177.
[24] W.D. Maxwell, *A History of Worship in the Church of Scotland*, London 1955, p. 65.

the eucharistic elements. Other Reformed churches adopted one of four different communion practices: ambulatory or walking communion, standing around the table, ministers delivering communion to people in their seats or sitting at tables. Contemporary evidence suggests that at both Neuchâtel and Geneva communion was received by walking past the table and receiving the bread from a minister at one end and the wine from a minister at the other. The continuation of this practice is attested to in the late eighteenth and early nineteenth centuries in the journals of the Swedish traveller, Jacob Björnståhl (1773), and the order of service at Geneva published by J.J. Paschoud in 1807.[25] It was also the initial practice of the Dutch Reformed Church before it was eventually replaced by sitting communion.[26] In Scotland, under Knox's influence, sitting communion was adopted immediately and the normal practice was to set up temporary tables when required, a practice continued to the present day in a small number of Scottish Presbyterian churches. The *Book of Common Order* of 1564 recommended monthly celebrations of Holy Communion but the General Assembly had provided for less frequent celebrations 2 years earlier, four times a year in town parishes and twice in country ones, and with a provision that it should not be celebrated on 'popish' festivals.[27] In practice, celebrations tended to be less frequent than this. This was partly a continuation of the pre-Reformation practice of annual communion at Easter and partly the result of a shortage of ministers. In 1583, the Perth kirk session settled for two celebrations a year.[28] By the early seventeenth century 'the pattern of the great communion season' had been established; communion services were staggered so that ministers and communicants travelled from neighbouring parishes to the church at which communion was to be celebrated, and this was preceded by days of fasting and preparation and concluded with a service of thanksgiving. Communion seasons were often the opportunity for religious revivals in the participating parishes.[29] In order to receive the sacrament, intending communicants had to be examined on the state of their spiritual lives and issued with a token to enable them to receive communion. On communion Sundays the area in which the tables were set up was fenced off from the rest of the church. The Ante-communion took place in the unfenced area and communicants passed through the fence at

---

[25] M. Lovibond, 'The Use of Spaces for Public Worship in the Early Reformed Tradition', Manchester PhD 2005, pp. 70–1, 117–18.

[26] See J.R. Luth, 'Communion in the Churches of the Dutch Reformation to the Present Day', *Bread of Heaven: Customs and Practices Surrounding Holy Communion*, eds Charles Caspers, Gerard Lukken and Gerard Rouwhorst, Kampen 1995, pp. 99–117.

[27] Burnet, *Holy Communion*, pp. 13–14, 17.

[28] Cowan, *Scottish Reformation*, p. 144.

[29] A.L. Drummond and J. Bulloch, *The Scottish Church, 1688–1843*. Edinburgh 1973, p. 49.

which the elders would receive their communion tokens.[30] Even so the Scottish church retained certain pre-Reformation liturgical practices abandoned by some other Reformed churches. For example, it was common to mix water with wine in the chalice, though that was usually done before the service began, and in many churches a type of unleavened shortbread was used instead of ordinary bread.[31] Depending on the number of communicants, communion services could be very long affairs, sometimes beginning as early as 3 a.m. or 4 a.m. on the Sunday morning and lasting until the afternoon, as communicants awaited their turn to sit at the tables. Generally speaking, the services and the church interiors lacked colour, though the latter 'were on occasion decorated with flowers' and the pulpit and precentor's desk were normally fitted 'with velvet, damask or brocade hangings'.[32]

3. The first episcopacy (1610–1638)

In 1603, James VI of Scotland succeeded to the throne of England as James I. James had always been uncomfortable with the quasi-democratic structure of the Church of Scotland and the power of its presbyteries, and looked enviously at other Protestant countries, such as England and Scandinavia, where the monarch could effectively control the established church through the bishops. There is no evidence that, before his accession to the English throne, James regarded the worship of the English church to be superior to that of the Scottish church; indeed in 1590 he had expressed his view that 'as for our neighbouring kirk in England, it is an evil said Mass in English, wanting nothing but the liftings'.[33] However, within a few years of his arrival in England, James had clearly changed his mind and in 1610 he began a process which endeavoured to produce a single Reformed church for the whole of the British Isles. In that year, three of the Scottish bishops, who only had Presbyterian orders, were consecrated by their English counterparts; a suggestion by the high church Bishop Andrewes of Ely that they should be re-ordained as well as was disregarded by Archbishop Bancroft of Canterbury on the grounds that 'otherwise it might be doubted if there was any lawful ordination in most of the Reformed Churches'.[34] The three newly consecrated Scottish bishops then consecrated the other diocesans. This created a theoretically unified episcopate for the whole of Britain and Ireland, with the possibility of translating Scottish bishops to England, Ireland or

---

[30] Burnet, *Holy Communion*, p. 56.
[31] Ibid., pp. 30–1; Cowan, *Scottish Reformation*, p. 147.
[32] Maxwell, *History of Worship*, p. 66.
[33] J.H.S. Burleigh, *A Church History of Scotland*, London 1960, p. 204.
[34] Ibid., p. 207.

Wales or *vice versa*. In practice, the only translations were those of a few Scottish bishops to Ireland.[35]

The second stage of James' process of ecclesiastical consolidation was the Articles of Perth. These required the reception of Holy Communion kneeling, provision for communion of the sick and private baptisms, the confirmation of children over the age of eight and the proper observation of the festivals and fasts of Christmas, Good Friday, Easter, the Ascension and Pentecost.[36] Not surprisingly there was a good deal of initial hostility to the draft Articles, especially the provision of kneeling to receive communion.[37] The five draft Articles were first presented to the synods in July 1617. Patrick Galloway, minister to the royal household, being asked for his opinion, expressed the view that, though kneeling was not acceptable and communion should be received sitting, holy days were indifferent, since several Reformed churches observed them, but that it would be best to celebrate them on the nearest Sunday. On 25 November 1617 the General Assembly, meeting at St Andrews, rejected both kneeling and the observance of holy days. In January 1618, James ordered the Privy Council to enforce the Articles and Good Friday was observed in both Edinburgh and Stirling. The feast of the Ascension was observed in Edinburgh on the Sunday following, but fewer than fifty communicants received kneeling. After further pressure from both James and the bishops the Articles were eventually approved, though with a significant minority voting against or abstaining, by the General Assembly, meeting at Perth, in August 1618 and they were ratified by the Privy Council that October. The Articles were generally disregarded and attempts to enforce kneeling were largely unsuccessful. Serious attempts were made to enforce the observance of Good Friday, Easter and Christmas, but the presbytery of Dunkeld insisted on meeting on 25 December 1623, thus making it impossible for the ministers to attend their own churches. There was some regional variation in the observance of the Articles. In north-east Scotland, always an area of religious conservatism, they were generally observed, while being almost completely disregarded in more radical religious areas such as Fife and Lothian. When some ministers tried to enforce kneeling, outraged laity attended neighbouring churches where the provision was not enforced.[38]

---

[35] See Nigel Yates, *The Religious Condition of Ireland 1770–1850*, Oxford 2006, p. 326. Bishops Knox and Leslie of The Isles were translated to Raphoe in 1611 and 1633, respectively and Bishop Maxwell of Ross to Killala in 1641. In 1693, the former archbishop of Glasgow, Alexander Cairncross, who had been deprived in 1687, was appointed bishop of Raphoe.

[36] Burleigh, *Church History*, pp. 213–14.

[37] Burnet, *Holy Communion*, p. 77.

[38] A.R. MacDonald, *The Jacobean Kirk, 1567–1625: Sovereignty, Polity and Liturgy*, Aldershot 1998, pp. 159–68.

The third and final stage of the policy of bringing the Protestant churches of the British Isles into line with one another was liturgical revision in Scotland. On the whole the English bishops took the view that the best option would be the replacement of the *Book of Common Order* with the *Book of Common Prayer*, but that view was not supported by some of the Scottish bishops. A draft prayer book had in fact been drawn up by Bishop Cowper of Galloway, who died in 1619. This book was closely modelled on the *Book of Common Prayer*. The office of Morning Prayer was virtually identical except that the versicles were omitted and a psalm sung instead of the *Te Deum*. The communion office was an interesting mix of the *Book of Common Prayer* and the *Book of Common Order*, but included provision for the reception of communion kneeling.[39] The case for the revision of the Scottish liturgy was later expressed in a pamphlet of 1639, the authorship of which was subsequently ascribed to Dean Balcanquall of Durham:

> the deformity which was used in Scotland, where no set or public form of prayer was used, but preachers, or readers, or ignorant schoolmasters prayed in the church, sometimes so ignorantly as it was a shame to all religion to have the majesty of God so barbarously spoken unto, sometimes so seditiously that their prayers were plain libels.[40]

In fact this was a highly biased and partisan view of the state of the Scottish liturgy but it did contain some grains of truth. In 1616, a committee of four was appointed to oversee liturgical revision. Their initial draft followed very closely the structure of the *Book of Common Order*, but provided a fixed table of psalms, epistles and gospels, and some lengthening of the set prayers. However, anti-Anglican feeling, induced by the Articles of Perth and anger at reports of the services in the Chapel Royal at Holyrood when James VI and I revisited Scotland, for the first time since 1603, in 1617, persuaded James that the time was not yet ripe for liturgical revision. On 17 May 1617 the services of the *Book of Common Prayer* were used in the Chapel Royal, with the clergy vested in surplices, and on 8 June the Holy Communion was administered, again according to the English rite, and with the communicants kneeling. The chapel itself had been fitted up with an organ and choir stalls.[41]

The question of liturgical revision was not raised again until 1629, by which date James had been succeeded by his son Charles I. Both Charles and his future archbishop of Canterbury, William Laud, thought that the Scottish

---

[39] W. McMillan, 'The Anglican *Book of Common Prayer* in the Church of Scotland', *RSCHS*, iv (1932), p. 142.
[40] Maxwell, *History of Worship*, p. 72.
[41] *Ibid.*, pp. 73–6.

church should adopt the *Book of Common Prayer*, but were reluctantly persuaded by John Maxwell, then minister of Edinburgh and later bishop of Ross, that a liturgy framed in Scotland would have a better chance of acceptance. In 1633, Charles, who continued his father's practice of having the English service sung, with organ and choir, in the Chapel Royal, instructed Dean Ballantine, who was also bishop of Dunblane, to preach in a surplice and to wear a cope at celebrations of Holy Communion, then the practice at cathedrals and collegiate churches in England. The bishops were also enjoined to encourage their clergy to wear surplices instead of black gowns 'when reading prayers, administering sacraments and burying the dead'.[42] Work on a new Scottish liturgy was begun by Bishop Maxwell in 1634 and completed by Bishop Wedderburn of Dunblane in 1636. It was published in May 1637 and ordered to be used in Scottish churches from Sunday 23 July, without being previously seen or approved by the General Assembly.[43] Although its use provoked riots at St Giles, Edinburgh and elsewhere, and was a major factor in leading to the decision of the General Assembly to abolish episcopacy in Scotland in 1638, opposition to the new book was not universal and there were parishes, especially in the conservative north-east of Scotland, in which it was used with the full support of both ministers and their congregations.[44] In 1644, both the English *Book of Common Prayer* and the Scottish *Book of Common Order* were replaced with the *Westminster Directory*. Unlike any of the liturgies in use in England or Scotland beforehand, the *Directory* was not a set liturgy but mainly a set of instructions to the minister on how to order the service.[45] Scoto-Catholic liturgists of the late nineteenth and early twentieth centuries regarded the introduction of the *Directory* as a liturgical disaster for Scotland, since it led to a widely held and inaccurate belief in the Church of Scotland that no form of set liturgy had been the historic practice in the Kirk since the Reformation. Although representatives of the General Assembly were involved in the discussions that drew up both the Westminster Confession of Faith and the *Directory*, the dominant voice in the deliberations belonged to English Puritans, both Presbyterians and Independents, many of whom disliked any form of set liturgy. The fact that the *Westminster Directory* has remained the standard of public worship in the Church of Scotland until the present time has led many churchmen to argue that the ability of the minister to frame his own service must be preserved as one of the essential characteristics of a Reformed liturgy. However, as W.D. Maxwell, one of the leading

---

[42] *Ibid.*, pp. 80–1.
[43] For the text of the communion office and a commentary on its composition, see W.J. Grisbrooke, *Anglican Liturgies of the Seventeenth and Eighteenth Centuries*, London 1958, pp. 1–18, 163–82.
[44] McMillan, 'Anglican Book', pp. 144–5.
[45] Text in *The Liturgy in English*, ed. B.J. Wigan, 2nd edn, London 1964, pp. 189–91.

Scoto-Catholic liturgists, has argued, the *Directory* was a breach of Scottish liturgical practice over the previous 80 years in which the first part of the morning service was almost entirely conducted by a reader, rather than the minister, strictly in accordance with the provisions of the *Book of Common Order*.[46]

The chief innovation of the *Directory*, formally adopted by the General Assembly in 1645, was the amalgamation of the, previously separate, readers' and ministers' services and, with it, the abolition of the post of reader. Before 1645 the reader had read the confession, the prayers for pardon and illumination and the lessons and led the singing of the psalm, before the minister had entered the church to preach the sermon, lead the intercession and, on sacrament Sundays, celebrate Holy Communion. The *Directory* created a service led entirely by the minister and with little participation by anyone else. It began with a summons to worship, a long introductory prayer to be composed by the minister, a reading from both the Old and New Testaments and one or more metrical psalms. The minister was then permitted to lecture on any part of the biblical texts that had been read beforehand. This was followed by a confession of sins, composed by the minister, a long sermon and the intercession, also composed by the minister. There were no texts as such, apart from the passages of scripture and the psalms, and the influence of the English Independents even ensured the omission of the Lord's Prayer, the Creed and the Ten Commandments, which were to be confined to catechizing services. When the Holy Communion was administered the closing psalm of the morning service became the offertory psalm, during which the elements of bread and wine were brought in and placed before the minister. This was followed by a long exhortation of the minister's composition, the fencing of the tables and the words of institution. There was then a prayer over the elements, composed by the minister, fraction and communion, which the communicants were to receive seated, either at the communion table or in their own pews. The service concluded with a prayer of thanksgiving, composed by the minister, a psalm and a blessing. Apart from joining in the psalms there was no congregational participation. The whole service was read by the minister and most of it was of his own composition.[47]

4. *The second episcopacy (1662–1689)*

Episcopacy, abolished in Scotland in 1638, was likewise abolished in the rest of the British Isles in 1645. With the restoration of Charles II in 1660

---

[46] Maxwell, *History of Worship*, p. 94.
[47] Ibid., pp. 102–5; Burnet, *Holy Communion*, pp. 110–11.

episcopacy was gradually reintroduced throughout the British churches. There were hopes in Scotland that this would not be the case but, despite early indications that he might tolerate a fully Presbyterian church in Scotland, Charles II eventually came to the conclusion that, in order to secure the unity of his kingdoms, a common method of church government, the episcopal one, was the best option. Only one of the former Scottish bishops, Thomas Sydserf of Galloway, was still alive in 1660 and he was translated to the diocese of Orkney, which he never managed to visit before his death in 1663. Four of the new bishops appointed – Sharp of St Andrews, Fairfoul of Glasgow, Hamilton of Galloway and Leighton of Dunblane – were summoned to London to be consecrated in Westminster Abbey on 15 December. Fairfoul and Hamilton had been episcopally ordained before 1638, but Sharp and Leighton had only Presbyterian orders. On this occasion, and ignoring the precedent of 1610, the English bishops insisted that they be ordained to both the diaconate and the priesthood before they could be consecrated. The remaining new Scottish bishops were consecrated in Holyrood Abbey on 7 May 1662 though without any requirement for prior ordination to the diaconate and priesthood if they only had Presbyterian orders.[48] Scottish ministers who had not been episcopally ordained were also allowed to continue in office and no attempt was made to impose the 1662 revision of the English *Book of Common Prayer* on the Church of Scotland.

There was indeed little change in Scottish worship after 1660. The majority of ministers still continued to use the *Directory*, though many also used the Creed, Lord's Prayer and the doxology to the psalms. The old office of reader was revived by the bishop and synod of Aberdeen in 1662. A few bishops and ministers used the *Book of Common Prayer* as revised in 1662. Bishop Leighton of Dunblane did so when officiating as dean of the Chapel Royal. The future Bishop Burnet of Salisbury claimed he had used it from memory as minister of Saltoun. Some bishops used the English ordinal to ordain. The *Book of Common Prayer* was still being used at Dumfries in 1692, and in the conservative north as late as 1712–1714 at Banchory and 1712–1720 at Contin. In 1665–1666, the bishops considered the possibility of introducing a new liturgy but, remembering the reception given to the 1637 one, thought better of it. However, in 1683 the diocese of Aberdeen set up a committee to draw up a new liturgy simply for use in that conservative diocese, later a hotbed of non-juring episcopalianism, and in 1685 it was reported that the text was nearing completion.[49] No attempt was made to introduce any 'popish' ceremonies such as 'Surplices,

---

[48] Burleigh, *Church History*, pp. 238–41.
[49] W.B. Foster, *Bishop and Presbytery: The Church of Scotland 1661–1688*, London 1958, pp. 125–32, 134; McMillan, 'Anglican Book', pp. 145–8.

Altars, Cross in Baptisms, nor the meanest of those things ... allowed in England'.[50] However, at St Machar's Cathedral in Aberdeen, Henry Scougal, professor of divinity at King's College, introduced a form of daily morning and evening prayer described by a subsequent commentator as 'reverent, serious and dignified'.[51]

Thomas Morer, an English chaplain serving in Scotland in the 1680s, has left a useful account of Scottish worship at this time. The service was begun by the precentor reading two or three chapters from the Bible. When the minister climbed into the pulpit the precentor set the psalms. The minister then pronounced a long confession of sins followed by the sermon. There was a further long prayer after the sermon containing petitions for the Royal family, the nation, the sick and other needs, concluding with the Lord's Prayer. A second psalm was then sung and the minister dismissed the congregation with the benediction. Sermons 'could not be read, but had to be delivered from memory' and they lasted, on average, an hour. Daily prayers were generally held in the larger churches, including fifteen in the diocese of Aberdeen in 1662. The observance of feasts was not generally reintroduced apart from that of Christmas. The bishop of Ross ordered all his clergy to preach on Christmas day 1668, sending a letter to this effect to each presbytery. By 1678 all ministers in the presbytery of Dingwall were doing so except 'Mr George Cumine who was tender for the tyme', but by 1684 all ministers in the presbytery were observing Christmas.[52] After 1660 the Scottish churches were ordered to hold at least one communion service each year. The bishops and synods of Aberdeen and Moray specified that this annual celebration should be at Easter. In 1685, the archbishop and synod of St Andrews required two celebrations a year. In practice, celebrations tended to be far more infrequent than the minimum required. It has been alleged that there were only two celebrations in the cathedral at Glasgow between 1660 and 1688; there were none at all in the Inverness-shire parish of Glenurquhart between 1647 and 1671. A visitation of Weem by the presbytery of Dunkeld in 1682 revealed that the minister there had never celebrated Holy Communion, though he had been admitted to the charge in 1664. The minister of Rattray was admonished by the presbytery of Meigle for only celebrating four times in 9 years. At the other extreme the future Bishop Burnet of Salisbury celebrated four times each year as minister of Saltoun. Celebrations of Holy Communion were always preceded by a service of preparation and followed by a service of thanksgiving.[53]

---

[50] Clare Jackson, *Restoration Scotland 1660–1690: Royalist Politics, Religion and Ideas*, Woodbridge 2003, p. 110.
[51] Maxwell, *History of Worship*, pp. 119–20.
[52] Foster, *Bishop and Presbytery*, pp. 134–5, 138–9, 144, 147.
[53] *Ibid.*, pp. 140–1; Burnet, *Holy Communion*, pp. 145–6.

5. Schism and reunion

With the enforced abdication and flight of James VII and II in 1688 all the Scottish bishops found themselves in the difficult position of some of their counterparts in England in being unwilling to break their oath to James, by taking one to William III and Mary II, while he was still alive. In this total episcopal vacuum, the new government decided that it would tolerate a fully Presbyterian church in Scotland, provided that room was made for all those ministers, including those with strongly episcopal sympathies, prepared to take the necessary oaths. Approximately 60 surviving ministers, ejected from their parishes for refusing to accept the episcopal settlement in 1662, were restored to their former, or other, charges, while somewhere between a 100 and 200 ministers of strongly episcopalian sympathies were 'rabbled' out of their parishes by parishioners who were exceptionally antipathetic to episcopacy, and a further 180 were deprived for refusing to take the oath to William and Mary. Nevertheless a significant number of ministers with strongly episcopalian sympathies, who were prepared to take the oath, survived, despite their contempt for what they called 'the General Assembly of the Presbyterians'. It was estimated that there were still 165 of these ministers in 1707 and many survived, undisturbed in their parishes, throughout the first quarter of the eighteenth century. One of the last was probably Archibald Lundie, minister of Saltoun, where Bishop Burnet had been one of his distinguished predecessors, from 1696 until his death in 1759.[54] One of the principal reasons for restoring episcopal ministers was the paucity of Presbyterians to succeed them. If all the Episcopalian ministers had been ejected, many charges would have been vacant in the early years of the eighteenth century.[55]

From 1690 the Church of Scotland became an established church very different from those in the rest of the British Isles. It was now both fully Presbyterian in government and as such enjoyed a freedom from government control not enjoyed by the other established, but still episcopal, churches. The General Assembly, which had had limited and disputed powers since the beginning of the Scottish Reformation and which had not functioned after 1660, was at last able to enjoy the authority over doctrine and worship which it had always sought. The only restriction placed on the Scottish church was the restoration of private patronage, abolished in 1690, under the Patronage Act of 1712 following the Act of Union of the Westminster and Scottish parliaments in 1707. Although the General Assembly expressed the view at the time that private patronage was 'grievous

---

[54] Burleigh, *Church History*, pp. 261–5; Maxwell, *Worship*, pp. 126–7.
[55] William Ferguson, 'The Problems of the Established Church in the West Highlands and Islands in the Eighteenth Century', *RSCHS*, xvii (1972), p. 18.

and prejudicial to this Church',[56] the legislation was not repealed until 1874. In the meantime, it was at least partially responsible for several schisms within the Church of Scotland, the most serious of which was the Disruption of 1843. Initially, however, the Church of Scotland as constituted in 1690 retained the allegiance of a majority of the people. The only groups outside it were the small bands of non-juring episcopalians, Roman Catholics and Cameronians, an extreme Calvinistic sect of the 1680s which refused to be in communion with the Church of Scotland, while it retained its 'erastian' connection with the state.

It was the patronage issue that brought about the first significant secession from the Church of Scotland when Ebenezer Erskine was suspended by the General Assembly for his attacks on it over the disputed appointment to the charge of Kinross in 1726–1732. The Secession Church was established in 1733. In 1743, one of the Secession ministers joined the one surviving Cameronian minister to form the Reformed Presbytery. In 1747, a more serious split in the Secession Church was caused by divisions over the Burgess Oath introduced at Edinburgh, Glasgow and Perth in 1745, at the time of the Jacobite rebellion, in order to exclude Roman Catholics from public office. The largest section of the Secession Church, known as the Anti-Burghers, refused to submit to the oath since it implied recognition of the established church, and those who were willing to take the oath were known as Burghers. In 1761, a further dispute over patronage, this time at Inverkeithing, led to the setting up of the Relief Church by the former minister of Carnock, Thomas Gillespie. Both the Burghers and the Anti-Burghers split into 'Auld Licht' and 'New Licht' factions over matters of doctrinal interpretation between 1799 and 1806. With the abolition of the Burgess Oath in 1819, the two branches of the 'New Licht', who were more liberal in their doctrine of salvation than the 'Auld Licht', united in 1820 to form the United Secession Church. In turn they united with the Relief Church, a body with an even more relaxed attitude to discipline and central church control, to form the United Presbyterian Church in 1847.[57]

The tensions within the Church of Scotland, which led to the Disruption of 1843, had their origins in the Evangelical Revival which swept across the whole of northern Europe and America in the eighteenth century.[58] The first of these revivals in Scotland had taken place at Cambuslang in 1742 and it

---

[56] Burleigh, *Church History*, p. 279.
[57] *Ibid.*, pp. 279–84; C.G. Brown, *Religion and Society in Scotland since 1707*, Edinburgh 1997, pp. 22–5, 28.
[58] See especially W.R. Ward, *The Protestant Evangelical Awakening*, Cambridge 1992, and David Bebbington, *Evangelicalism in Modern Britain: A History from the 1730s to the 1980s*, London 1989; useful for the later phases of the Evangelical Revival is Ian Bradley, *The Call to Seriousness: The Evangelical Impact on the Victorians*, London 1976.

was followed by a series of revivals in individual parishes, and sometimes a larger area, in the late eighteenth and early nineteenth centuries: at Croy, near Inverness, in 1766–1771, and later at Tongue (1773), Ardclach (1776), Kilbrandon and Kilchattan (1786), Skye (1806–1812) and Lewis (1824). As in other parts of Europe these revivals were built around highly emotional preaching by itinerant preachers, and were looked at askance by the majority of 'moderate' ministers and laity in the Church of Scotland. The failure of the established church in Orkney to respond to the Evangelical Revival encouraged the setting up of not just Secessionist Presbyterian churches, but also Baptist, Congregationalist and Wesleyan Methodist missions in the islands. A Secessionist Presbyterian Society was established in Kirkwall in 1790 and a church opened there in 1796. There were Evangelical missions by Baptist and Congregationalist missionaries in Arran and Bute from 1800, Skye from 1805 and Lewis in the 1820s, the last two competing with Evangelical revivals within the Church of Scotland.[59] Compared with its success in England and Wales, and to a lesser extent in Ireland, Methodism enjoyed comparatively little success in Scotland despite extensive preaching tours in the 1740s and 1750s by both John Wesley and George Whitefield.[60]

The growth of the Evangelical party in the Church of Scotland after 1800, and its charismatic leadership under Thomas Chalmers,[61] resulted in enormous tensions between them and the Moderate party over the relationship between church and state, and the view of the Evangelicals that the church's Moderate leadership was not putting sufficient pressure on the state for the removal of such irritants as private patronage. Two other very important irritants, as noted in more detail in Chapter 3, were the difficulty in persuading the British government to fund Chalmers's campaign for church extension in Scotland and the poor drafting of legislation to enable the establishment of new *quoad sacra* parishes for newly built churches. In 1843, this tension came to a head when Chalmers and about 190 ministers and elders walked out of the General Assembly protesting that it was not free from state control. Across Scotland 451 ministers joined the new Free Church of Scotland as opposed to the 752 who remained in the established church.[62] In much of highland Scotland the figure was much higher than this in proportional terms, though there has been a good deal of recent academic discussion of the raw statistics:

---

[59] D.E. Meek, 'Evangelical Missionaries in the Early Nineteenth-Century Highlands', *Scottish Studies*, xxviii (1987), pp. 1–34.
[60] Brown, *Religion and Society*, pp. 36–7.
[61] See the splendid study by S.J. Brown, *Thomas Chalmers and the Godly Commonwealth in Scotland*, Oxford 1982.
[62] Drummond and Bulloch, *Scottish Church*, p. 249.

The precise extent of the Highland exodus into the Free Church in 1843 is open to debate. In certain areas of the Highlands, such as Argyll, the Established Church retained considerable strength. ... In the north and west of the region, though, where the crofting system prevailed most strongly, the Free Church became the church of the vast majority. In some cases, notably Lewis, Harris, Sutherland and Ross-shire, the Free Church attracted over 90 per cent of the people. Yet it is significant that only 72 ministers from the Highland synods of Argyll, Glenelg, Ross, Sutherland, and Caithness joined the Free Church while 79 remained in the establishment. This demonstrates that the ministry – unlike the general Highland population – was fairly equally divided between evangelicals and moderates in 1843.[63]

In 1845, there were only 13 Free Church ministers in the western highlands and islands for an estimated population of 167,283 the majority of whom attended Free Church services. Across Scotland, however, the Free Church had about 700 congregations within a few months of the Disruption and had raised £366,719 to provide new churches and manses.[64] The collapse of the established church in some parts of the highlands and islands was phenomenal. At Durness (Sutherland) there were 134 baptisms in the Free Church in 1843–1848 compared with hardly any in the parish church. In Lewis, only 450–700 people out of a population of 17,000 remained in the Church of Scotland; in the parish of Lochs it was only one person.[65]

In 1876, the majority of the Reformed Presbyterian congregations joined the Free Church, but this was more than compensated for in 1893 when a section of the Free Church, concerned about the Declaratory Act of 1892 by which the holding of an orthodox Calvinist interpretation of the Westminster Confession was made optional, set up the Free Presbyterian Church. Initially only two ministers joined this new church, but more significant were the 4,000 lay members of the Free Church who also joined. By 1900 this new church had a total of 75 charges and mission stations, of which 70 were in the Highlands and Islands (Ross and Cromarty 16, Western Isles 13, Skye 12, Sutherland 11, Inverness-shire 7, Argyll 5, Caithness 5 and Aberdeenshire 1) with two congregations in Glasgow and one each in Dumbarton, Edinburgh

---

[63] A.W. MacColl, *Land, Faith and the Crofting Community: Christianity and Social Criticism in the Highlands of Scotland, 1843–1893*, Edinburgh 2006, p. 21.

[64] Drummond and Bulloch, *Scottish Church*, p. 251.

[65] P.L.M. Hills, 'The Sociology of the Disruption', *Scotland in the Age of the Disruption*, ed. S.J. Brown and M. Fry, Edinburgh 1993, pp. 47–8; Douglas Ansdell, *The People of the Great Faith: The Highland Church 1690–1900*, Stornoway 1998, p. 63.

and Greenock.[66] In 1900, the Free Church was again divided when the majority of its ministers voted to unite with the United Presbyterian Church (itself the union of the Relief and Secession churches in 1847) to form the United Free Church. Although only 19 out of 239 ministers in the four Highland synods of the Free Church remained in the Continuing Free Church (hence known as the 'Wee Frees'), over 90 of the Highland congregations did so and overall a third of the laity. Within a few months of the schism the section of the Free Church that had entered the United Free Church claimed 245 congregations in the Highlands and Islands compared with 119 for the 'Wee Frees'. However, the latter group had declined to 105 by 1905, even though in the previous year a court case brought by the Continuing Free Church had eventually resulted in a House of Lords judgement, which awarded it the property of the pre-schism Free Church. In lowland Scotland, the Continuing Free Church had an almost minimal presence; the United Free Church had 862 congregations compared with only 19 belonging to the Continuing Free Church.[67] Both the Free Church and the Free Presbyterian Church have suffered further schisms in recent years. In 1988, there was a schism in the Free Presbyterian Church when one of its most distinguished members, Lord Mackay of Clashfern, was disciplined for attending a Roman Catholic requiem mass. More than half the members left to form the new Associated Presbyterian Churches. In 1996–1997, a Free Church 'Defence Association' was set up in Lewis, prior to a formal schism in the Free Church, after charges of sexual assault had been brought against a professor in the Free Church College. Although the charges were dismissed, there was a widespread belief that these charges had been instigated by a group of Free Church conservatives determined to remove the professor 'because of his liberal views on doctrine and worship'. When their efforts failed they took the first steps towards the creation of a new Free Church (Continuing).[68]

By far the most significant event in the history of Scottish Presbyterianism since 1900 was, however, the reunion of the United Free Church with the Church of Scotland in 1929.[69] This union was the culmination of a number of earlier unions between some of the smaller Presbyterian churches which aimed at reversing the trend of the previous two centuries in which various groups – the Secession, Relief and Free Churches – had left the Church of Scotland, as it saw the majority of the members of all three bodies reunited with their mother church. From 1929 the majority of Presbyterians in

---

[66] Brown, *Religion and Society*, p. 29; Ansdell, *People of the Great Faith*, p. 78; A.I. MacInnes, 'Evangelical Protestantism in the Nineteenth-Century Highlands', *Sermons and Battle Hymns*, ed. Graham Walker and Ian Gallagher, Edinburgh 1990, p. 63.
[67] *Loc. cit.*; Ansdell, *People of the Great Faith*, pp. 196–7.
[68] Brown, *Religion and Society*, p. 31.
[69] For the process of reunion see D.M. Murray, *Rebuilding the Kirk: Presbyterian Reunion in Scotland 1909–1929*, Edinburgh 2000.

Scotland have been members of the established Church of Scotland. The remaining groups of Presbyterians, including those of the United Free Church who refused to join the 1929 union, are very small indeed. This has, however, created an enormous surplus of ecclesiastical plant in Scotland as the uniting churches brought their buildings with them. In the intervening years, there have been strenuous attempts to deal with the problems of surplus plant. Churches and other buildings have been demolished, secularized and passed over to other religious bodies. In the process, a number of significant buildings have been lost or altered beyond recognition, though much of this, certainly in the last 40 years, has been as a result of declining congregations, a factor that has affected nearly all the churches of Western Europe. In the chapters that follow, we will look at the important heritage of post-Reformation church building in Scotland, chiefly for the Presbyterian churches, but also for the episcopal and Roman Catholic churches, small minorities in 1690, which were to see their fortunes change in the nineteenth century, and whose buildings are now as much a part of the Scottish architectural heritage as those of their Presbyterian competitors in a religiously pluralist society.

2

SCOTTISH CHURCH INTERIORS 1560–1690

1. *The adaptation of pre-reformation buildings*

Compared with England and many parts of mainland Europe, churches in pre-Reformation Scotland were generally on the small side. They were rarely designed to hold the whole population of a parish, certainly not seated, and were therefore ill-designed for post-Reformation worship of a type that involved extensive preaching, and therefore a requirement for the congregation to be seated.[1] The poor survival of pre-Reformation churches and the treatment of most of the cathedrals and larger parish churches in the post-Reformation period has, in the past, led to allegations that there was a whole-scale destruction of medieval buildings in the late sixteenth century. This was not, however, the case, though, as Gordon Donaldson has pointed out, it was a fact that many churches in Scotland were in poor condition after 1560 and therefore needed either extensive repairs or complete replacement.

> The suggestion that the reformers, as a matter of deliberate policy, destroyed parish churches, or had any desire to destroy parish churches, must be met by ridicule. They inherited the result of perhaps a generation of neglect, dilapidation and destruction, and their concern was not the demolition but the repair of churches required for parochial purposes.[2]

Indeed this objective had been clearly stated in the First Book of Discipline (1560) under the heading 'For Reparation of the Kirkes'.

---

[1] Todd, *Culture of Protestantism*, p. 45.
[2] Donaldson, *Scottish Reformation*, pp. 96, 99.

> Least that the word of God and ministration of the Sacraments by unseemlinesse of the place come in contempt, of necessity it is that the Kirk and the place where the people ought publickly to convene, be with expedition repaired with dores, windowes, thack, and with such preparation within as apperttaineth as well to the Majestie of God, as unto the ease and Commodity of the people.[3]

This requirement was reinforced by parliamentary legislation in 1563, and in 1568 action was taken against the parishioners of Alford for refusing to repair their church as they had been ordered. Relatively few new churches were built before 1600. Indeed the majority of pre-Reformation churches, repaired and often enlarged, remained in use until replaced in the great wave of church building in Scotland in the late eighteenth and early nineteenth centuries.[4]

There is no doubt that some cathedrals and large churches were treated in a somewhat cavalier fashion in the immediate post-Reformation period, but even here the action, which succeeding generations of Scottish antiquarians were to deplore, has to be placed in a practical contemporary context.

> The precise fate of a cathedral depended to some extent on whether it was necessary as a parish church. Where there was no centre of population around the cathedral and neither the need nor the resources for the maintenance of the whole building ... or where the population was served by an adequate parish church ... the cathedral was wholly or partly neglected from the outset. But where the cathedral was necessary for worship and there was a population with resources to maintain it, the cathedral was preserved.[5]

The truth of this statement is indeed documented by the fate of Scotland's thirteen pre-Reformation cathedrals. Those at Elgin and St Andrews were completely abandoned, and allowed to fall into ruins, as both towns had parish churches adequate to house the inhabitants. The cathedral at Fortrose was also abandoned in 1720, and that at Whithorn, where only the nave had remained in use, in 1822, when new, and more practical, parish churches replaced them. In other places it was found necessary to maintain only parts of the building: the naves at Aberdeen and Brechin; the chancels at Dunblane

---

[3] James Whyte, 'The Setting of Worship', *Studies in the History of Worship in Scotland*, ed. Duncan Forrester and Douglas Murray, 2nd edn, Edinburgh 1996, p. 141.
[4] Donaldson, *Scottish Reformation*, pp. 99–100.
[5] Ibid., p. 97.

and Dunkeld; and the chancel and transepts at Dornoch.[6] At Iona an attempt to convert parts of the cathedral into a parish church were abandoned and the building was not restored, and indeed largely rebuilt, until the early twentieth century. At Lismore the attempt to preserve part of the cathedral to serve as a parish church was more successful.[7] Only two of Scotland's cathedrals remained completely intact, though that at Glasgow was eventually divided into three separate churches: the crypt was used as Barony parish church from 1595; in 1635 the cathedral choir was walled off to form the church of the Inner Kirk congregation, and enlarged with galleries in 1657; in 1647 the five western bays of the cathedral nave were walled off and galleries constructed to form the church of the Outer Kirk congregation.[8] At Kirkwall, although only the choir was used for parochial worship, the rest of the building continued to be maintained and its roofs remained intact.[9]

Similar fates to that which befell Glasgow cathedral were also witnessed in some of the larger parish churches, those of St Nicholas at Aberdeen, St Mary at Dundee, St Giles at Edinburgh (briefly a cathedral in the seventeenth century), St John Baptist at Perth and the Holy Rude at Stirling being similarly divided into two or more churches. This was not the practice in the Netherlands and Switzerland, where medieval churches remained intact even if not all their parts were used for worship. Nor was it the case in England, where a permanent communion table was retained in the chancel, even if it might be moved to a more convenient location for the celebration of Holy Communion.[10] Although the Scottish reformers rejected the idea of a permanent communion table, placed in the chancel, the notion that they were reluctant to have permanent seating installed in churches, preferring parishioners to bring their own stools with them – it was the stool allegedly thrown at the celebrant of the 1637 liturgy in St Giles' Cathedral, Edinburgh, that was supposed to have sparked the campaign that resulted in the abolition of episcopacy in 1638 – is not supported by the surviving evidence. Margo Todd describes the late sixteenth century in Scotland as

> an era of pew-building. Kirk session minutes are cluttered with petitions for permission to construct 'seats' or 'desks' – pews with attached lecterns and sometimes canopies – for members of eminent families.[11]

---

[6] Peter Galloway, *The Cathedrals of Scotland*, Edinburgh 2000, *passim*.
[7] *BS Argyll and Bute*, pp. 363–5, 509–19.
[8] *BS Glasgow*, pp. 108–35.
[9] *BS Highland and Islands*, pp. 311–27.
[10] *BFW*, pp. 28, 31.
[11] Todd, *Culture of Protestantism*, p. 318.

Seating capacity in churches was increased by the erection of lofts (galleries) or 'degrees', benches banked in ascending height. Seating arrangements tended to reflect the social structure of the local community in Scotland as much as they did in England and Wales.[12] Seating and lofts in churches were generally erected by families, for themselves and their servants, at their own expense. Redundant chancels were frequently used by the principal landowner for the construction of handsome pews or lofts for use his own use and that of his family.[13] It may have been the case that before 1690 some of the poorer parishioners did bring their own stools with them to church, and place them in the unpewed parts of the building, but certainly by the eighteenth century the evidence of surviving church seating plans suggests that this practice had died out by then.

In addition to the installation of seating, Andrew Spicer has noted through his detailed examination of burgh and visitation records, much evidence of church repairs being carried out in the sixteenth century, especially in the towns. In the diocese of Dunblane in 1586, the visitors noted that the churches at Fowlis Wester and Tullyallan were furnished with seats, pulpits and communion tables, but that the church at Kincardine lacked 'a decent pulpit, communion table, honest settis for the pepill and a place for publict penitentis'.[14] Later on the newly established presbyteries took on the responsibility for ensuring that each parish had a church in proper repair. In 1600, the Presbytery of Aberdeen note that the church at Drumoak was now 'watter tight and wind tight' but that repairs were still needed to the walls and steeples. At Maryculter money needed to be raised for the 'reparatione and glassing' of the church.[15]

2. *Comparisons with other reformed churches*

We have already noted the different attitudes in Scotland to chancels compared with that in other Reformed churches in the Netherlands and Switzerland, and the 'quasi-reformed' Church of England before the Laudian transformation of that church in the early seventeenth century. The Scottish church differed from these Reformed churches in other ways. It was by far the most deeply iconoclastic of those churches in the Zwinglian and Calvinist tradition, eschewing virtually every form of decoration or symbolism as 'popish' and creating church interiors of extreme severity. In the Netherlands, when they

---

[12] *Ibid.*, pp. 46, 320; *BFW*, p. 37.
[13] Foster, *Bishop and Presbytery*, p. 124; Ian Lindsay, *The Scottish Parish Kirk*, Edinburgh 1960, pp. 38–9.
[14] Andrew Spicer, *Calvinist Churches in Early Modern Europe*, Manchester 2007, p. 48.
[15] *Ibid.*, p.76.

remodelled a medieval church, they often left the chancel screen intact or even created a new one, so that what had been the chancel at the east end of the church, could be used as a chapel for smaller events or as a meeting space.[16]

Sometimes the chancel was used as the place for laying out the communion tables. Dutch Reformed churches were normally furnished with painted boards inscribed with the Ten Commandments, Creed and Lord's Prayer. An exceptionally elaborate one of 1687 at Poortugaal is in the form of a triptych with the Commandments on the central panels and the Creed and Lord's Prayer on the inside of the doors. Post-Reformation pulpits were frequently elaborately carved, one at Augsbuur incorporating figures of Moses and Aaron displaying the Ten Commandments. Painted glass was permitted in the windows, with good examples of seventeenth- and eighteenth-century painted glass in the windows of the Oude Kerk at Amsterdam and at churches in Akkrum, Appingedam, Broek, Edam, Egmond aan den Hoef and Schermerhorn.[17] At Gouda, the surviving painted glass includes not only the, largely heraldic, windows installed after the Reformation, but also a number of pre-Reformation windows in which the content was considered to be wholly scriptural. At Naarden, the magnificent sixteenth-century painted roof, incorporating the judgement of souls and scenes of heaven and hell, together with scenes from the passion, death, resurrection and ascension of Christ, and from the Old Testament illustrating similar events that appeared to foretell them, such the ascension of Elijah into heaven, also survived the Reformation and remains intact. A similar conservatism was the case in Switzerland and it was compared, unfavourably, with what the author described as the 'mangling' of churches in Scotland.[18] A painting of the interior of Basel Minster in 1650 shows the pre-Reformation stalls intact in the choir.[19] At the former cathedral in Lausanne, the south portal, with its statues of the 12 apostles, was also left intact by the reformers.[20] In Hungary, the Calvinist churches were painted with scriptural texts, and the furniture – pulpit, minister's seat, gallery fronts and pews – tended to be painted as well, often in quite garish colours. As in Scotland, seating in Hungarian churches, as at Nádasdaróc, where it dates from 1687, was

---

[16] Richard Kieckhefer, *Theology in Stone: Church Architecture from Byzantium to Berkeley*, Oxford 2004, pp. 49–50.

[17] C.A. van Swigchem, T. Brouwer and W. van Os, *Een Huis voor het Woord: Het Protestantse Kerkinterieur in Nederland tot 1900*, The Hague 1984, pp. 154, 166, 174, 288, 290.

[18] A.L. Drummond, *The Church Architecture of Protestantism*, Edinburgh 1934, pp. 21–2.

[19] Lovibond, 'Use of Spaces', p. 98.

[20] Bernard Reymond, *L'Architecture Religieuse des Protestants*, Geneva 1996, p. 199.

distributed on the basis of social position, gender and age and the front seats were secured for the most eminent families of the congregation often on a hereditary basis. Two galleries, one across each of the short walls, was the norm, one being used by young men and the other by young women.[21]

Canopied seats for important people and tiered benches for the rest of the congregation was also the norm in Dutch churches in the seventeenth and eighteenth centuries. In the Netherlands, the canopied seats were normally placed against the pillars of the nave, or occasionally against the outer walls of the aisles, in a position where they had a clear view of the pulpit.[22] In Scotland the only surviving example of such a canopied pew is the magistrate's pew erected at St Columba's, Burntisland, in 1606 [Plate 1].[23]

In England, action against the deliberate destruction of pre-Reformation

Plate 1 Magistrates' Pew of 1606 at St Columba's, Burntisland

---

[21] Balázs Dercsenyi, Gábor Hegyi, Ernö Marosi and Bela Takács, *Calvinist Churches in Hungary*, Budapest 1992, p. xxxiii.
[22] Lovibond, 'Use of Spaces', p. 230; Van Swigchem et al., *Een Huis voor het Woord*, pp. 98–9, 116.
[23] *BS Fife*, p. 112.

furnishings had been taken by Archbishop Parker of Canterbury in 1566. He ordered the rood screens to be maintained *in situ* but all above the beam, the loft and the figures of Christ with Our Lady and St John, to be removed and replaced with the Royal Arms. When not in use for the communion service, the communion table was to be placed against the east wall of the chancel and the Ten Commandments, Creed and Lord's Prayer were to be inscribed on panels placed behind and above the table. Some relaxation of this requirement was made in 1604 when it was ordered that the table be placed

> in so good sort, within the church or chancel, as thereby the minister may be more conveniently heard of the communicants in his prayer and ministration, and the communicants also more conveniently, and in more number, may communicate with the said minister.[24]

From the 1620s this relaxation was reversed by the Laudian bishops, who ordered the altar to be placed against the east wall of the chancel and railed in, and for the Holy Communion to be celebrated with the altar still in this position, the celebrant standing at the north end of the table. The Canons of 1604 also ordered churches to be provided with 'a convenient seat ... for the minister to read service in' and for the provision of a stone font for baptism.[25]

The one Reformed church in which iconoclasm similar to that in Scotland seemed to be prevalent was that of France. The new churches built for the Reformed congregations in France in the seventeenth century were basically large spaces for a pulpit and seating. The plan of the church at Rouen before its destruction after the Revocation of the Edict of Nantes, which had guaranteed French Protestants freedom of worship since 1598, in 1685, shows a twelve-sided building with galleries supported on pillars. The two Reformed churches shown in a plan of La Rochelle in 1620 were, respectively, square and hexagonal. At Charenton, near Paris, an illustration of 1648 shows a rectangular church with a double row of galleries around all four sides of the interior and the pulpit placed against one of the short walls.[26] These were all theatre-type buildings, totally devoid of any 'popish' ornamentation, in which the pulpit took the place of the stage.

There was greater similarity between Scotland and the Reformed churches in Europe on the matter of internal arrangement in the post-Reformation period. Apart from the Church of England, most abandoned the use of a

---

[24] G.W.O. Addleshaw and F. Etchells, *The Architectural Setting of Anglican Worship*, London 1948, p. 109.
[25] *BFW*, pp. 31–4.
[26] Reymond, *L'Architecture Religieuse*, pp. 53–4, 100, 143.

font, preferring instead to baptize from 'a ewer or basin set on a table or bracketed from the pulpit'.[27] The latter was the standard practice in Scotland, though a late eighteenth-century bowl on a stand is preserved at Ceres (Fife).[28] There was also general agreement about the relationship of the pulpit to the seating, with the preferred arrangement before 1700 being either the placing of the pulpit on one of the long sides of the nave or the creation of a T-plan interior with seating facing the pulpit from three different directions. As we shall see, such arrangements were very common in Scotland until well into the nineteenth century. They were replicated in the Netherlands, Switzerland, Hungary and other parts of the British Isles. Pulpits were placed in the middle of the long sides of the nave at St Peter's, Leiden, the Grote Kerk at Hoorn and the Westerkerk and Zuiderkerk at Amsterdam. There were similar arrangements in Switzerland, shown in nineteenth-century illustrations of the former cathedral of St Peter and the church of St Gervase at Geneva, and the former collegiate church at Neuchâtel, and an eighteenth-century plan of the church at St Imier.[29]

One major difference in the internal arrangement of churches within what might be termed the north-western manifestation of the Reformed tradition, compared to that in south-eastern Europe, was that for communion. Bernard Reymond may slightly over-emphasize this point when he states that Scotland and the Netherlands were the exception rather than the norm in the Reformed tradition in not having a permanent communion table placed in a central position in their buildings,[30] but it certainly was the case that Calvinists in France, the Netherlands and Scotland eventually opted for sitting communion around temporary tables, adopted also by Presbyterians in Ireland and Puritans in England and Wales, whereas their co-religionists in Hungary, Switzerland and the southern parts of Germany adopted the permanent communion table which the congregation walked past to receive communion. In Switzerland, where it was common also to have a font for baptism placed in a central position in the church, it was not unusual for the font to be used as the base of the communion table and for an oval board to be placed over it when communion took place. This was the case in the church at Chavornay. More usual, however, was for the font and communion table to stand separately, either in front of the pulpit or in the middle of the seating.[31]

---

[27] Lovibond, 'Use of Spaces', p. 70
[28] See Appendix C/24.
[29] Bernard Reymond, *Temples de Suisse Romande*, Yens and St Gingolph 1997, pp. 28, 32, 41, 47.
[30] Reymond, *L'Architecture Religieuse*, p. 31.
[31] *Ibid.*, pp. 31–2.

The Nieuwe Kerk at Emden, built in 1647, is an early European example of a T-plan church, of which there were more or less contemporary Scottish examples at Anstruther Easter (Fife), Careston (Angus), Dunlop (Ayrshire), Kirkmaiden (Dumfries and Galloway) and Pitsligo (Aberdeenshire).[32] It is important at this point to note that George Hay was incorrect in believing that the T-plan design 'must be regarded as a peculiarly Scottish manifestation'.[33] Apart from some examples in mainland Europe, including Lutheran ones at the Nykirken in Bergen and Valleberga (Sweden), T-plan churches are common in Ireland – for Church of Ireland and Roman Catholic buildings as well as Presbyterian ones – England and Wales. The earliest English example, Little Hadham (Herts), shown in a plan of 1692, and still substantially intact, may date from the very end of the sixteenth century and is therefore older than any known Scottish example of this arrangement.[34] Placing the pulpit on one of the long walls was also not an uncommon Anglican arrangement, and can still be seen in surviving seventeenth-century examples at Wilby (Norf), refitted after a fire in 1637–1638, Bramhope (Yorks) of 1649, Balinderry (Antrim) of 1664–1668 and Disserth (Powys) of c. 1687.[35]

Only one church in Scotland built before 1690 departed from either the long-wall or T-plan arrangements and this was St Columba's, Burntisland. The parishioners had petitioned for a new church in 1589 and the new building was probably in use by 1596. It was built as an exact square, the four central pillars supporting a later belfry and steeple. Between about 1600 and 1630 the four 'aisles' around the central space acquired galleries or lofts erected by the town's trade guilds. The body of the church has been much altered over the years, with a mix of eighteenth- and nineteenth-century box pews and a central space re-ordered in 1926 with a new pulpit, font and communion table [Plate 1]. Previously the central space had been occupied by a series of table pews with movable divisions.[36] In the Netherlands, a new type of Reformed church, designed as an octagon, was developed during the seventeenth century, but it was not replicated in Scotland until late in the following century. These early Dutch examples included the Marekerk of 1638–1640 in Leiden, the Oostkerk of 1646–1667 in Middelburg and the churches of 1653 at Sappemeer and 1682 at St Annaparochie.[37] Another important difference between Dutch and Swiss churches on the one hand, and Scottish churches on the other, was that many

---

[32] Lovibond, 'Use of Spaces', p. 144; *SPC*, pp. 53–5.
[33] *Ibid.*, p. 52.
[34] *BFW*, pp. 93–6; see also Yates, *Religious Condition of Ireland*, pp. 232–6.
[35] *BFW*, p. 79.
[36] *BS Fife*, pp. 110–12, Plates 18 and 19; *SPC*, pp. 32–4, Plates 2, 29b and 43b.
[37] Lovibond, 'Use of Spaces', p. 231; Van Swigchem et al., *Een Huis voor het Woord*, p. 112.

of the former made provision for an organ whereas no such requirement was even considered in Scotland before the nineteenth century. The use of an organ was much debated by the various Reformed churches and nowhere more enthusiastically than in the Netherlands, where town churches were the property of the municipality and, in a sense, 'loaned' to the minister to conduct Sunday worship. Whereas many ministers deprecated the use of organs in worship as 'popish' and unscriptural, the municipalities preferred to retain the organs, at least for non-ecclesiastical use. A visitor to the Grote Kerk in Rotterdam in 1679 noted two organs,

> one small single and one double and very large one with great variety in it. On this, the organist playes several voluntryes each Saturday after 6 in the afternoon. And on Sundays he plays the tune of the psalme immediately before it is sung but playes not while they are singing.[38]

This rather unsatisfactory compromise and a growing realization by many within the Dutch Reformed Church that congregational singing was improved by organ accompaniment rather than relying on the competence of a *voorsanger*, the Dutch equivalent of the Scottish precentor, resulted in more and more churches adopting use of the organ in worship, a situation which had become virtually universal within the Netherlands, even in village churches, by the end of the eighteenth century. A good example of this development was the Westerkerk in Amsterdam. Built as a new church between 1620 and 1638, it was designed without any provision for an organ. However, in 1685–1686, a gallery was built across one of the short walls specifically to house an organ.[39]

3. *The first new churches in Scotland*

Work on the arrangement of Scottish church interiors before 1690 is almost entirely speculative. There are no surviving interiors from the seventeenth century, and with the possible exception of the church at Inverallan,[40] no surviving plans or illustrations of such interiors. Apart from the church at Burntisland, very few new churches were built in Scotland in the late sixteenth century. The exceptions were Kemback (Fife) 1582, Kilmaveonaig

---

[38] Centre for Kentish Studies, Maidstone, U951 C24, Journal of a tour to the Netherlands, 1679.
[39] Kieckhefer, *Theology in Stone*, p. 51; Lovibond, 'Use of Spaces', p. 242; Reymond, *L'Architecture Religieuse*, p. 106.
[40] NAS, GD248/85/1. The plan is undated but is in a bundle of materials dating from the late seventeenth and early eighteenth centuries.

(Perthshire) and Greenock, both 1591, and Prestonpans (East Lothian) 1595. Only fragmentary remains of the first and last of these churches survive. The church at Prestonpans was financed by the minister and by Lord and Lady Preston. After 1600, the pace of new church building increased, with new churches at Dirleton (1612), Dairsie (1621), Anwoth (1627), Portpatrick (1629), Auchterhouse (1630), Kingsbarns (1630), South Queensferry (1633), Anstruther Easter (1634) and Elie (1639).[41] One of the most interesting of these new churches was that of the Greyfriars, Edinburgh, built between 1612 and 1620. Whereas the church at Burntisland had attempted to create a building which radically departed from the pre-Reformation model of the rectangular building, Greyfriars was extremely traditional in its design, an aisled rectangle with the pulpit placed in the middle of one of the long sides of the nave. In 1718, Greyfriars was enlarged to accommodate two separate congregations, but the dividing wall between them was removed, and the churches refurnished, in 1938.[42] James Kirk sees this programme of church building as a 'sign of consolidation and confidence' within the Church of Scotland, one that even extended to the highland parishes with new or repaired churches at Ardclach, Convinth, Edinkillie, Kiltarlity, Kincardine, Kingussie and Urquhart and Glenmoriston.[43]

At St Giles', Edinburgh, raised to cathedral status to serve the new diocese of Edinburgh in 1633, much work was done on the interior, the dean having visited the cathedral at Durham to see how the interior of his own cathedral might be improved. This work was carried out in 1636–1637. Repairs were also carried out at the cathedrals at Dornoch, Dunkeld and Kirkwall in 1630s, as well as at the church of Holy Trinity, St Andrews, which had been designated to replace the former cathedral of the diocese.[44]

Despite the lack of surviving evidence, the assumption has been that Scottish churches, in general, probably looked in the seventeenth century much like they did in the eighteenth. According to G. D. Henderson, the average church was

> a bare hall with probably one or two lofts or galleries, the pulpit in the middle . . . with a sandglass attached, and a ring for holding the basin of water on baptismal occasions; beneath the pulpit the lattron or reader's desk; somewhere close by the stool of repentance or pillar or pillarie; in some churches also a special seat for the elders; the rest of

---

[41] Todd, *Culture of Protestantism*, pp. 46–7; Foster, *Church Before the Covenants*, p. 174.
[42] Lindsay, *Scottish Parish Kirk*, pp. 42–3.
[43] James Kirk, 'The Jacobean Church in the Highlands' 1567–1625', *The Seventeenth Century in the Highlands*, ed. L. MacLean, Inverness 1986, p. 40; *Patterns of Reform*, p. 476.
[44] Spicer, *Calvinist Churches*, pp. 82–5.

the church divided into sections where stood the 'dasks' of the various heritors and their tenants and in some churches . . . a part set aside for women. . . . When Communion was observed the middle of the church was cleared to make room for the long table round which the members gathered.[45]

By the 1620s, these arrangements were at variance with the requirements of the Articles of Perth but there is not much evidence to indicate that Scottish churches were altered to accommodate a more Anglican type of liturgy. The church at Dairsie, built by Archbishop Spottiswoode of St Andrews in 1621, was an exception. Here a rectangular building was divided into a nave and a separate raised chancel with a screen displaying the Royal Arms, but none of the original furnishings survive.[46] When James VI and I had the royal chapel at Holyrood repaired before his visit to Scotland, 'organs . . . were sent up from England'. By Whit Sunday 1617 the chapel

> had been fitted out with an altar, candles and an organ. Choristers sang the service, the English liturgy was used and the bishops and nobles knelt to take Communion.[47]

There is some evidence that a few other Scottish churches might have also adopted quasi-Anglican furnishings and liturgical arrangements. In 1642, Principal William Guild of Aberdeen was 'busy with the destruction of a timber screen at St Machar's Cathedral'.[48] Architectural evidence, however, suggests that such examples were untypical. The ground plan of Durness church, built in 1619, only two years earlier than Dairsie, shows one of the earliest examples of the typical Scottish T-plan arrangement with the pulpit placed centrally on the long wall and all the seating arranged to face it.[49]

In addition to the need for new churches in the early seventeenth century, a number of existing churches were also in need of extensive repairs. In 1611, a visitation by Archbishop Gladstanes of St Andrews revealed that, out of nineteen churches for which there was a report on the fabric, five needed urgent repairs and fourteen were in good repair. In the presbytery of Ellon in 1607, there were only two churches fit for worship. In 1617 the Scottish parliament required

---

[45] D. Henderson, *Religious Life in Seventeenth Century Scotland*, Cambridge 1937, pp. 154, 193.
[46] *BS Fife*, p. 169.
[47] MacDonald, *Jacobean Kirk*, p. 158.
[48] Henderson, *Religious Life*, p. 192.
[49] David MacGibbon and Thomas Ross, *The Ecclesiastical Architecture of Scotland from the Earliest Times to the Seventeenth Century*, 3 vols, Edinburgh 1897, iii, p. 558.

that all the paroche kirkis within this Kingdome be prowydit off Basines and Lavoiris for the Ministratioun of the sacrament of Baptisme and of Couppes tablis and table Clothes for the ministratioun of the holy Communione.

No fewer than 43 parishes in Scotland still retain communion vessels made in the early seventeenth century.[50] The surviving accounts for Brechin cathedral in 1638–1642 'feature an extraordinary amount of repairs to the windows of the kirk. It would seem that nearly every window in the kirk received new glazing'. The pulpit stood 'in the middle bay of the south arcade'. In 1615, a new central chandelier was purchased to light the cathedral and the kirk session accounts record regular amounts for cleaning this chandelier and the purchase of candles. In 1649, the floor of the cathedral was 'levelled and paved'. Arrangements for communion comprised two long tables in the middle of the nave and a small cross-table used by the minister. The cross-table was bought in 1619 and the long tables renewed and given new benches, at a cost of four pounds, in 1658.[51] Some of the woodwork in the church at Lyne (Borders) dates from the 1640s, including two canopied pews, against the back wall of the nave, and a pulpit

> which, it is usually stated, was made in Holland. Lyne is distant from the sea and must have been difficult of access; for which reason, amongst others, we doubt whether there is any truth in the tradition. The pulpit, which is circular, in plan, is quite simple in design, and its construction would not present a formidable task to a Scottish country wright, judging by other examples of woodwork made in Scotland about this time.[52]

These included the almost contemporary pulpit, on a stone base and with a low backboard, made for St Cuthbert's, Edinburgh, in 1651–1652, and the surviving pulpits of 1655 at Ayr and c.1687 at Yester.[53]

4. *Scottish churches in the late seventeenth century*

An English visitor to Scotland has recorded his opinion of the nation's churches in the late seventeenth century.

---

[50] Foster, *Church before the Covenants*, pp. 173, 175–6.
[51] D.B. Thomas, *The Kirk of Brechin in the Seventeenth Century*, Perth 1972, pp. 57, 67–8, 78.
[52] MacGibbon and Ross, *Ecclesiastical Architecture*, iii, p. 591.
[53] *Ibid.*, iii, p. 563; *SPC*, p. 185.

In the country, they are poor and mean, covered no better than their ordinary Cottages. . . . But in the Boroughs and Cities, they are Brick'd and Tile'd, and well enough furnished with Galleries and other Conveniences for the Parishioners. The Precentor's Desk is under the Pulpit, and under him the Stool of Penance, or rather a bench for five or six to sit on, to be seen by the Congregation, and bear the Shame of their Crimes. . . . Chancels they have none, nor Altars.[54]

Arrangements of this type for penitential discipline, though practised by other Protestants, seem to have been peculiar to Scotland. Few examples of penitents' platforms still survive, though they do at Bourtie (Aberdeenshire) and Duirinish (Highland),[55] but there are more surviving examples, mostly in the southern lowlands, of the jougs, 'an iron collar . . . secured by a chain to the wall of the kirk', in which penitents accused of breaches of church discipline, 'such as drunkenness, immorality, sabbath-breaking', were displayed before being brought into church to stand or sit on the penitents' platform and being publicly rebuked by the minister.[56] The distinction between rural and urban churches, as far as the maintenance of church fabrics was concerned, reflected a state of affairs which was not fully addressed until the nineteenth century. In 1665, the minister of Lochbroom complained to the presbytery of Dingwall that 'he has not a convenient meeting place for preaching, the Kirk of Lochbroom being unthatched' and in 1681 the same presbytery noted that 'their churches were Werie ruinous'.[57] However, at Brechin, extensive improvements continued to be made to the cathedral: 'in 1676 the West Window alone was repaired . . . at a cost of £160, and within a year another £100 was spent on . . . the other windows'. The kirk session accounts show that between 1661 and 1677 the pulpit and precentor's desk were 'draped in green silk'. Brackets were attached to the pulpit for the baptismal bowl and the sermon glass. The former was renewed in 1673 at a cost of £28 and a new sermon glass was bought for £14 in 1668. During the late seventeenth century thirty new pews were erected in the cathedral, paid for by their owners, though this resulted in a situation where 'the new pews threatened to trespass upon the free space in the centre of the nave reserved for the communion tables'. There were also eight lofts in the cathedral, one reserved as a royal pew in case the monarch should visit the cathedral, one belonging to the Earl of Panmure, and the remainder allotted to the city's trade guilds.[58] Another town church in which

---

[54] Foster, *Bishop and Presbytery*, p. 122.
[55] See Appendix B/7 and C/2.
[56] *SPC*, p. 240.
[57] Foster, *Bishop and Presbytery*, pp. 123–4.
[58] Thomas, *Kirk of Brechin*, pp. 57, 66, 69–72.

considerable refurbishment took place in the late seventeenth century was St Michael's, Linlithgow, which was re-seated in 1671–1672. Only the nave was used for worship with burials taking place in the chancel and transepts. The pulpit was placed in the middle of the south side of the nave with 19 pews facing east, 26 facing south and 10 facing west. There were also five lofts, three on the north side, allocated respectively to the king, the Earl of Linlithgow and the burgh magistrates, and two each side of the pulpit assigned to the town's trade guilds. In 1672, a further trade guild loft was erected across the west end of the nave.[59]

Compared with England and Wales, where religious changes during the seventeenth century meant both the destruction of many furnishings in the 1640s and 1650s, and their replacement during the last four decades of the century, the pattern of church design and furnishing in Scotland was much less disrupted. The evidence is that few churches altered their internal arrangements to create more Anglican interiors, and therefore there was no need for church interiors to be altered with the abolition of episcopacy. Indeed certain aspects of church arrangement in Scotland, such as the division of large buildings for the use of separate congregations, were imported to England. At Exeter, in the 1640s and 1650s, the cathedral choir was used by the Presbyterians and the nave by the Independents.[60] After the restoration of episcopacy in 1660–1662 churches in England and Wales had to be returned to their pre-1640 liturgical arrangements. In particular, Anglican bishops and archdeacons insisted that churches must have a permanent altar and that it must be placed against the east wall of the chancel and railed in. In the diocese of Rochester Archdeacon John Warner used his 1670 visitation to order several churches to place their altars in the correct position and to install altar rails. At Brenchley, he ordered 'the seats at the upper end of the chancel to be removed and the communion table to be sett up there and railed in as formerly'. Several Anglican churches were also provided with new chancel screens in the late seventeenth century and even later, with screens of 1727 at St Paul's Walden (Herts), 1729 at Crowcombe (Som), 1796 at Thorpe Market (Norf) and 1821 at Haccombe (Devon).[61]

Just as no attempt was made during the second episcopacy to impose an Anglican liturgy on the Church of Scotland, no attempt was made to alter existing church interiors. Indeed the consistency with which Scottish churches were arranged and furnished between the late seventeenth and the early nineteenth centuries makes it difficult to date them without specific documentary evidence. What is even more remarkable, as we shall see, was that post-1690 episcopalians operating outside the Church of Scotland

---

[59] John Ferguson, *Ecclesia Antiqua* Edinburgh 1905, pp. 85–6.
[60] Drummond, *Architecture of Protestantism*, p. 41.
[61] *BFW*, pp. 33–4.

maintained an attitude to church arrangement which made their buildings virtually indistinguishable from Presbyterian ones. Even when a fixed communion table was introduced, it was normally placed in the middle of the church, in front of the pulpit and precentor's desk, as it was in some Anglican churches in Ireland, such as Clonguish or Timogue,[62] or at Old Devonshire Church, Bermuda, until 1767.[63] There is no doubt that the classic Scottish church interior, which we will examine in much greater detail in the next two chapters, was created in the seventeenth century, and it is unfortunate that no complete building, and indeed remarkably few individual furnishings, should survive from this deeply formative period in Scottish religious history.

---

[62] Yates, *Religious Condition of Ireland*, pp. 232, 234, 369–60.
[63] *BFW*, p. 97.

3

PRESBYTERIAN CHURCH INTERIORS 1690–1860: WORSHIP AND THE CARE OF BUILDINGS

1. Presbyterian worship

The Church of Scotland, as constituted in 1690 without bishops, had as its liturgical standard the *Westminster Directory* of 1644. The *Directory* was not a liturgy in the sense that Knox's *Book of Common Order* had been or the Anglican *Book of Common Prayer*, in use in England, Ireland and Wales, was. It was no more than a guide to the minister; though the way individual ministers interpreted the document seems to have been fairly standard, so that a worship norm can be established without difficulty. It was perhaps ironic that the Church of Scotland should have based its worship on an English Puritan model, having deliberately rejected a book composed by Scottish clergy, albeit the despised bishops, in 1637–1638. There is no doubt that later Scottish liturgists regretted this and would have preferred the Church of Scotland either to have amended the 'bishops' book by removing its doctrinally unacceptable elements, or to have returned to the Genevan model of Knox's *Book of Common Order*. In 1694, the General Assembly passed an Act which recommended that 'ministers.... read and open up to the people some large and considerable portion of the Word of God'.[1] The result was the 'lecture' or a detailed exposition of a frequently fairly short, passage of Scripture, as the chief feature of the service after the sermon.[2] This pattern lasted until well into the nineteenth century. Sunday worship at Redgorton in 1843 comprised a psalm, opening prayer,

---

[1] Maxwell, *History of Worship*, p. 128.
[2] Henry Sefton, 'Revolution to Disruption', *Studies in the History of Worship*, ed. Forrester and Murray, p. 80.

lecture, sermon, second prayer and closing psalm.[3] The general posture of the congregation was sitting, except for standing for prayer, and men kept their hats on. Ministers abandoned the traditional Genevan gown, associated with episcopal practice before 1690, for blue cloaks and three-cornered hats, though the Geneva gown was beginning to be re-introduced at the same time that Episcopalians were beginning to replace the black gown, except for preaching, with the surplice in the early nineteenth century.[4] When there were two Sunday services the congregation frequently retired to a local hostelry for refreshment, unless their homes were nearby. The lairds used the retiring room behind their lofts as places of refreshment and relaxation between services.[5] The people were summoned to worship by the ringing of the church bell. At the second ringing of the bell the congregation entered the church and the service began with a psalm led by the precentor, the precentor singing the line and the congregation repeating it. At the third ringing of the bell the minister entered and after a long extempore prayer began the lecture: 'in a non-stop solo performance the minister proceeded from the lecture to prayer to the sermon proper'. After the sermon there was a further long extempore prayer, a psalm and the benediction. If there was an afternoon service the pattern tended to follow that of the morning, but with the omission of the lecture. In some parishes, the afternoon service was replaced with public catechizing.[6]

Holy Communion was celebrated very infrequently in most churches between 1690 and 1860. Some ministers refused to celebrate at all on the grounds of there being too few parishioners 'worthy' to receive the sacrament or the churches being out of repair. The Orkney island of Shapinsay had not had a celebration for 50 years in 1795 and possessed no communion cups, cloths or tables. At Muckhart there was no celebration between 1734 and 1786. These were, however, fairly extreme cases. The usual pattern was once or twice, occasionally four times, a year. Parishes frequently joined forces for communion services, making them very large affairs indeed. At Culross (Fife) in 1708 the communicants came from 19 or 20 neighbouring parishes as well as Culross itself. It is, however, a myth that communion was celebrated in the churchyards because of lack of space in the churches. Communicants did, however, wait in the churchyard for their turn to receive communion and tents were frequently erected to shelter the ministers who preached to them. At some services there might be as many as 30 sittings for

---

[3] A.L. Drummond and J. Bulloch, *The Church in Victorian Scotland 1843–1874*, Edinburgh 1975, p. 179.
[4] Maxwell, *History of Worship*, pp. 129–31.
[5] Sefton, 'Revolution to Disruption', p. 82.
[6] W.P.L. Thomson, 'The Eighteenth Century Church in Orkney', *Light in the North*, ed. H.W.M. Cant and H.N. Firth, Kirkwall 1989, p. 61.

communion and the service could take all Sunday. Communion services normally lasted at least an hour, sometimes two, and occasionally even four.[7] Open-air communion was a feature of the secessionist Presbyterian churches and not the established Church of Scotland, apart from a few examples, subsequently highly mythologized, of Covenanters' communion services in the seventeenth century. Holy Communion did not just comprise the Sunday set apart for the sacrament, but a period of 5 days known as the 'communion season'. It consisted of

> Thursday, the fast day. Friday was the day of self-examination and the fellowship meeting. Saturday was a day of preparation at which the tokens would be distributed. The Sabbath was the day of communion and the Monday was a day of thanksgiving. ... Lord Teignmouth described a Skye Communion in Sleat in the early nineteenth century. He described the tables as made of long planks of wood about two feet in breadth ... covered by a white cloth ... the ministers took their places at the head of the tables and gave a short message, distinct from the sermon, before the bread and the wine was passed round. When this was done, the ministers would address each table again and those at each table would then rise to make way for others who would again be spoken to and served by the ministers.[8]

One reason, in addition to their length, for the infrequency of communion services was the cost of holding them. At Cadder, as late as 1852,

> there being no allowance by the Heritors for defraying expenses connected with the dispensation of the sacrament of the Lord's Supper, the session agreed to allow the minister the sum of 5 pounds for each occasion.[9]

Communion services were generally more frequent in urban parishes than rural ones but the practice was very similar. John Wesley noted that at St Cuthbert's Edinburgh, in 1764,

> two long communion tables were set on the sides of one aisle covered with tablecloths. Each table had four or five and thirty. Three ministers sat at the top behind a cross table.[10]

---

[7] Burnet, *Holy Communion*, pp. 225–7, 233.
[8] Ansdell, *People of the Great Faith*, pp. 114–15.
[9] MLGA, CH2/863/3, 14 March 1852.
[10] Drummond and Bulloch, *Church in Victorian Scotland*, p. 179.

The whole process was 'simple in form, solemn in character, and inordinately long'.[11]

Another feature of Scottish worship was the total lack of music in the services. The metrical psalms were sung to one of twelve common tunes, following the practice of lining, the congregation repeating the line sung by the precentor. Any attempt to introduce new tunes was almost universally resisted, though Thomas Bruce's *Common Tunes*, published in 1726, added eight new tunes to the traditional twelve. The title of the psalm tune to be sung was normally given out by the precentor by placing the title of the tune on a card at the front of his desk. These psalm-tune cards and their holder still survive in the church at Glenbuchat (Appendix C/3). The office of precentor was frequently combined with that of reader, the person responsible for leading worship in the absence of a minister, and also that of schoolmaster. At Heriot in 1759 the precentor was also the schoolmaster, 'session-clerk, beadle, and grave-digger, and yet his whole income does not exceed £8 per annum'. He normally occupied a desk below the pulpit and 'quite commonly wore a black stuff gown, and sometimes even bands'.[12] During the eighteenth century dissatisfaction with the state of church music in Scotland grew, as it had done a century earlier in the Netherlands. However, whereas the Dutch had replaced their *voorsanger* with organ accompaniment, the solution adopted in Scotland was to replace the precentor with a professional choir and choirmaster. The first Scottish church to do this was Monymusk, under the influence of the principal heritor, Sir Archibald Grant, second baronet, in 1748. This innovation could, however, be controversial. When a choir began to sing the psalms at St Nicholas West, Aberdeen, in January 1755, the kirk session passed a resolution stating that such an arrangement should not be continued 'and they appoint their precentors to sing only, in all time coming, the twelve tunes commonly sung in churches in Scotland'. However, by the same date, in addition to Monymusk, choirs had been successfully introduced in ten other Aberdeenshire parishes: Cluny, Kemnay, Midmar, Kintore (where the choir loft was erected in 1754), Fintray, Rayne, Old Meldrum, Kennethmont, Towie and Drumoak.[13] A choir was introduced at Paisley Abbey in 1807 and the *Paisley Abbey Congregational Psalmody* published in 1850.[14] In the western highlands and islands of Scotland, services were held in both English and Gaelic. The

---

[11] G.R. Cragg, *The Church and the Age of Reason 1648–1789*, 2nd edn, Harmondsworth 1966, p. 85.
[12] Millar Patrick, *Four Centuries of Scottish Psalmody*, London 1949, pp. 121, 123, 129–30, 133–4. See also D. Johnson, *Music and Society in Lowland Scotland in the Eighteenth Century*, Oxford 1972.
[13] Patrick, *Four Centuries*, pp. 150, 153, 160.
[14] *Ibid.*, pp. 193–4.

normal practice was one service each Sunday in each language but at Tongue there were two Sunday services in Gaelic and only one in English.[15]

Dissatisfaction with the state of worship in the Presbyterian churches of Scotland, which extended well beyond the state of church music, had begun by the late eighteenth century. The length of extempore prayers, lectures and sermons was the main problem. Some extempore prayers could last 15 or 20 minutes and the sermon usually lasted for at least 50 minutes. In an effort to provide a better structure for the church's services, Henry Robertson, minister of Kiltearn 1776–1815, published *The Scottish Minister's Assistant* in 1802. It contained three forms of marriage service, forms for baptism with six discourses, six discourses for the fencing of communion tables, six communion addresses, two exhortations to conclude the communion service, two prayers over the elements, a form of ministerial ordination, a form of prayer for visiting the sick, four sets of prayers for before and after the sermon and three sets of family prayers, morning and evening. In 1829, A. G. Carstairs, minister of Anstruther Wester 1805–1838, published *The Scotch Communion Office*, containing services for each of the 5 days of the traditional communion season. In 1843, William Liston, minister of Redgorton 1812–1864, published *The Service of the House of God*, which provided forms of service for Sundays, fast days, communion, ordination, baptism and marriage. This was quickly followed by Alexander Brunton's *Forms for Public Worship in the Church of Scotland*, published in 1848. Brunton, minister of New Greyfriars, Edinburgh, between 1803 and 1809, and subsequently minister of the city's Tron Church, provided four forms of Sunday service, services for parochial visiting, baptism, communion, marriage, the ordination and induction of ministers and the ordination of elders.[16]

There was also an attempt to increase the frequency of communion. John Erskine, minister of New Greyfriars, Edinburgh, 1758–1767, and Old Greyfriars 1767–1803, published *An Attempt to Promote the Frequent Dispensing of the Lord's Supper* in 1783. This advocated a minimum of four communion seasons, with preparatory fasts, each year.[17] Acts had indeed been passed even earlier by the General Assembly of the Church of Scotland, encouraging more frequent communion, in 1712, 1724 and 1751.[18] These attempts were, however, largely unsuccessful until fairly well into the nineteenth century. Evangelicals, in particular, were moving

---

[15] C.W.J. Withers, *Gaelic in Scotland 1698–1981*, Edinburgh 1984, p. 177.
[16] Drummond and Bulloch, *Church in Victorian Scotland*, p. 180; J.A. Laws, 'Aids to Public Worship in Scotland 1800–1850', *RSCHS*, xiii (1959), pp. 174–7.
[17] *Ibid.*, p. 173.
[18] John MacInnes, *The Evangelical Movement in the Highlands of Scotland 1688–1800*, Aberdeen 1951, p. 101.

in a different direction by aiming to restrict communion to the truly worthy. The impact of this on some highland and island parishes can be seen in the statistics contained in Table 3. In some parishes, such Barvas and Stornoway in Lewis, fewer than a tenth of the attenders at the parish church were considered worthy to be admitted to communion. This attitude was reflected by the kirk session of Cadder in 1820 when it

> took into consideration the arrangement necessary for the orderly celebration of the Holy Communion. . . . They were particularly anxious that every thing . . . should be conducted with decency and order and, especially that none should be allowed to partake of the Gospel Feast but such as produced testimonials if strangers and such as they thought in Christian Charity worthy if parishioners.[19]

Gradually, however, some parishes did begin to introduce more frequent communion services. At Eastwood, in 1854,

> the session on the recommendation of the moderator unanimously and cordially agreed to have a third annual dispensation of the sacrament of the Lord's Supper in the parish church. . . . They also resolved that whatever services they might agree to have upon the occasion, they would not lay upon the parish the obligation of a general fast.[20]

Attitudes were beginning to change but only very slowly.

One major change, pioneered in the first quarter of the nineteenth century, was the abandonment of the traditional practice of receiving communion at tables. In an effort to reduce the length of the communion service, distribution to the people in their own seats began at St John's, Glasgow, in 1824. Although the practice was condemned by the General Assembly of the Church of Scotland in both 1825 and 1826, it gradually spread throughout the established church and was widely adopted by the Free Church of Scotland after 1843. A later innovation took place in 1857 when, after the reopening of Old Greyfriars Church in Edinburgh after a fire, the minister

> invited the congregation to kneel for prayer and to stand for praise, and the prayers were read from a printed liturgy which he had composed.

Previously Scottish congregations had sat throughout most of the service.

---

[19] MLGA, CH2/863/3, 3 August 1820.
[20] MLGA, CH2/119/3, 27 December 1854.

Table 3 Comparison of attenders and communicants in selected highland and island parishes in 1837

Presbytery	Parish	Attenders	Communicants
Islay and Jura	Kildalton	600	235
	Kilarrow	1,400	449
	Kilchoman	1,500	202
Lorn	Kilbrandon	1,100	450
	Oban	560	360
	Duror	300	170
Skye	Sleat	900	222
	Kilmuir	700	81
	Duirinish	750	350
Lewis	Lochs	1,000	120
	Stornoway	1,200	45
	Barvas	450	12
Tongue	Eddrachillis	350	70
	Durness	350	70
	Tongue	1,000	108

Source: MacInnes, A. I. (1990), 'Evangelical Protestantism in the nineteenth-century highlands', *Sermons and Battle Hymns: People and Protestant Culture in Modern Scotland*, Ed. Graham Walker and Tom Gallagher, Edinburgh, p. 50.

The minister, Robert Lee, was condemned by his own presbytery but in 1859 the General Assembly permitted the new liturgical postures but not the use of a printed form of service, which it described as 'an innovation upon and contrary to the laws and usages of the Church in the celebration of public worship'.[21] There was further pressure after 1800 for the reform of church music. Here the initiative had been taken by some of the secessionist Presbyterian churches. The Relief Church was the first to adopt the practice of singing hymns in addition to metrical psalms in worship, publishing its first hymnal in 1794. The United Presbyterian Church, a merger of the Relief and Secession churches, published a hymnal in 1852, whereas the Church of Scotland did not do so until 1870, and the Free Church until 1873.[22] In 1807 St Andrew's, Glasgow, attempted to introduce the use of an organ to accompany the singing. The minister and congregation had first petitioned Glasgow town council to permit the installation of an organ behind the pulpit in 1806. The minister, William Ritchie, had attended universities in Germany and the Netherlands and had, therefore, witnessed the use of

---

[21] Drummond and Bulloch, *Church in Victorian Scotland*, pp. 190, 193; Ian McCraw, *Victorian Dundee at Worship*, Dundee 2002, p. 96; W.M. Bryce, *History of the Old Greyfriars*, Edinburgh 1912, p. 148.
[22] Patrick, *Four Centuries*, pp. 218–19.

organs in Reformed churches. The council refused its consent without the permission of the presbytery of Glasgow. However, the minister and congregation got around the prohibition by acquiring the council's consent to certain minor alterations to the building, during which a small chamber organ was installed, designed to assist psalmody practice. It was not used during worship until 23 August 1807, when it was used at the Sunday afternoon service. The presbytery condemned this innovation as 'contrary to the law and constitution of our Established Church', and on 7 October Ritchie gave the presbytery an assurance that the innovation would not be repeated. In the following year, he left Glasgow to become Professor of Divinity and minister of St Giles at Edinburgh and no further attempt was made to introduce an organ at St Andrew's until 1866. Attempts were made by some members of the congregation of the Roxburgh Place Relief Chapel in Edinburgh to introduce an organ from 1813, but were resisted by the minister and a majority of the congregation until 1829 when an organ was at last installed. The Relief Synod condemned the installation as illegal and unscriptural and demanded its removal, but the minister and congregation eventually left the Relief Church for the established church, having abandoned their organ, in 1833.[23] Whereas attitudes to organs were eventually to change, in both the Church of Scotland and the Free Church, after 1860, there remained areas, notably the western highlands and islands, where 'the singing of metrical psalms, unaccompanied musically but led by a precentor, remained a readily identifiable feature ... throughout the nineteenth century',[24] and in some areas even into the present day.

2. *The care of church buildings*

Most Scottish churches rebuilt in the seventeenth and eighteenth centuries were generally rebuilt on the foundations of their medieval predecessors. This meant that, in the majority of cases, they still remained too small to seat the whole population of their respective parishes. At Smailholm the church could seat only 200 out of a population of 551 in 1755; at Dalmeny it was 200 out of 1,103, at Carnock 140 out of 583 and at Gladsmuir 340 out of 1,415. The old church in the parish of Tranent with a population of 2,732 could only seat 200, but even its replacement was only designed to seat 446. The population of Jedburgh (5,816) worshipped in the one-roofed aisle of the former abbey church. There were only eleven churches in Edinburgh,

---

[23] Drummond and Bulloch, *Church in Victorian Scotland*, p. 187; James Inglis, 'The Scottish Churches and the Organ in the Nineteenth Century', Glasgow PhD 1987, pp. 58–72, 86–94.
[24] MacInnes, 'Evangelical Protestantism', p. 52.

including three in the High Kirk of St Giles, for a population of nearly 50,000. Even by the middle years of the nineteenth century the city's churches could only accommodate about a third of the population. There were only seven churches in Glasgow, including three in St Mungo's Cathedral, for a population of 27,000.[25] In most parishes, the responsibility for the maintenance of the existing churches and the erection of new ones lay with the heritors or principal landowners, who taxed themselves for the purpose. In some cities and towns, such as Edinburgh, the council took on these responsibilities. It was possible to erect chapels-of-ease as a means of increasing church accommodation but the regulations for the erection of such buildings were tightly constrained by the General Assembly of the Church of Scotland in 1798. The decision could only be taken by the General Assembly and not the presbytery; the qualifications of the proposed minister had to be approved beforehand; the amount of the ministerial stipend and security for its payment had to be agreed; no ecclesiastical area or separate kirk session could be established in connection with the new place of worship; the minister was not a member of presbytery and the congregation was subject to the discipline of the kirk session of the parish church. As a result of these restrictions only 27 chapels-of-ease were built in Scotland between 1799 and 1826.[26] Where town councils were responsible for church maintenance there were frequently complaints that they did so at a profit to themselves either through high pew rents or other means. At Glasgow, where these responsibilities ceased in 1857, the town council re-seated the interior of St Mungo's Cathedral at a cost of £2,500 in 1855. They also maintained the cathedral at an annual cost, including cleaning and the payment of vergers, of about £200. However, they received a good deal more than this annual sum by charging visitors for admission to the cathedral. The charge of 2d on Saturdays and 6d on weekdays produced an income of £307 13s 0d from a total of 16,034 visitors in 1855.[27]

By far the best snapshot of the state of Scottish parish churches in the period between 1690 and 1860 is provided by the entries, mostly by the parochial ministers, in the *Statistical Account of Scotland* for 1791–1799. In many cases, there is no detailed description of the parish church but in somewhat over half the cases there is. Altogether, of the 886 parish churches in Scotland, 262 had been built since 1700, 331 were noted as being in good repair and 134 as being in poor repair. There was, however, a wide variation between different parts of Scotland, as Table 4 shows. In the county of

---

[25] Drummond and Bulloch, *Scottish Church*, pp. 73–4; Gordon Donaldson, *The Faith of the Scots*. London 1990, pp. 123, 136.
[26] Burleigh, *Church History*, pp. 319–20.
[27] G.E. Todd, *The Book of Glasgow Cathedral: A History and Description*, Glasgow 1898, pp. 174–5.

Table 4 Churches recorded as new built and in good or poor repair in the *First Statistical Account of Scotland* 1791–1799

County	Number of Parishes	Built since 1700	In good repair	In poor repair
Aberdeenshire	81	24	32	11
Angus	54	13	15	6
Argyll*	35	10	12	11
Ayrshire	47	16	22	3
Banffshire	26	5	7	8
Berwickshire	32	10	9	3
Bute	4	1	2	–
Caithness	10	2	3	4
Clackmannanshire	4	2	2	1
Dumfriesshire	43	21	16	7
Dunbartonshire	12	4	3	–
East Lothian	24	6	11	1
Fife	61	6	15	7
Inverness-shire*	31	11	15	6
Kincardineshire	19	8	10	4
Kinross-shire	4	2	3	–
Kirkudbrightshire	28	10	12	4
Lanarkshire	40	11	15	6
Midlothain	33	5	9	6
Moray	19	9	5	3
Nairnshire	4	2	2	–
Orkney	16	5	3	6
Peeblesshire	16	4	5	–
Perthshire	78	18	35	13
Renfrewshire	17	10	7	2
Ross and Cromarty*	33	12	18	6
Roxburghshire	31	9	11	6
Selkirkshire	5	–	1	–
Shetland	12	8	8	2
Stirlingshire	25	7	7	5
Sutherland	13	4	8	1
West Lothian	12	3	2	2
Wigtownshire	17	4	6	–
Total	886	262	331	134

* The counties of Argyll, Inverness-shire and Ross and Cromarty included both mainland and island parishes: Argyll, mainland 25, islands 10; Inverness-shire, mainland 19, islands 12; Ross and Cromarty, mainland 29, islands 4.

Kinross-shire, 75 per cent of the churches were in good repair; the figure was over 60 per cent in both Shetland and Sutherland; over 50 per cent in Kincardineshire and Ross and Cromarty; and over 40 per cent in the counties of Ayrshire, Bute, East Lothian, Inverness-shire, Kirkcudbrightshire, Nairnshire, Perthshire and Renfrewshire. The counties with the fewest number of churches in poor repair, in all cases below 10 per cent, were Ayrshire, Berwickshire, Dunbartonshire and Sutherland. At the other end of the scale the county with the highest proportion of churches in poor repair was Caithness at 40 per cent; the figure was over 30 per cent in Argyll, Banffshire and Orkney and 20 per cent or above in Clackmannanshire, Kincardineshire and Stirlingshire. Some of the more detailed descriptions of church interiors, in good or poor repair, have been reproduced in Appendix A. In general terms, the defects of churches tended to fall into one or more of three main categories: irregular and shabby seating; leaking roofs and general dampness; and, especially, the lack of heating, either by stoves, or through the proper maintenance of ceilings, doors and windows, which made them very cold during the winter months. In a few places, the church was little better than a ruin. The blame for this tended to be laid at the doors of the heritors, some of whom had declined to pay for the necessary repairs. In other parishes, however, it was clear that the heritors had dug deeply into their own pockets to maintain and rebuild churches. Nevertheless there is little doubt that the evidence of the *Statistical Account* was such as to encourage a massive programme of church repairs and rebuilding during the first quarter of the nineteenth century. When the *New Statistical Account* was published in 1845, significant improvements had taken place in the condition of churches in those parts of Scotland which had reported a large number of churches as being out of repair in the 1790s. It is possible that the naming and shaming of heritors by ministers in the previous *Statistical Account* had had the desired effect of ensuring that they did not wish to suffer the same fate in future. Table 5 shows a comparison between the two accounts. In Argyll, Banffshire and Caithness the improvement was extremely marked, though much more marginally so in Orkney.

The condition of churches in Orkney, in comparison to those in Shetland where a high proportion of churches were in good repair, remained a cause for concern over many years. Even in St Magnus's Cathedral at Kirkwall, where the roofed nave, aisles and transepts were used solely for burials,[28] worship took place in the partitioned off choir in which individuals had

Table 5 Comparison of condition of churches in selected Scottish counties in 1791–1799 and 1845

County	Churches in good repair		Churches in poor repair	
	1791–1799 (%)	1845 (%)	1791–1799 (%)	1845 (%)
Argyll	34.3	64.7	31.4	17.6
Banffshire	26.9	69.6	30.8	4.3
Caithness	30.0	60.0	40.0	20.0
Orkney	18.8	22.2	37.5	27.8

Source: SAS, passim; NSA, passim.

---

[28] OA, OCR/14/95, plan of burials 1769.

erected their own pews and galleries, frequently painted by them in 'garish colours'.[29] In 1791–1799, the churches at Evie and Rendall (Appendix A/57) had both been in ruins; that of Hoy and Graemsay (Appendix A/58) had been only partly rebuilt by the heritors; the church at Deerness (Appendix A/60) was roofless and that at St Andrews in a very dilapidated state; the churches of both Eday and Stronsay (Appendix A/61) were in a similarly poor state of repair. By 1845 the churches of St Andrews and Deerness were in good repair, but there were no reports on those at Evie and Rendall, Hoy and Graemsay or Eday and Stronsay. Several other churches were now noted as being in poor condition. At Stromness 'the roof almost every year requires repairs ... being much exposed to violent storms'.[30] At Sandwick, even though a new church was built in 1836, it was no longer in good repair

> for being founded partly on the foundation of the old church, and partly on soft sand, the wall cracked so far, that the arch of a window came down, and that again being rebuilt, it has again cracked in such a manner, that it gives little prospect of durability.[31]

Accommodation for parishioners in the churches was a serious problem at South Ronaldsay and Burray.

> If a small loft were put in each end of the south church, and the present seats repaired, the accommodation would be complete, and the attendance much better. North parish should have accommodation for 1,020; but the actual accommodation is only for 414, at 18 inches each; and there is no accommodation for the island and parish of Burray. About 40 years ago, the church in the island and parish of Burray fell into ruins ... and it has not since been repaired. ... In 1832, the parishioners offered to put a loft in the North Church to accommodate 250 people. Lord Dundas, as chief heritor, consented; but some of the other heritors discouraged the proposal. Baptists have, in consequence, invaded the parish.[32]

It was not until some years after this that a mission was built on Burray, with the appointment of a minister in 1872, the building of a manse in 1874 and the eventual creation of a *quoad sacra* parish in 1904.[33]

---

[29] Thomson, 'Eighteenth Century Church', pp. 64–5.
[30] *NSA*, xv, p. 36.
[31] *NSA*, xv, p. 63.
[32] *NSA*, xv, pp. 194–5.
[33] S.D.B. Picken, *The Soul of an Orkney Parish*, Kirkwall 1972, p. 83.

Elsewhere the complaints about church accommodation and repair were few and far between in the New Statistical Account. At Gigha and Cara, 'as the floor . . . is considerably lower than the ground outside, it [the church] is damp and uncomfortable in winter, and at all seasons in wet weather'.[34] At Marnoch

> the church . . . is still little fitted for comfort. It is one of those old-fashioned barn-looking houses, which are now very properly disappearing, to make way for more improved places of worship.[35]

A church had at last been built in Barra and there were now 65 Protestant families in the island compared with 306 Roman Catholic ones.[36] However, on South Uist there was still

> no parish church. About 18 years ago the late incumbent, with the consent of the Presbytery, agreed to have the walls of the old-house roofed and thatched, for a temporary place of worship, until circumstances should render it necessary to build a parish church. Measures are now in progress for this purpose, as the present house is in a ruinous state.[37]

South Uist, however, still had three Roman Catholic places of worship as it had had in the 1790s.

The condition of churches in Scotland in the late eighteenth and early nineteenth centuries may have been bad but it needs to be put into context. Descriptions of churches in Wales by Richard Fenton in 1804–1813, Theophilus Jones in 1805–1811 and E.H. Hall in 1809–1811 paint a similar picture to that of those in Scotland, as Table 6 shows. In his description of the Breconshire church of Merthyr Cynog, Theophilus Jones indulges in similar language to that in the Statistical Accounts.

Table 6 Descriptions of churches in Wales in the early nineteenth century

State of churches	Fenton (%)	Jones (%)	Hall (%)
Churches in good repair	48.0	17.6	63.6
Churches in moderate repair	12.0	57.4	4.6
Churches in poor repair	40.0	25.0	31.8

---

[34] *NSA*, vi, p. 406.
[35] *NSA*, xiii, p. 387.
[36] *NSA*, xiv, pp. 214–15.
[37] *NSA*, xiv, p. 195.

This church, like most of the other county churches in Breconshire, and I fear in Wales, resembles a large barn, into which something like pens for sheep have been thrown in disorderly regularity to rot when they become unfit for use . . . in most of them the windows are broken, the tiles out of repair, so that the rain penetrates and falls upon the heads of those who have a sufficiency of devotion to frequent them on wet days . . . many of them are dark and gloomy.[38]

The church building and restoration programmes in Wales and Scotland in the first half of the nineteenth century were designed to remedy very similar problems. One of the major problems was getting churches heated in winter. At Cadder, in 1839,

the Moderator having reported it to be the opinion of competent tradesmen, that if it were possible to procure the use of the vault under the Session House the heating of the church by means of a stove might be easily and efficiently accomplished; the Session do hereby appoint the Moderator to write to Mr Stirling, whose private property it is, requesting the loan of said vault for the above object, and that during the pleasure of the family of Keir, or until they shall require it for any other purpose.[39]

A letter from Mr Stirling's factor, dated 19 February 1839, acceded to the request and stated that Mr Stirling would himself meet the cost of installing the stove.

The problems of replacing inadequate buildings resulted in an energetic debate about whether rebuilding or restoration was the most economic option to pursue. At Kilsyth in 1810 the kirk session considered this in relation to the need for an increase in church accommodation, since the population of the parish was now 3,000, having increased by 600 in the previous 20 years. There were 680 parishioners on the communicants' roll and the church could only accommodate 450. Although the heritors agreed to meet to consider the views of the kirk session nothing appears to have been done and no further debate on the matter was recorded.[40] In 1821, the Campsie kirk session approved a meeting of the heritors 'for the purpose of considering of the propriety of building a new church or repairing the old one', but after much discussion, in which rebuilding was favoured over restoration, decided to defer the launching of a rebuilding programme until

---

[38] Glanmor Williams, W.M. Jacob, Nigel Yates and Frances Knight, *The Welsh Church from Reformation to Disestablishment 1603–1920*, Cardiff 2007, pp. 278–9.
[39] MLGA, CH2/863/3, 20 January 1839.
[40] MLGA, CH2/216/6, 22 June and 23 September 1810.

at least 1825.[41] In other parishes, frequent repairs and alterations were carried out to the fabric and furnishings. This was the case at Eastwood in the 1850s.

> Plans for the alteration of the seat for the Band and Sir John Maxwell's seat in the parish church were submitted and approved of and the session resolved to recommend the execution of them to the heritors.[42]
>
> The session resolved to make a subscription throughout the parish to defray the expenses which had been incurred in making the recent alterations of the sittings in the parish church, which had been rendered necessary for the comfort of the congregation.[43]
>
> Plans for the alteration of the pulpit and communion tables were submitted to the meeting and approved of with the view of being immediately executed. The moderator was instructed to receive the consent of the Heritors to the same and a committee of the whole session was appointed to carry this . . . into effect.[44]
>
> The session authorized the moderator to procure a new carpet for the pulpit stair, and a new Bible, and Chair for the mission room and cloth to cover the pulpit there.[45]

In addition to these improvements to the furnishings, the kirk session also recorded its gratitude to Sir John Maxwell for the presentation of four silver communion cups to the church, to replace those that had been stolen.[46]

Restorations of four of the largest of Scotland's churches took place from the late eighteenth century. At Paisley Abbey in 1788–1789, 'a new roof of plaster was constructed . . . galleries and seating renewed. The front seats in the galleries were reserved for the chief heritors, and adorned with armorial bearings.'[47] At St Mary's, Haddington, a reordering of the seating and galleries took place in 1810–1812. The pulpit and precentor's desk were retained in the middle of the south arcade of the nave, but new, uniform, box pews installed throughout. Each box pew had a table which could be turned into a series of long tables on sacrament days. The galleries ran around all four sides of the interior of the nave, the chancel remaining in its ruinous condition.[48] At St Michael's, Linlithgow, the roof was found to be in a poor

---

[41] MLGA, CH2/51/3, 9 September 1821.
[42] MLGA, CH2/119/3, 4 September.
[43] *Ibid.*, 30 December 1854.
[44] *Ibid.*, 5 October 1855.
[45] *Ibid.*, 6 February 1857.
[46] *Ibid.*, 15 November 1855.
[47] A.R. Howell, *Paisley Abbey*, Paisley 1929, p. 43.
[48] R.K. Marshall, *Ruin and Restoration: St Mary's Church*, Haddington 2001, pp. 31–2.

state of repair in 1808, and a full-scale restoration was carried out in 1812–1813. This involved the complete refurnishing of the building, with the main body of seating being moved from the nave to the chancel. Uniform box pews were installed with a gallery around three sides of the interior. A canopied pulpit was placed in the middle of the chancel's apse with a series of table pews in front of it. Although the total cost of the restoration had been estimated at £2180, the actual expenditure was almost double this at £4117 14s 8d.[49] The major restoration of the period was, however, that of St Mungo's Cathedral, Glasgow. The first step towards this had been taken with the removal of the Barony congregation from the crypt to the new Barony church in 1798. The Inner Kirk was reordered in 1805, when the pulpit was moved from the south choir arcade to the east end of the choir and galleries erected across the west end of the choir and both choir aisles. This was the arrangement shown in an engraving of 1822 [Plate 2]. In 1835–1836, the congregation of the Outer Kirk in the nave was relocated to the new St Paul's Church, leading to the demolition of the dividing wall between the two churches and the opening out of the whole cathedral. The new St Paul's Church had been built by Glasgow town council at a cost of £8000.[50] The 1835–1836 alterations coincided with the earliest antiquarian study of the cathedral, with drawings of its interior showing monks worshipping in the pre-Reformation cathedral, by James Collie.[51] Such antiquarian studies were to have an impact on other buildings. One of the earliest of these antiquarian restorations was carried out at Coldingham Priory, where the restoration of the church was completed on 7 December 1855 [Plate 3].

> The galleries, pews, and whole contents were gutted out . . . the whole of the beautiful architectural decorations have been cleared of the unseemly coating of white. . . . There are now no galleries, and the character and arrangement of the pews and fittings is in conformity with the building. The pulpit is placed against the south wall, near the centre of the church, and the pews are arranged across this area, to the right and left of the pulpit, those in front of the pulpit being placed longitudinally from west to east. . . . The sum contributed by the Board of Works towards the expenses of this undertaking was L.625, and the amount incurred by the heritors, as originally agreed to, was L.843.[52]

---

[49] Ferguson, *Ecclesia Antiqua*, pp. 100–16.
[50] Chalmers, *Cathedral Church*, pp. 21–3; Todd, *Book of Glasgow Cathedral*, pp. 170, 172.
[51] James Collie, *Plans, Elevations, Sections, Details and Views of the Cathedral of Glasgow*, London 1835.
[52] W.G. Hunter, *History of the Priory of Coldingham from the Earliest Date to the Present Time*, Edinburgh 1858, pp. 101–4.

Plate 2 Engraving of the interior of the choir of Glasgow Cathedral in 1822 (Glasgow University Library, Special Collections)

By ecclesiological standards in England such a restoration still fell short of what was required, but it was a notable achievement in Scotland, where the ecclesiological movement did not begin to impact fully on the Presbyterian churches until the last quarter of the nineteenth century.

3. *Church extension and new buildings*

By the early nineteenth century the problem of church accommodation, and ease of access to religious buildings, had become acute. Apart from re-buildings of existing churches, few new churches had been built and these mostly in the cities and large towns. By far the greatest need for new churches was in the highlands and islands, where many parishes were

Plate 3 Engraving of the interior of Coldingham Priory Church as restored in 1855 (Glasgow University Library, Special Collections)

exceptionally large and the parish churches inaccessible to many of the inhabitants. This situation had been largely created by the uniting of parishes in the seventeenth century to cope with a shortage of ministers. The united parishes of Appin, Duror, Glencoe and Lismore were served by a single minister in the 1660s. There were only two ministers and parishes in Lewis in 1688. After 1700 the process of dividing such parishes began but it was still inadequate to meet the pastoral needs of the inhabitants. New parishes were created at Lochs and Uig on Lewis in 1722, at Applecross in 1724 and Glenshiel in 1726. The Small Isles parish was disjoined from Strath in 1720, followed by Sleat and Portree in 1726. The previous parish had covered two-thirds of Skye and the islands of Canna, Eigg, Muck, Raasay and Rhum. Tongue and Eddrachillis were separated from Durness and made separate parishes in 1724; Gigha and Cara were separated from Killean in 1726; and Barra from South Uist in 1733. By that date the process began to be abandoned though the Islay parishes of Kilchoman and Kilarrow were separated in 1769.[53] As a temporary measure, to improve pastoral oversight in such vast parishes, the first Royal Bounty scheme, in 1724,

---

[53] MacInnes, *Evangelical Movement*, pp. 42–3.

provided a thousand pounds annually to support missionaries and catechists in the highlands and islands, but the sum was not increased to £2,000 until 1830. The Scottish Society for Promoting Christian Knowledge, founded in 1701 and incorporated in 1709, also funded missionaries, catechists and schoolteachers in these areas.[54] However, the problems remained serious. Boswell and Johnson, in their visit to the western highlands and islands in 1773, noted that there was no church on Raasay, but that the minister of Portree preached occasionally in the laird's house. There was also no church on Coll and worship was conducted in a private house by the minister of Coll and Tiree.[55]

Churchmen in Scotland were not slow to notice that the British government was giving large annual grants to the Irish Board of First Fruits to build churches and glebe houses for the Church of Ireland, and from 1818 established a Church Building Commission to provide financial support for building new churches in places of growing population in England and Wales. They pressed the British government for similar support for the Church of Scotland, arguing that, in the highlands and islands particularly,

> the zeal and activity of Roman Catholic priests in the islands and some mainland districts was preventing further reclamation from Rome, and . . . in some districts Catholicism had gained ground within the last few years.[56]

In 1823, Parliament passed legislation enabling the building of forty churches and manses, at a cost not to exceed £50,000, with no individual church and manse costing more than £1,500 together, in the highlands and islands and a further, unspecified, sum to permit the payment of stipends to the new ministers. The scheme was managed by a Commission that initially identified 60 districts in 54 parishes in which churches and manses might usefully be erected.[57] In fact the Act resulted in 'the construction of 43 churches and manses and the endowment of 42 ministers', this last costing £180,000.[58] The commission appointed the celebrated engineer Thomas Telford to oversee the work and he appointed three surveyors to supervise the building contracts. It was one of these surveyors, William Thomson, who seems to have been responsible for the actual design of the

---

[54] MacInnes, 'Evangelical Protestantism', p. 44.
[55] F.A. Potter and C.H. Bennett, *Boswell's Journal of a Tour to the Hebrides with Samuel Johnson, LLD*. London 1936, pp. 143, 255–6, 282.
[56] I.F. MacIver, 'Unfinished Business? The Highland Church Scheme and the Government of Scotland', *RSCHS*, xxv (1995), p. 384.
[57] MacInnes, 'Evangelical Protestantism', p. 45.
[58] MacIver, 'Unfinished Business', pp. 395–6.

buildings. There were two standard designs, both T-plans, without galleries to seat 312 and costing £600, and with galleries to seat an additional 250 and costing £948.[59] Only three of these churches still survive in more or less their original condition: Portnahaven (Appendix C/12), with galleries, and Croik (Appendix C/32) and Quarff (Appendix C/63), without them. Like the additional churches erected under the General Assembly's provisions of 1798, these 'parliamentary' churches were only chapels-of-ease, and did not provide the parochial infrastructure that the new districts needed. In 1834, the General Assembly endeavoured to rectify this deficiency by passing the Chapels Act, under which these new chapels-of-ease would become the parish churches of new *quoad sacra* parishes, exercising their own ecclesiastical discipline, with their own kirk sessions, and with their own ministers being members of the presbytery. However, some heritors saw the Act as threatening their rights of presentation. When the Act was tested in the courts it was found to be illegal. This decision, in 1842, was one of the factors that brought about the Disruption of 1843. It was a body blow to the *quoad sacra* parishes; in addition to the chapels-of-ease erected since 1798 and the 'parliamentary' churches of the 1820s, the Church of Scotland had itself begun a major campaign of church extension in 1834, led by Thomas Chalmers, with the intention that those new churches would be designated *quoad sacra* parishes. Between 1834 and 1841 no fewer than 222 new churches had been built by the Church of Scotland, increasing its plant by a fifth.[60]

The collapse of the legislation that had underpinned the Church of Scotland's church extension programme, followed a year later by the Disruption, resulted in very few churches being built by the established church until the 1860s. By contrast, the new Free Church, within 4 years of its establishment, had obtained 725 sites 'upon which churches were either already built or in the process of erection'. The idea that the Free Church had difficulties in obtaining sites, resulting from the opposition of the heritors, is largely a fiction. In 1847, only 35 sites had been refused in such circumstances throughout the whole of Scotland. In Aberdeen, the departing Free Church congregations initially either erected temporary wooden buildings, or made arrangements to share the buildings of Congregationalist or Secessionist Presbyterian congregations, or rented public halls for their services. However, permanent new churches were built very quickly in 1844–1845, most of them costing between one and two thousand pounds, raised mostly by their respective congregations. However, the Free Church, became more unwilling to create new charges and erect new buildings after

---

[59] *BS Argyll and Bute*, p. 34; *BS Highland and Islands*, p. 37.
[60] S.J. Brown, *The National Churches of England, Ireland, and Scotland 1801–1846*, Oxford 2001, pp. 191–7, 217–27, 355–6.

the initial 'exertions' of the 1840s. Only 25 new Free Churches were built in the 1850s, including four in Edinburgh and eight in Glasgow. By 1870 the Free Church had 859 churches and 719 manses.[61]

We can conclude this chapter by saying that, though the Presbyterian churches in Scotland, and particularly the established Church of Scotland, were suffering problems in relation to church buildings that were not satisfactorily addressed until the early years of the nineteenth century, these were not problems that were unique to Scotland. In the next chapter, we will look in more depth at the way in which Scottish Presbyterian churches were designed to meet the needs of Presbyterian worship – their liturgical arrangement – and at developments in their furnishings between 1690 and 1860.

---

[61] A.L. Drummond and J. Bulloch, *The Church in late Victorian Scotland 1874–1900*, Edinburgh 1978, pp. 162–3; MacInnes, 'Evangelical Protestantism', p. 56; A.A. MacLaren, *Religion and Social Class: The Disruption Years in Aberdeen*, London 1974, pp. 105–8; Donaldson, *Faith of the Scots*, p. 137.

4

PRESBYTERIAN CHURCH INTERIORS 1690–1860: FURNISHINGS AND LITURGICAL ARRANGEMENT

Unlike Anglican, Lutheran and Roman Catholic churches, churches in the 'Reformed' tradition required rather less in the way of church furniture. In Scotland, neither a fixed communion table, nor a font was in liturgical use. Communion was celebrated at temporary tables, though in the course of time these became an integral part of the seating arrangements. Baptism was administered in bowls, which, as a matter of convenience, tended to be fixed by a bracket to the pulpit. The essential furniture for a Scottish Presbyterian church was thus a pulpit for the minister, a desk for the precentor and seating for the congregation. This led to a simplicity of liturgical arrangement that has few counterparts in Europe, though it was replicated to some extent in some of the other churches of the 'reformed' tradition.

1. *Liturgical arrangement*

Between 1690 and 1860, all Scottish Presbyterian churches fell into one of three categories of liturgical arrangement. The earliest type was the rectangular building with the pulpit on one of the long walls (Type A). A slightly later, but still early, arrangement was the T-plan with seating facing the pulpit from three directions (Type B). The third, and generally latest, type of building was a rectangular one with the pulpit on one of the short walls (Type C). During the nineteenth century, buildings of the first type were frequently 'turned' so that they became buildings of the third type. The reasons for doing this are not entirely clear. Possibly it was to make the building feel more like a church and less like a meeting house. In terms of acoustics, it could cause problems since in the long-wall arrangement the congregation seated against the outer walls was normally closer to the pulpit and precentor's desk than it was in the short-wall arrangement. Other, less popular, types of building – the Greek cross, circular, square, elliptical or octagonal – were essentially variants on one of the three types listed earlier. Table 7 identifies the relative popularity of these three traditional arrangements on the basis of extant seating plans and surviving buildings. As can be seen the popularity of the long-wall arrangement grew less after 1800 whilst that of the short-wall arrangement, largely unknown before the end of the eighteenth century, rapidly increased thereafter. The T-plan arrangement, by contrast, remained popular throughout, notably so after 1860 in those churches still designed on traditional lines and uninfluenced by the Scoto-Catholic movement of the late nineteenth century.

2. *The long-wall arrangement*

This arrangement, particularly popular during the eighteenth century, is shown in the surviving plans of the church at Inverallan, of the Barony Church at Paisley [Plate 4], of the East Church at Stirling and St Cuthbert's, Edinburgh, as well as in the water-colour drawing of the interior of St Giles's, Elgin, in c.1770 [Plate 5]. Even the important, and, in terms of their design, very advanced town churches of St Nicholas West at Aberdeen (1755) and St Andrew at Dundee (1774) followed this arrangement.[1] St Nicholas West, which still retains the majority of its eighteenth-century furnishings, still has its elaborate canopied pulpit in the middle of one of the nave arcades [Plate 6]. The plan of the church at Inverallan, which dates from about 1700 and appears to be the earliest surviving plan for any Scottish church, shows the long-wall arrangement in a simple country building. It was a long rectangular building with two side windows, two doors and two middle windows on either side of the pulpit, on the entrance wall. There was also a desk for the precentor in front of the pulpit, and all seating faced inwards from the short walls so that those sitting immediately opposite the pulpit were doing so sideways on. The more normal latter arrangement was for these seats to face directly towards the pulpit. A wide central

Table 7 Relative popularity of different liturgical arrangements for Presbyterian Churches in Scotland

Period	Type A (%)	Type B (%)	Type (C)
Before 1800	77.8	22.2	–
1801–1820	40.0	30.0	30.0
1821–1840	23.3	69.4	13.3
1841–1860	38.1	28.6	33.3
After 1860	13.3	53.4	33.3

[1] Drummond and Bulloch, *Scottish Church*, p. 73.

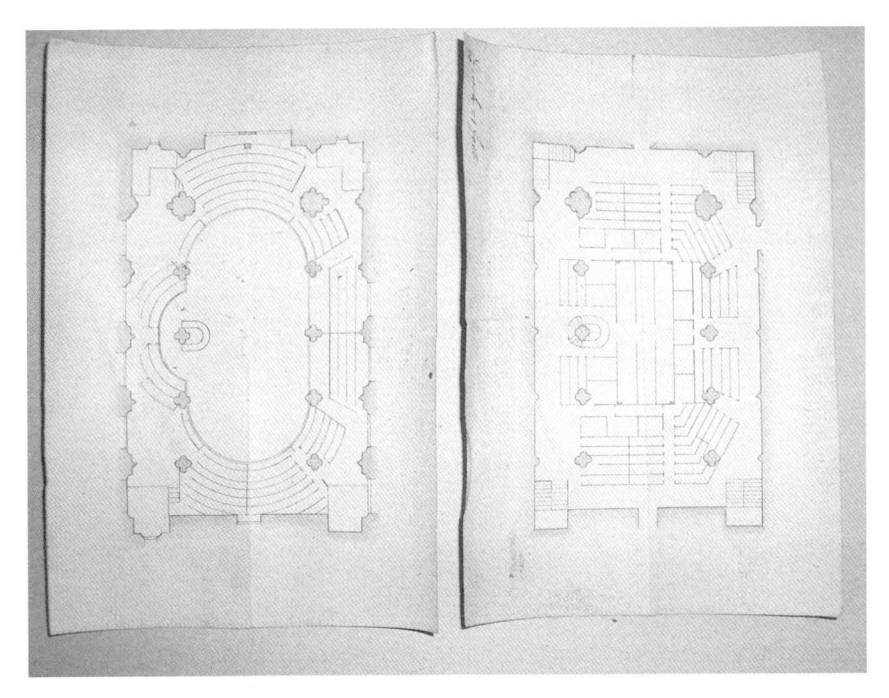

Plate 4 Seating plans of the ground floor and galleries at the Barony Church, Paisley, 1789 (Stirling Archives)

Plate 5 Watercolour drawing of a service at St Giles's, Elgin, c.1770 (Elgin Museum)

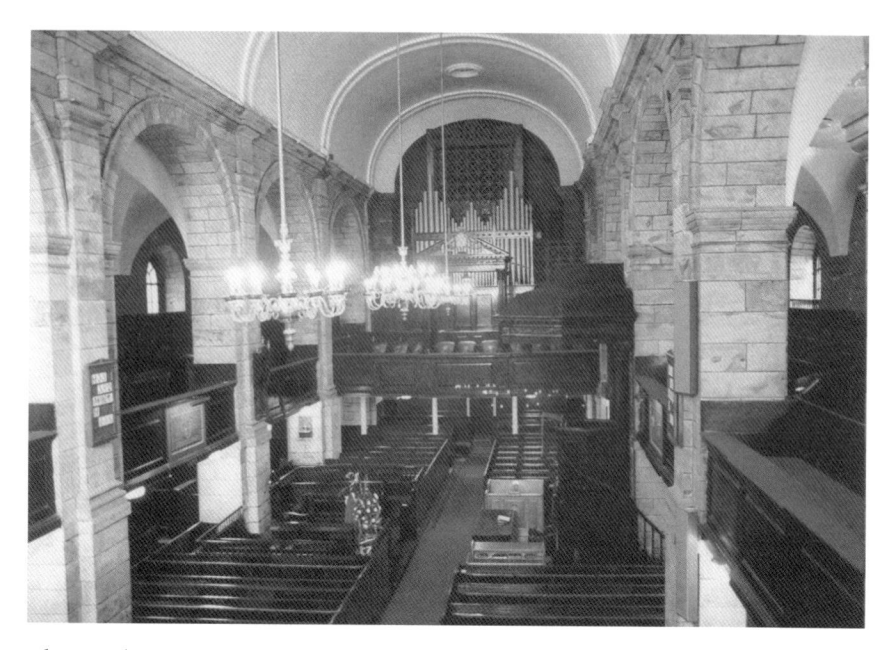

Plate 6 The interior of St Nicholas West Church, Aberdeen, rebuilt and refurnished in 1755

passageway between the two rows of seating was almost certainly intended to provide space for the setting up of temporary communion tables on Sacrament Sundays. At each end of the building were staircases to two L-shaped lofts, but with no gallery across the central part of the interior. The plan is in three sections, with the elevation of the building at the top, the loft plan in the middle and the ground floor plan at the bottom.[2]

Three late-eighteenth-century plans show the long-wall arrangement in town churches at Edinburgh, Paisley and Stirling. That of St Cuthbert's, Edinburgh, dated 1779, shows pulpit and precentor's desk in the middle of one of the long walls. On the ground floor there were two blocks of box pews facing the pulpit against the long wall. The other seating is arranged in three blocks: the middle block opposite the pulpit has three sets of square pews, the one directly in front of the pulpit being occupied by the elders, as it still is at St Nicholas West, Aberdeen; the two side blocks have two sets of long pews each. All the pews on the ground floor were assigned to individuals or groups. Around three sides of the interior were a double set of seven-sided galleries. In the lower gallery only a small proportion of the seating was assigned, and in the upper gallery about half the seating was assigned; the seating in the galleries was arranged in seven blocks to coincide

[2] NAS, GD248/85/1, Item 15.

with the composition of the gallery fronts.[3] The series of plans for the East Church at Stirling show the arrangement of the church as it was in 1802 before the proposal for turning it into a short-wall arrangement and several abortive arrangements for reordering between 1789 and 1799. The plan of the church as it was showed the pulpit in the middle of the north arcade with box pews, most fitted with tables, arranged quite irregularly through the rest of the building.[4] The 1789 plan retained the pulpit in its long-wall position but reordered the seating so that it was more regular, with semicircular blocks in the eastern apse and at the west end and with a gallery around four sides of the interior.[5] The 1797 plan proposed even a more radical semi-circular seating arrangement throughout the church, but with the pulpit still retained in the long-wall position.[6] The 1799 plan retained the four-sided gallery, but proposed curved fronts, and re-ordered the seating so that the arrangement was no longer semicircular. Seating was even placed behind the pulpit and precentor's desk, still in the middle of the north arcade. There was an oblong table pew on either side of the pulpit and five table pews along each side of the central passageway.[7] The final proposal, in 1802, was to turn the interior so that all the seating faced the pulpit in the middle of the apse, with a semicircular arrangement of seating for the elders on either side and a precentor's desk in front. A table for the minister to celebrate Holy Communion was placed in a small semicircular raised area below the pulpit and precentor's desk and there were two oblong table pews at the front of the central block of seating and two smaller ones in each of the side aisles.[8] The seating plan of the Barony Church at Paisley, dated 1789, was endorsed on the reverse.

> The plan of the Barony Church of Paisley newly seated and repaired in the most elegant manner. The Building of the Church and Gothick pillars and size is in every respect the same as the East Church in Stirling and by the new improvement holding more Sitters and better hearing than before.[9]

The plan is in two sections, one showing the ground floor and the other, the gallery arrangement. Seating was provided by a mixture of box pews and open benches facing the pulpit on one of the long walls. Three rows of

---

[3] NAS, RHP 20589.
[4] SA, MP/SB/258.
[5] SA, MP/SB/262/11.
[6] SA, MP/SB/262/8.
[7] SA, MP/SB/262/1 and 2.
[8] SA, MP/SB/258.
[9] SA, MP/SB/257.

seating in front of the pulpit were clearly communion pews. The gallery ran around all four sides of the building, forming an ellipse behind the pulpit but still fitted up with seating.

Apart from St Nicholas West, Aberdeen (Appendix C/1), there are two other surviving late-eighteenth-century examples of the long-wall arrangement, at Glenbuchat (Appendix C/3) and Southend (Appendix C/13), and early nineteenth-century ones at Kildrummy (Appendix C/4), South Ronaldsay (Appendix C/47) and Channelkirk (Appendix C/52). The arrangement remained popular between 1820 and 1860, and there are very late examples of it at Torosay (Appendix D/3) and Lochalsh (Appendix D/8). The church of 1806 at Bourtie (Appendix C/2), which was square, can be seen as a combination of both the long- and short-wall arrangements. The long-wall arrangement is also shown in the surviving plan of the church at Ellon in 1828. Here there were table pews each side of the pulpit with rows of seating between them and the short walls. There were three blocks of seating against the long wall opposite the pulpit, facing across the central passageway in the middle and one block set sideways against the long wall at each end of the building.[10] The long-wall arrangement had the advantage of placing the pulpit and precentor's desk in the middle of the building where the minister could be easily heard from all parts, but it had the disadvantage that some parts of the congregation could be awkwardly placed in relation to the pulpit and precentor's desk and that sight lines could be poor. This was a disadvantage also discovered by Anglicans who had largely abandoned the arrangement long before Presbyterians.[11]

3. The T-plan arrangement

We have already noted that this arrangement had been adopted in parts of Scotland from the early seventeenth century, and was by no means confined to Scotland as some earlier writers have suggested. The great advantage that the T-plan had over the long-wall arrangement was that it retained the pulpit and precentor's desk in the middle of the building, thus ensuring audibility, but that it also greatly improved visibility by aligning the seating so that all of it was directly focussed on the liturgical centre of the building. An excellent eighteenth-century example of the T-plan arrangement survives at Golspie (Appendix C/36) and the East Church at Cromarty, though partly refurnished, is another good early example of the arrangement. It is also shown in the surviving plans of the church at Kippen, near Stirling, and of St David's, Ramshorn, in Glasgow. The Kippen plan dates

---

[10] NAS, RHP 45480.
[11] *BFW*, pp. 77–84.

from 1779. The pulpit and precentor's desk are placed in the middle of the long wall with two large square box pews each side of the pulpit and five square pews on the opposite side. The remainder of the seating in the cross-aisle and in the transepts opposite the pulpit is regular and appears to be simple open benches. There are lofts in all three projections. Those at each end of the cross-aisle are clearly accessed by external staircases, that in the transept by an internal one. There are two square box pews at the front of each loft and behind them open benches, as in the body of the church.[12] At St David's, Ramshorn, the interior, shown in a surviving plan of 1824–1826, was dominated by an exceptionally handsome canopied pulpit, shown in a separate drawing.[13] The pulpit was approached by a double staircase and had a desk for the precentor in front; this was placed on a platform approached by seven steps, with a further seven steps leading from the platform to the pulpit. Pews were, as usual, placed in all three projections, but the arrangement was not typical of churches of this type. In the transept opposite the pulpit, there were four blocks of pews, a double one in the middle and two side blocks separated from the central one by passageways. In the cross-aisle the pews were arranged so that they faced the long wall in one half of the area, but with the pews adjacent to the long wall facing sideways on to the pulpit and precentor's desk. The passageways in the cross aisle, except in front of the pulpit and precentor's desk, were placed against the outer walls so that there were two blocks of pews facing the long wall, an incredibly economical arrangement which increased the seating capacity of the church. There was a five-sided gallery across the three projections, rather than separate lofts, with all the seating facing the gallery fronts. All the seating in the church was rented, the annual pew rents ranging from 5s to 12s 6d on the ground floor, with the cheapest seats being opposite the pulpit (so that the occupants would have had to crane their necks to see the minister), and between 2s and 14s in the gallery. The most expensive seats were those in the front of the gallery, which clearly had the best view of the pulpit and precentor's desk.[14]

Good early-nineteenth-century examples of T-plan arrangements survive at Spott (Appendix C/20), Fogo (Appendix C/54) and Torphichen (Appendix C/63). Torphichen has lofts in all three projections; Fogo lofts accessed by external staircases, and containing family pews, at each end of the cross aisle; and Spott has no lofts. Later T-plan churches without lofts or galleries are the parliamentary churches at Croick (Appendix C/32) and Quarff (Appendix C/63), the early gothic parish church at Tynron (Appendix C/18) and the very handsome Free High Church at Oban (Appendix C/10).

---

[12] NAS, GD 259/4/7.
[13] MLGA, D/TC/13/602.
[14] MLGA, D/TC/13/603.

Interesting variants of the T-plan were the cruciform arrangements formerly found at Thurso (Figure 1), before the building of the new parish church in 1833, and still extant at Lauder (Appendix C/56; Figure 2). In both of these, seating faced the pulpit from four, rather than three, separate directions. T-plan arrangements remained popular throughout the nineteenth century with late examples at Kinneff (Appendix D/1), Luss (Appendix D/2), Kirkmaiden (Appendix D/5) and Canisbay (Appendix D/7).

4. *The short-wall arrangement*

The earliest example of the short-wall arrangement appears to have been the new church of St Andrew, Glasgow, designed by Allan Dreghorn, and built between 1739 and 1756. The church was much influenced by James Gibbs's St Martin's-in-the-Fields, London, and had a galleried interior with much elaborate rococo plasterwork and a tall wine-glass pulpit and matching

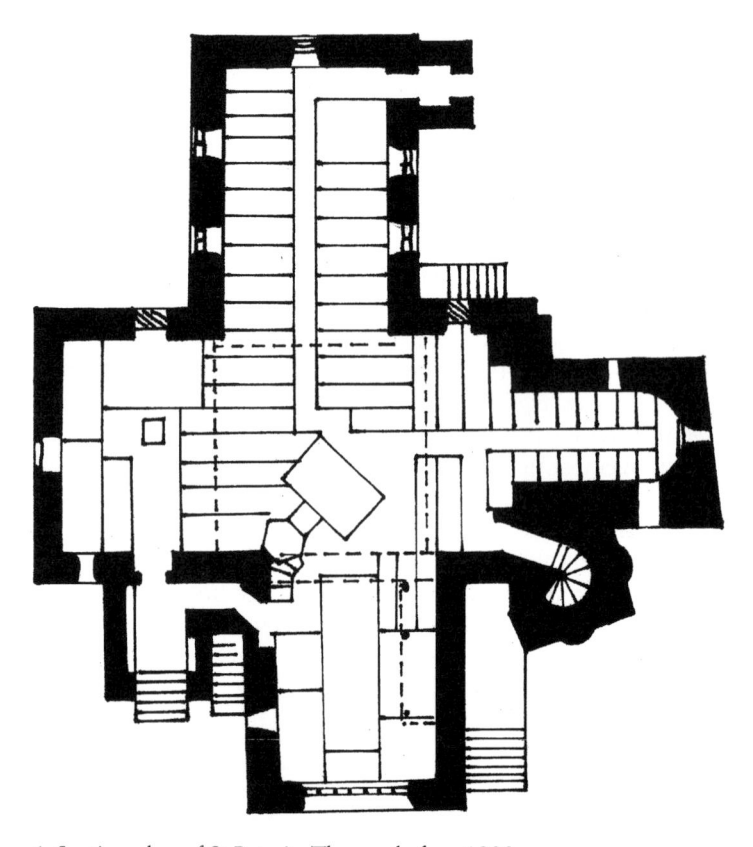

Figure 1 Seating plan of St Peter's, Thurso, before 1833

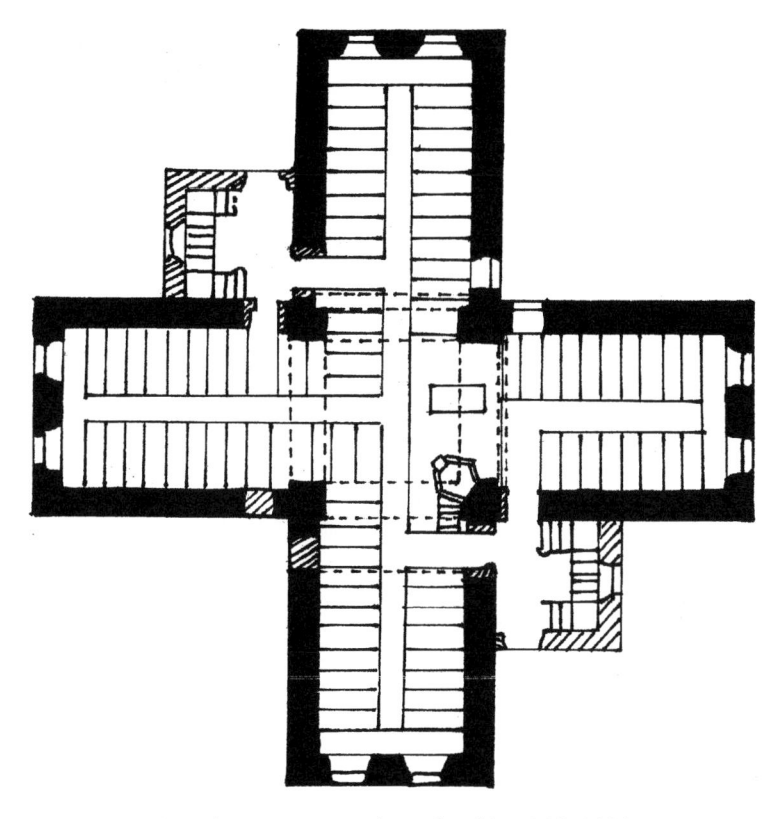

Figure 2 Seating plan of St Mary's, Lauder, refitted in 1820–1821

precentor's desk placed directly in front of a shallow chancel,[15] emulating the design of many Anglican eighteenth- and early nineteenth-century town churches in which the altar was placed behind the pulpit and reading desk.[16] Indeed George Hay has postulated in his plan of St Andrew's that this Anglican arrangement was replicated with a communion table placed in the apse,[17] but this seems highly unlikely as fixed communion tables were a thing of the future in Presbyterian Scotland. The church was repewed in 1874, though preserving its original plasterwork, but is no longer in ecclesiastical use, having been secularized to operate as a concert hall. There appear to be few other examples of the short-wall arrangement before 1800, but there are surviving early nineteenth-century examples at Ceres (Appendix C/24; Figure 3), Eriboll (Appendix C/34) and Rogart (Appendix C/41). The

---

[15] Drummond and Bulloch, *Scottish Church*, p. 73; *BS Glasgow*, pp. 452–3.
[16] *BFW*, pp. 84–93.
[17] *SPC*, pp. 101–3, Fig. 36.

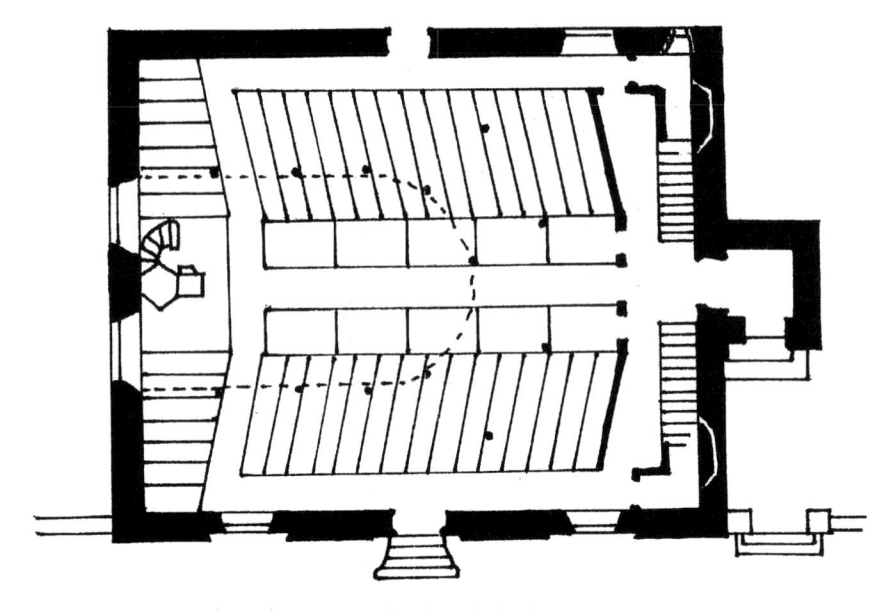

Figure 3 Seating plan of Ceres Parish Church, built in 1806

arrangement is also shown in the plans of churches at Dalgetty and Govan, both of which date from 1830. At Dalgetty, the pulpit and precentor's desk were placed in the middle of the short wall opposite the entrance, with a baptism pew, incorporating a table, in front of them. On each side of the pulpit were two table pews, with two further seats behind each table pew. In the body of the church were four blocks of seating, the middle two being separated from the side ones by narrow passageways. All but two of the seats, those directly in front of the pulpit marked 'poor people', were assigned to the parish's three principal heritors and the plan includes a list of those properties that leased their pews from the heritors. The two seats behind one of the table pews flanking the pulpit were assigned to the minister and his family. The church also had a U-shaped gallery around three sides of the interior, with four rows of seating at the back and two at the sides. As with the ground-floor seating, it was all assigned to the three principal heritors.[18] The seating of the church at Govan shows the short-wall arrangement with four blocks of pews, two in the middle and one against each side wall, separated as at Dalgetty by narrow passageways. At the pulpit end of the side blocks, the pews face inwards, towards the pulpit. There were stairs against the entrance wall, either side of the tower, to a five-sided gallery around the whole interior except for the pulpit wall. In this plan

---

[18] NAS, GD172/628.

the only seating marked was that allocated to the City Council, Hutcheson's Hospital and the Trades House; Hutcheson's Hospital was allocated 77 sittings, 60 in the body of the church and 17 in the gallery, whereas the other bodies were each allocated 42, half on the ground floor and half in the gallery.[19] A virtually identical arrangement was shown in a much later plan of 1884, before the demolition and rebuilding of the parish church, though in this one the allocation of other seating in the building is clearly marked.[20]

The short-wall arrangement remained popular after 1840. It is to be seen in the extant arrangement at Lochbroom (Appendix C/40; Figure 4) and in three of the early Free Churches where the original furnishings are extant: Altnaharra (Appendix C/31), Halladale (Appendix C/37) and Stornoway (Appendix C/70), a particularly impressive example of the arrangement. There are also splendid late nineteenth-century examples in Church of Scotland churches at Sleat (Appendix D/9) and Northmavine (Appendix D/14) and an early twentieth-century one in the Free Church at Urquhart (Appendix D/12). The short-wall arrangement was adapted from about 1870 to form the pulpit-platform composition, popular among English and Welsh nonconformists, which then began to be introduced into Scottish Presbyterian churches. This involved the enlargement and lowering of the pulpit, first seen in Scotland in the former Free Church at Altnaharra, the placing of a fixed communion table with seats for the ministers and

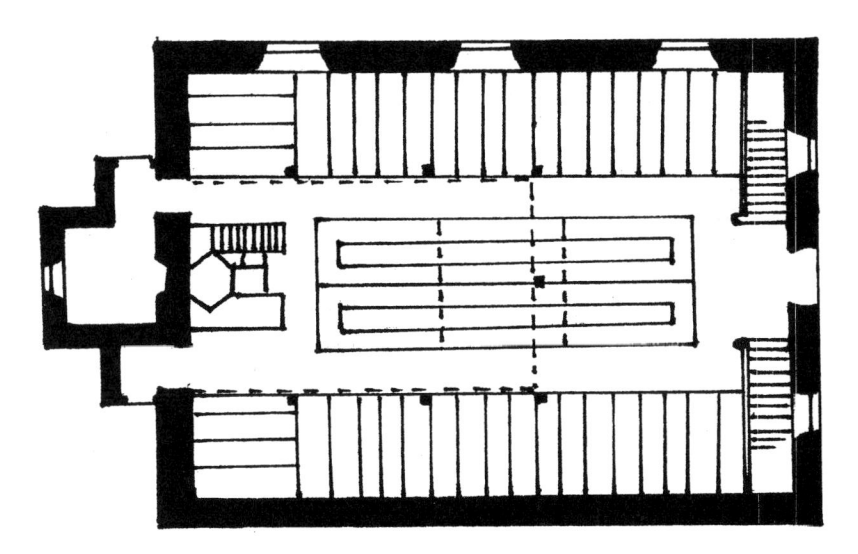

Figure 4 Seating plan of Lochbroom Parish Church, built in 1844–1845

[19] MLGA, D/TC/13/604.
[20] MLGA, CH2/1277/104.

elders in front, and frequently that of an organ behind them, organs being acceptable to some Scottish Presbyterians from the 1860s. Good examples are the late nineteenth-century refurnishing of the church of c.1840 at Belhaven (East Lothian), the 1877–1878 reseating of the 1767–1769 round church at Bowmore (Islay), the Wellington Church of 1882–1884 in Glasgow, and the handsome Arts and Crafts interiors of 1896–1898 at Dryfesdale parish church in Lockerbie and St Andrew's, Stranraer, both in Dumfries and Galloway.

5. *Experimental church planning*

In addition to the three main types of Presbyterian churches in Scotland before 1860, there were a number of experimental designs from the middle years of the eighteenth century, as there were in other parts of the British Isles and throughout Europe. Probably the earliest was the parish church at Hamilton [Plate 7]. This was designed by William Adam in 1732 and comprised a circle with four projecting arms in the shape of a cross. The pulpit, precentor's desk and baptism pew were placed in the section of the circle nearest the entrance portico, but with some seating behind them, with the loft of the Duke of Hamilton, seats for his servants and a retiring room placed immediately opposite. Seating filled the other projections, with a circular gallery and a space in the middle of the circle for the communion tables. There were also the circular church of 1767–1769 at Bowmore (Islay), octagonal churches of 1773 at Kelso and 1780 at Dreghorn, and the elliptical church of St Andrew in the New Town of Edinburgh, designed by Andrew Frazer and built between 1785 and 1789. The last of these needs to be compared with a Swiss example of an elliptical building, dated 1780–1782, at Horgen. Here the pulpit is on one of the long walls of the ellipse, and the font in the middle of the four blocks of pews facing the pulpit. Note that, compared with the general plainness of Scottish church interiors, the church at Horgen has extremely elaborate Baroque plasterwork.[21] There were other Swiss examples of octagonal or elliptical churches at Villars-le-Grand, Sonvilier, La Fusterie in Geneva, Chêne-Pâquier (constructed as early as 1667), Oron-la-Ville, Chêne-Bougeries, La Chauds-de-Fonds and St Sulpice. At Oron-la-Ville the church, built in 1678–1679, originally had the pulpit on one of the long walls; in 1825 the interior was 'turned' and the pulpit placed opposite the entrance on one of the short sides of the ellipse.[22] None of the Scottish churches retain their original liturgical arrangement or more than a small part of their original

[21] Reymond, *L'Architecture Religieuse*, pp. 107, 109.
[22] Reymond, *Temples*, pp. 110–35.

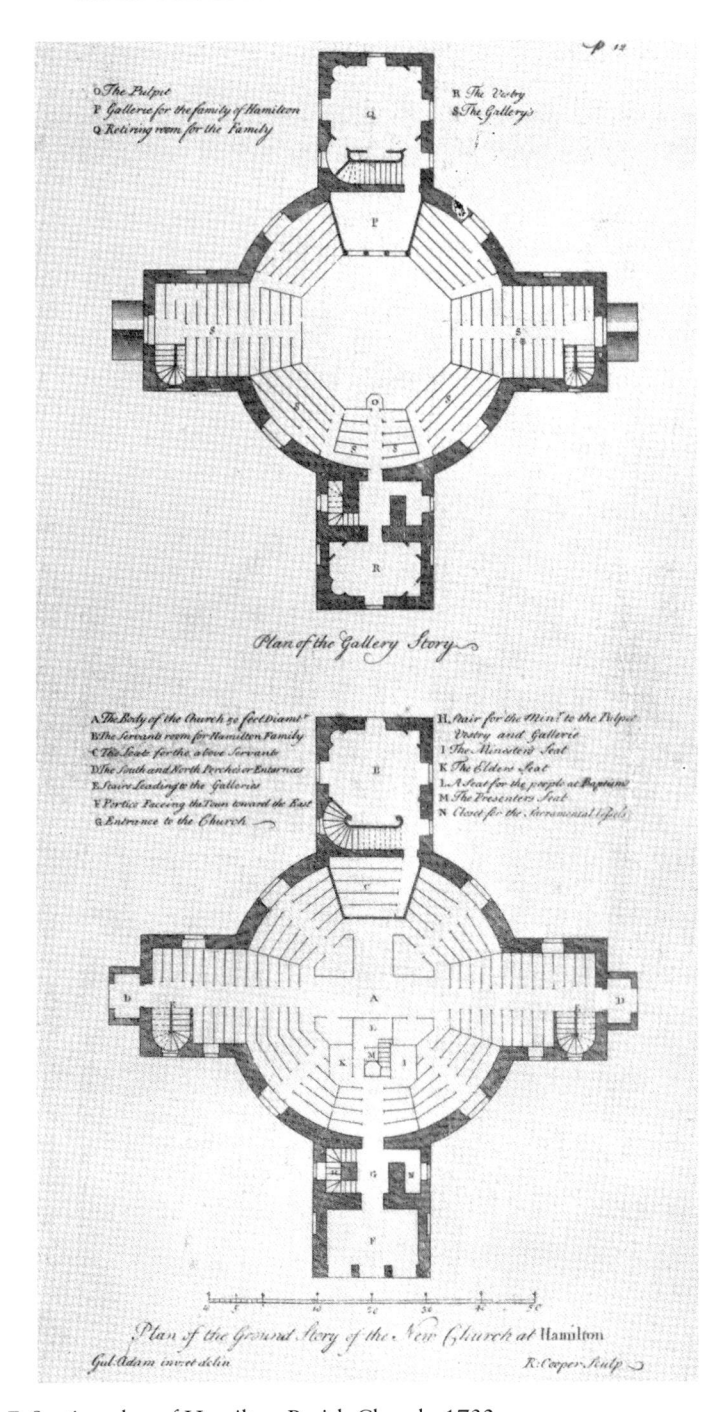

Plate 7 Seating plan of Hamilton Parish Church, 1732

furnishings; St Andrew's, Edinburgh, retains its original pulpit and galleries. Later examples were the octagonal churches at Perth (St Paul's, 1807) and Glenorchy (1811), both of which have also been refurnished, and the modified octagonal arrangement at St Stephen's, Edinburgh (Figure 5), which was designed by W. H. Playfair and completed in 1828. Here the church was externally square but internally octagonal; it was reordered by David Rhind in 1880. In each case, the liturgical arrangement is, in effect, a variation of the long or short-wall arrangement, the pulpit and precentor's desk being placed against one wall of the circle or octagon, or, at St Andrew's, Edinburgh, the long side of the ellipse. One of the intentions of these experimental designs was the seating of as large a congregation as possible,

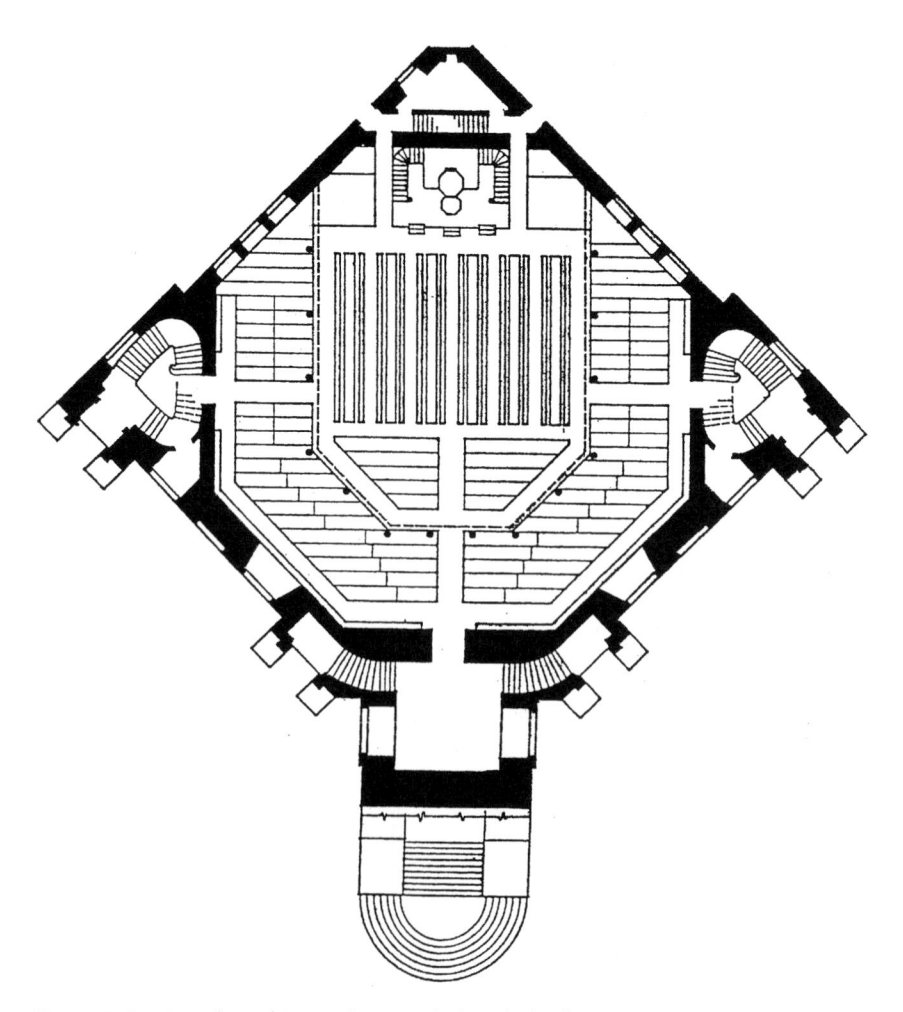

Figure 5 Seating plan of St Stephen's, Edinburgh, built in 1828

preferably as many as 1,500, within a reasonable distance of the pulpit and precentor's desk.[23]

Another, and very unusual, experimental church was the new one eventually erected at Inveraray between 1795 and 1802. The original plans for the church in the new town being built by the Dukes of Argyll were drawn up by John Adam in 1758, and were for a circular church, much influenced by his father's designs for the church at Hamilton in 1732. However, the church at Inveraray was designed to provide for both English- and Gaelic-speaking congregations, so the circle was divided by an internal wall, thus creating two semicircular interiors, both with a semicircular gallery along the outer walls of the building. This church was never built and the design of the one that was came from Robert Mylne. This was also a double church, with an internal wall between the two congregations, but was rectangular rather than circular, with entrance facades at each end, north and south, and the pulpits placed back to back against the internal wall. Both had precentor's desks in front and behind them a staircase, accessible from both churches, leading to the spire in the middle of the roof. Box pews were placed against the side walls and the spaces between the entrance doors and the pulpits were filled with benches. There were also galleries across both entrance walls. The original plan was to add semicircular entrance porticos to both churches in the side walls, east and west, but these were never built.[24] Although the church survives it has been much altered. The English church remains in use for worship but has been completely refurnished, and the Gaelic church is now used as the church hall.

6. *The pulpit and its appurtenances*

The pulpit was by far the most important piece of furniture in any Scottish Presbyterian church before 1860, and was the one piece of furniture which could afford to be elaborate and therefore a work of beauty in its own right. Normally the pulpit had both a backboard and a tester or canopy, often with a crown or domed top. The backboard incorporated a seat for the minister and the tester assisted the projection of the minister's voice into the church. In front of the pulpit was a precentor's desk and both the pulpit and desk were usually decorated with velvet hangings, as was the case with Anglican pulpits and reading desks in the pre-ecclesiological period. In addition the pulpit normally supported two brackets, one for the baptismal bowl

---

[23] *SPC*, pp. 92–9, 122–7; I.G. Lindsay and D. Walker, *Georgian Edinburgh*, Edinburgh 1973, pp. 29–30, 32.
[24] I.G. Lindsay and M. Cosh, *Inveraray and the Dukes of Argyll*, Edinburgh 1973, pp. 165–7, 282–7.

Plate 8 Pulpit and precentor's desk at St Modan's Church, Ardchattan, built in 1838–1839 (Royal Commission on the Ancient and Historical Monuments of Scotland)

and the other for the sermon glass, which allowed the minister to time his sermon; unlike English and Welsh nonconformist chapels, Scottish Presbyterian churches before the middle of the nineteenth century, were not normally provided with clocks on the galleries facing the pulpit. Relatively few Scottish churches still retain the full pulpit complement, though there are good examples at Bourtie (Appendix C/2), Ardchattan (Plate 8; Appendix C/6), Croick (Appendix C/32) and Laggan (Appendix C/39). Pulpits, lacking precentor's desks but retaining the brackets for both baptismal bowl and sermon glass, survive at Durisdeer (Appendix C/16) and Kilmany (Appendix C/28). A number of churches in which the seating has been altered retain pre-1860 pulpits. Those that incorporate a precentor's desk survive at Duirinish (Appendix B/10), Plockton (Appendix B/16), Makerstoun (Appendix B/18) and at Applecross in Wester Ross, where the former parish church of St Maelrubha was rebuilt in 1816–1818. There are also two surviving examples of three-decker pulpits at Dyke and Fort George. The Dyke pulpit dates from the rebuilding of the church in 1781 and its lowest desk would have been occupied by the beadle; other examples previously existed at Fintray, Inverkeithny, Sanquhar and Yarrow, but they were never very common. The Fort George chapel was part of a military barracks and the services in it followed those of the Anglican *Book of Common Prayer*, so the placing of a three-decker pulpit (common in other Anglican churches) in it is hardly surprising. The chapel dates from 1767.[25] Apart from their pulpits both the church at Dyke and the chapel at Fort George have been completely refurnished, and the church at Dyke has had a false ceiling inserted at gallery level which cuts off the pulpit canopy. Other churches that retain eighteenth- or early-nineteenth-century pulpits, but have otherwise been significantly altered and either wholly or partly seated, include Livingston (West Lothian), where the pulpit dates from 1732 and the canopy from 1837, Edinkillie (Moray) of 1741, Kirkintilloch (Dunbartonshire) of 1782, Mochrum (Dumfries and Galloway) of 1794 and Tarves (Aberdeenshire) of 1798. At least a further nine churches have pulpits dating from between 1820 and 1850.[26]

7. Seating: from box pews to open benches

In most parts of the British Isles until the middle years of the nineteenth century, seating in both Anglican churches and nonconformist chapels, and even a few Roman Catholic ones, was almost invariably provided by box pews. This was not the case in Scotland, as Table 8 shows, where the provision of seating by open benches rather than box pews had become relatively common even before 1800 and the most popular method of seating churches by the 1820s. The reasons for this are not entirely clear. There is certainly no evidence that similar theological arguments, to the effect that all seating should be open and therefore equal, used by the Free and Open Seating lobby in England and Wales from the 1840s, were being advocated in Scotland a generation earlier. The likelihood is that in a country where those responsible for church maintenance, the heritors, were frequently accused of

Table 8 Provision of box pews or open benches in Scottish Presbyterian Churches before 1860

Period	Box pews (%)	Open benches (%)	Mixed seating (%)
Before 1800	50.0	25.0	25.0
1801–1820	53.8	23.1	23.1
1821–1840	25.0	57.1	17.9
1841–1860	26.9	65.4	7.7

---

[25] *SPC*, p. 186.
[26] Foss (Perth and Kinross) 1821; Dunscore (Dumfries and Galloway) 1823–1824; Eskdalemuir (Dumfries and Galloway) and Daviot (Highland) both 1826; Ardnamurchan (Highland) 1827–1829; Kirkcowan (Dumfries and Galloway) 1834; Resolis (Highland) 1838–1840; Penninghame (Dumfries and Galloway) 1841; and Langholm (Dumfries and Galloway) 1842–1846.

being too mean to carry out their responsibilities adequately, open benches were preferred to box pews as a means of saving expense on reseating schemes. They tended, of course, to make the occupants colder in winter, since box pews had the great advantage of keeping out draughts. Nevertheless, for whatever reason, Scotland appears to have been the first country in Europe to begin to abandon box pews for open benches in its churches. That does not mean that box pews went instantly out of fashion. They were still being installed in a quarter of seating schemes up to 1860, and there were churches fitted with them even later than this. When the church at Kirkmaiden (Appendix D/5) was reseated in 1885, it was reseated with a mix of box pews and open benches. Churches that retain box pews even though their other furnishings have been replaced include the churches at Canonbie (Dumfries and Galloway), where they date from 1821–1822, Dunnet (Highland) of 1836–7, Colintraive (Argyll and Bute) of 1840, Polmont (Falkirk) of 1844–1845 and Strathmiglo (Fife) of 1848–1849.

Seating could be a very contentious issue: where one sat in church tended to reveal one's social position in the community, especially when it involved the payment of pew rents. At Campsie in 1850,

> the Moderator called the attention of the Kirk Session to the many complaints which had lately been made to him in person, who after having occupied unchallenged for years seats in the Church, had been forcibly ejected from them. He mentioned one family who in consequence of this, and their inability to get other sittings in the church appropriated to them, had become Dissenters: and that several heads of families had intimated to him, that unless some plan was adopted by which they might procure seats which they could occupy unchallenged, they feared that they would have to give up their communion with the Church.

In order to resolve this problem the minister proposed that each heritor should be asked to provide a list of the seats allocated to his tenants at the building of the church and to indicate 'which and how many of these seats he wishes to be retained'. Heritors should not allocate seats to people who did not attend church regularly and give power to the kirk session to sub-allocate for one year the seats originally allocated to them which are no longer to be appropriated to their use or that of their tenants. The kirk session agreed with those proposals, to allow those currently occupying pews to continue to do so, and to allocate any other seats to those who applied for them.[27]

---

[27] MLGA, CH2/51/4, 1 July 1850.

Detailed records of the allocation and renting of pews survive for the parishes of Kippen in 1779 and Alloa in 1819. At Kippen, the box pews on the ground floor of the church were allocated as follows:

Mr Campbell's family seat
Mr Wright's family seat
Mr Leakie's family seat
Mr Forrester's family seat
Mr Downes' and Mr Provan's family seat
Mr Galbraith's and Mr Gourley's family seat
Killorn family seat
Mr Campbell's and Mrs Harvie's family seat
The minister's seat

Of the open benches on the ground floor of the cross-aisle, nineteen were allocated to the Gartmore estate, three belonged to Sir James Campbell, one to Mr Wright and three jointly to Mr Forrester, Mr Harvie and Mr Leakie. In the transept opposite the pulpit, ten benches were allocated to the Gartmore estate, one belonged to Arnprior and two to Mr Erskine. There were also lofts at each end of the cross-aisle and in the transept. In one of the cross-aisle lofts, there were family seats for Arnprior and Mr Monteath with, behind them, two open benches allocated to Arnprior, one to the Gartmore estate and four were 'allotted to Mr Monteath by the heritors'. In the other cross-aisle loft there were family seats for Mrs Stirling and Sir James Campbell with, behind them, four open benches allocated to Mr Stirling and six to Sir James Campbell. In the transept loft, there were family seats for Gartmore and Mr Erskine with, behind them, five open benches allocated to Gartmore and two to Mr Erskine.[28]

The Alloa seating scheme is recorded in a small booklet entitled

Scheme of the Division of the seating in the new Church of Alloa made by Archibald Rennie, Esq., Sheriff Substitute of Clackmannanshire on the 15th and 16th day of July 1819 in the process of Division at the instance of John Francis Erskine of Mar and others

It lists each seat, the number of sittings, the value of each pew and the price of each sitting. Most pews had between six and ten sittings but there were also some larger pews. The price of each sitting varied between £1 11s 0d and £9 15s 0d. One pew containing 33 sittings was reserved for the use of baptism parties. Seatholders in the church included the Hon. George

---

[28] NAS, GD259/4/7.

Abercromby, the Earl of Mansfield, Lady Charlotte Erskine's trustees, Mr Erskine of Mar and a number of leading tradesmen in Alloa. There were also seats for the elders and the schoolmaster and his family, as well as a seat for the minister's family. Two of the seatholders, William Lemon and Charles Honeyman, were described as labourers. There were 137 pews in the body of the church and 30 in the gallery.[29]

8. Laird's lofts

The provision of galleries or lofts for the important families in the parish was widespread throughout Europe, especially in its Protestant churches, between the seventeenth and the nineteenth centuries. Scotland has a number of particularly handsome surviving laird's lofts of which the earliest are the Forbes loft of 1634 at Pitsligo (Aberdeenshire) and the Ker of Cavers loft of 1661 at Bowden (Scottish Borders). Between 1690 and 1840 elaborate laird's lofts were erected in a number of churches: the Hopetoun loft of c.1700 at Abercorn (West Lothian), the Crauford loft of c.1705 at Kilbirnie (Ayrshire), the Reay loft of 1728–1729 at Tongue (Appendix D/10) and the Sutherland loft of 1739 at Golspie (Plate 9; Appendix C/36). At St Nicholas West, Aberdeen (Appendix C/1), the rebuilding of 1752–1755 included the erection of an elaborate loft for the Lord Provost and members of the City Council.[30] By the late eighteenth and early nineteenth centuries, though laird's lofts were still being erected in churches, they tended to be more modest affairs. Good examples include those of 1828 at Glenbuchat (Appendix C/3), of 1848 at Murroes (Appendix C/5), of 1825 at Durisdeer (Appendix C/16), of 1830 at Yester (Appendix C/21), of c.1860 at Whalsay (Appendix C/66) and of 1803 at Torphichen (Appendix C/68). Occasionally, instead of lofts, canopied pews were constructed for the principal families in the parish. There are good examples at Crossmichael (Appendix C/14) and Dunrossness (Appendix C/59). Laird's lofts were erected as late as 1875, for Sir James Colquhoun, at Luss (Appendix D/2), though that for the Macdonalds at Sleat (Appendix D/9), where the church was rebuilt in 1876–1877, consists solely of the front pew in the gallery opposite the pulpit. Some lofts, particularly for the more important families, were provided with heated retiring rooms where the laird and his family could partake of refreshments, provided by his servants, between the morning and afternoon services.

---

[29] SA, CH2/942/45
[30] *SPC*, pp. 190–5.

Plate 9 Sutherland Loft of 1739 at St Andrew's, Golspie

9. Communion arrangements

Until at least the middle years of the eighteenth century, the practice in Scotland was for temporary tables to be brought into the churches on communion Sundays and be covered with white cloths. This practice was maintained even later by Presbyterians in Ireland, and is still the practice of some churches belonging to the Non-Subscribing Presbyterians, which retain by far the largest number of substantially unaltered eighteenth- and early nineteenth-century Presbyterian churches in Ireland. There are still a few Presbyterian churches in Scotland where the traditional practice has been retained, or even re-introduced, but generally it has been abandoned. Once the practice of erecting temporary tables had been abandoned, two arrangements were adopted for permanent or semi-permanent communion tables in the churches. Permanent tables usually comprised either one or two tables running the length of the church, either in front of the pulpit in buildings with a long-wall arrangement, or between the pulpit and the entrance in buildings where the pulpit was on one of the short walls. Kilmodan (Appendix C/9) and Croick (Appendix C/32) are good examples of the first type of church with their long communion tables *in situ*; there were probably similar arrangements at Nesting (Appendix C/62) and Quarff (Appendix C/63) but the surviving long tables are no longer *in situ*. South Ronaldsay (Appendix C/47) had an unusual arrangement, a square table in front of the pulpit, and long tables between it and the two short walls. There was another unusual arrangement at Rogart (Appendix C/41), where the long table is placed in a pew to one side of the pulpit. Good examples of the second type of church are Ardchattan (Plate 10; Appendix C/6) and Lochbroom (Appendix C/40). At Ardchattan, there is a single long table running from the pulpit and precentor's desk to the short entrance wall with benches on each side. A similar arrangement existed at Scarista, Harris (Appendix B/11) until it was completely refurnished in 1994, and still survives at Howmore, South Uist, where the church was built in 1858, though the other furnishings appear to have been somewhat modified. A single long communion table, with benches either side, has also been

Plate 10 Long communion table and benches at St Modan's Church, Ardchattan, built in 1838–1839 (Royal Commission on the Ancient and Historical Monuments of Scotland)

retained at Carsphairn (Dumfries and Galloway), though the rest of the church was refurnished when an apsidal sanctuary was added in 1931–1932. At Lochbroom, there are two long communion tables, both with benches each side, down the middle of the church between the pulpit and precentor's desk and the short entrance wall. By the latter part of the nineteenth century, shorter or even square communion tables were replacing the long tables in some churches. At Tongue (Appendix D/10), four tables were installed in 1861–1862, one each side of the pulpit and two in front of the Reay loft. At Sleat (Appendix D/9), rebuilt in 1876–1877, a large square communion table was placed in the pew directly in front of the pulpit and precentor's desk.

The second type of communion arrangement was less permanent and somewhat more practical when communion was only celebrated once or twice a year, if that. This was to create a series of ordinary box pews with moveable partitions which could be turned into long table pews on sacrament days. This type of arrangement can still be seen at Glenbuchat (Appendix C/3), Durisdeer (Appendix C/16), Spott (Appendix C/20) and Ceres (Appendix C/24). Even later a more convenient variant of this arrangement was for the front pews in the church to have hinged ledges, which could be opened up to form narrow communion tables when required. This type of arrangement survives in the early Free Church at Halladale (Appendix C/37). The movement from the 1820s to cease communion at long tables, and instead to deliver the sacrament to communicants in their own seats, meant that tables could be completely abandoned. This was the case in the very handsome Free Churches at Oban (Appendix C/10) and Stornoway (Appendix C/70), both of which were designed without any fixed or even semi-fixed communion tables. At Stornoway a communion board was, and still is, placed over the front pews for Holy Communion, but by the late nineteenth century many churches were installing permanent communion tables in front of the pulpit. A good example of a traditional interior furnished with such a table is Kinneff (Appendix D/1), where the church was refurnished in 1876. In churches where it became the practice to communicate people in their seats, the pews used for communion were draped with white cloths, and this practice is still maintained in many churches in Scotland. It is in fact a survival of the pre-Reformation houseling cloths used to drape the altar rails and to prevent any of the consecrated bread falling on the ground. It is perhaps ironic that one of the most Protestant of the 'reformed' churches of Europe should retain this interesting vestige of Catholic practice.

10. Penitent's platforms

One of the features of Presbyterianism in Scotland from the sixteenth to the nineteenth centuries was the maintenance of discipline which involved the public 'reproof, punishment, confession and absolution of penitents'. During the sixteenth and seventeenth centuries this discipline could be very severe. Maxwell records that in 1594 the kirk session of Glasgow authorized the making of 'a cart ... to cart harlots through the Town', and also 'a pulley ... on the Bridge, whereby adulterers may be ducked in the Clyde'. The kirk session administered the Correction House at which in 1635 it was stipulated that the occupants 'both men and women ... be whipt every day during the Session's will'.[31] These may have been fairly extreme examples but the use of the 'jougs', an iron collar on a chain attached to the outside wall of the church in which offenders were displayed before the Sunday service, was commonplace. Examples of 'jougs' survive in several Scottish churches, mostly in the lowland areas: at Sorn in Ayrshire, Garvald in East Lothian and Eckford, Mertoun and Oxnam in the Scottish Borders, the Eckford 'jougs' dating from 1718.[32] Display in the 'jougs' was just the first part of the penitential discipline; thereafter the offender was brought into church and made to stand or sit on a special platform, on which was either a stool or a pillory, throughout the service during which the minister formally rebuked him or her for their misdemeanours. Examination of the records of kirk sessions shows that the majority of business dealt with until the second half of the nineteenth century was discipline cases, usually involving moral lapses. One of the most common was prenuptial fornication, very easy to prove if the wife gave birth less than nine months after the wedding had taken place. The sentence depended on the gravity of the offence. In the seventeenth century, offenders might be sentenced to the 'jougs' and the penitent's platform for between 3 and 26 Sundays, occasionally even up to 39 or 52 Sundays, and might also have to pay a fine to the kirk session, which provided a useful source of parochial income. Offenders were normally made to wear sackcloth as a sign of their repentance. On the last Sunday on which they occupied the penitent's platform, as well as receiving a further rebuke from the minister, they were formally absolved after they had knelt down and made a full confession of their sins.[33] Penitent's platforms were a significant article of furniture, usually next to the pulpit, in Scottish Presbyterian churches before the nineteenth century but are now exceptionally rare. Good examples survive at Bourtie (Appendix C/2) and

---

[31] Maxwell, *History of Worship*, p. 145.
[32] *BS Lothian*, p. 207; *BS Borders*, pp. 249, 561, 604.
[33] Maxwell, *History of Worship*, pp. 146, 148–50, 152.

Duirinish (Appendix B/10), where they date from 1806 and 1832, respectively.

11. Linen chests and mortcloths

Before the second half of the nineteenth century, most Scottish churches were not provided with vestries and the arrangements for storing the communion plate and linen are not clear. They may have been kept in the Session House or the manse or possibly in a cupboard in the church. At a meeting of the Campsie kirk session in 1812, the minister,

> Mr Lapslie further stated that there is a necessity of a small chest to hold the clothes belonging to the communion service and that of baptisms; and he likewise stated that there formerly belonged to the parish of Campsie a Pulpit Bible ... the pulpit Bible which he now useth being his own property and much tattered and worn out in the course of 29 years. The Session therefore taking the circumstances into consideration, and considering it highly honourable for such a parish as Campsie to possess a pulpit Bible in property, as formerly, desired Mr Lapslie to take the remaining 18/1 of Isobel Cowan's fine ... and the remaining £2 of Sir C. Edmondstone's [the heritor's] allowance to purchase immediately a chest to hold the Communion Clothes, and an excellent Pulpit Bible to be the property of the parish: and whatever more money may be requisite for these purposes, to take it from the first fine which shall come into the hands of the Session.[34]

Parishes were also concerned about the state of their mortcloths or funeral palls. These 'were hired for funerals, the charge depending on the grandeur of the cloth used', the finest being of 'black velvet with silk fringes, ... and the revenue so derived went into the parish poor relief funds',[35] to supplement the offerings made at the end of Sunday services. At Kilsyth, in 1816, a committee was appointed to inspect the mortcloths. There were eight altogether:

> fine large mortcloth given out at 8/-
> at 5 shillings cotton fringes
> large one at four shillings
> youth's one at 3/6
> smaller one at 3/-

[34] MLGA, CH2/51/3, 10 May 1812.
[35] *SPC*, p. 238.

child's one at 2/-
old one gratis for poor
old one out of repair.[36]

At Campsie in 1822

> the Session . . . took into consideration the state of the parish mortcloth and finding that it is above 30 years since it was bought, and that the parishioners are complaining that it does not become the parish of Campsie to have no better mortcloth for the use of the inhabitants . . . they therefore unanimously approve the materials and the form of the mortcloth furnished by Wilson Stow and Co for the parish of Greenock, and give orders to Mr Donald Fleming to purchase such a mortcloth and at as low a rate as possible.[37]

Five months later, having purchased both a small and large mortcloth, which cost with carriage and a chest for their storage £31 6s 2½d, 'the Session' authorized 'the Grave Digger to charge for the use' of the smaller one 'at the rate of one shilling and sixpence sterling until further orders'.[38] By 1831, the parish clearly owned three mortcloths as 'the Session now resolved that the Hire for the best Mortcloth should be reduced to 5/-, the next to 3/6 and the small one to 1/3'.[39]

One of the features of Scottish Presbyterian church furnishings and liturgical arrangement between 1690 and 1860 was the consistency of both. Apart from the few experiments with square, circular, octagonal or elliptical churches, the two basic types of building design in existence for a century beforehand, the long-wall arrangement and the T-plan, remained popular for the next 170 years. From the end of the eighteenth century, the short-wall arrangement began to increase in popularity as did the replacement of box pews by open benches, but a visitor to Scotland in 1690 would have noticed very little change in the design of either church furnishings, or in liturgical arrangement, if he had been transported back there in 1860. Indeed, as we have seen, these traditional types of Scottish Presbyterian interior were still being provided for some congregations up to the First World War, with examples of 1907 at Urquhart (Appendix D/12) and 1910 at Lochalsh (Appendix D/8). After 1860, as we shall see in Chapter 6, the situation in Scotland began to change. Presbyterians then began to abandon their traditional furnishings and liturgical arrangements and to adopt either

[36] MLGA, CH2/216/6, 19 September 1816.
[37] MLGA, CH2/51/3, 3 November 1822.
[38] *Ibid.*, 6 April 1823.
[39] *Ibid.*, 2 December 1831.

the pulpit platform arrangement favoured by English and Welsh nonconformists or, perhaps even more significantly, the ecclesiological innovations that had been adopted by Anglicans, even in Scotland, and by Roman Catholics outside Scotland, from the 1840s. Although Scotland was one of the last countries in Europe to be influenced by the revival of medievalist church architecture, the impact of that movement was to be considerable by the last two decades of the nineteenth century and the first three decades of the twentieth.

5

ROMAN CATHOLIC AND SCOTTISH EPISCOPALIAN CHURCH INTERIORS 1690–1860

Three groups in Scotland declined to accept the religious settlement of 1690: a small group of extreme Presbyterians, normally known as Cameronians, who rejected any form of state church; those Roman Catholic recusants who had never been part of the Church of Scotland; and those continuing Episcopalians who operated outside the established church. Until the early nineteenth century, when the present Scottish Episcopal Church was effectively established, the Episcopalian picture in Scotland was complicated. Some episcopally ordained ministers, who were at best lukewarm to the Presbyterian establishment, remained in the Church of Scotland, supported by their congregations. Outside the Church there were two groups of Episcopalians: those who were non-jurors (and who suffered the same political disabilities as Roman Catholics), ministered to by the bishops ejected in 1690 and their successors; and groups of Episcopalians ministered to by English, Irish or Welsh clergy, who had taken the oaths required by law and, therefore, enjoyed legal protection. These two groups had little contact with each other until the Scottish bishops agreed to abandon their opposition to the Hanoverian monarchy, after which a gradual merger of the two groups took place. The non-juring Episcopalians, however, to some extent made common cause with the, just as aggressively Jacobite, Roman Catholics, to such an extent that, in the words of Callum Brown, unlike the rest of the British Isles, 'in Scotland Episcopalianism has always been seen as resting on the Catholic side of the Protestant-Catholic divide'.[1] In this chapter, we will consider Roman Catholic and Episcopalian worship, and the impact it had on their buildings, between 1690 and 1860.

---

[1] Brown, *Religion and Society*, p. 35.

1. *Roman catholics*

Roman Catholicism in Scotland in the eighteenth century was strongest in some parts of the western highlands and islands. It was alleged in 1720 that in

> Moydart, Knoydart, Arisaig, Morar, Glengarry, Braes of Lochaber ... the Western Isles of Uist, Barra, Benbecula, Canna, Egg [sic] ... nothing is professed but the Roman Catholic religion.[2]

In all these areas surviving communities of Roman Catholics had been strengthened during the early seventeenth century by the work of missionary priests from Ireland.[3] In order to care for the various groups of Roman Catholic recusants in Scotland vicars-apostolic, on the model of those in England and Wales, had been established with the appointment of Thomas Nicholson as vicar-apostolic for the whole of Scotland in 1697. This arrangement was not really satisfactory. The two groups of Roman Catholics, those in the north-west highlands and islands, with their links to the Roman Catholic church in Ireland, and those in the lowlands, based on the estates of a small number of recusant landowners, with much more in common with similar groups of recusants in England and Wales, had no common culture, and in 1727 it was decided to split the Scottish vicariate, with Hugh MacDonald being consecrated as vicar-apostolic to the Scottish *Gaidhealtachd* in 1731.[4] In 1768, the new vicariate established a seminary on Lismore for the training of priests to serve the Gaelic-speaking Roman Catholic communities of the western highlands and islands.[5] Even in the late eighteenth century the strength of Scottish Roman Catholicism was still in this area. It was estimated that there were between 1,200 and 1,250 Roman Catholics in Barra, between 2,300 and 2,500 in South Uist, between 848 and 894 in Moidart, between 739 and 824 in Arisaig and between 1,340 and 1,400 in North Morar and Knoydart. There had been, however, an extreme shortage of priests with only one for every 1,250 laity before 1750. This situation was partly rectified by the establishment of the Lismore seminary, with the numbers of priests to serve the Gaelic-speaking Roman Catholic community increasing from ten in 1750 to 22 by 1810. By contrast there

---

[2] Michael Mullett, *Catholics in Britain and Ireland, 1558–1829*, Basingstoke 1998, p. 170.
[3] Kirk, *Patterns of Reform*, p. 476.
[4] Mark Dillworth, 'Roman Catholic Worship', Forrester and Murray (eds), *Studies in the History of Worship*, p. 137; Mullett, *Catholics in Britain and Ireland*, p. 105.
[5] C. Johnson, *Developments in the Roman Catholic Church in Scotland 1789–1929*, Edinburgh 1983, p. 41.

were only five Roman Catholics altogether in the counties of Ayrshire, Bute, Dunbartonshire, Lanarkshire, Renfrewshire and Wigtownshire in the 1780s, and a further five in Glasgow. The main presence of Roman Catholics in the lowlands was on the estates of recusant families such as those at Drummond Castle, Stobhall, Terregles and Traquair.[6] Whereas Roman Catholicism in the southern lowlands, and even in the north-east, where there were considerable groups of Roman Catholics in Aberdeenshire and Banffshire, was strongly controlled by the recusant landed families which had ensured its survival, in the western highlands and islands the Roman Catholic faithful 'were almost uniformly peasants'.[7] Indeed the strength of Roman Catholicism in the southern parts of the Western Isles in the 1790s is attested to by the entries in the statistical accounts.[8]

Worship in this recusant church was deliberately low key, and the congregations worshipped either in the private chapels of recusant landowners, or in domestic buildings adapted for worship. One of these still survives, at Tynet, Moray (Plate 11; Appendix C/45), complete with many of its furnishings, and gives a good insight into the state of Roman Catholic worship and church building at this time. The private chapel at Traquair (Appendix C/58) was originally in one of the upper rooms of the house, with accommodation for a priest, but was relocated in one of the service wings in the 1820s. Even so, compared with many contemporary buildings in other parts of the British Isles, it is an exceptionally modest construction with little in the way of opulent furnishings. Roman Catholic worship in eighteenth-century Scotland was similar. The normal service comprised 'a sermon, long vernacular prayers and a Low Mass in Latin'.[9] Any form of musical accompaniment to the services had been prohibited by Bishop Hay and it was not until the early years of the nineteenth century that Roman Catholic services included music, or that their churches were equipped with organs. Roman Catholic churches in which organs had been introduced by the 1820s included those at Aberdeen, Banff, Edinburgh, Fochabers, Glasgow, Greenock and Paisley.[10]

---

[6] Mullett, *Catholics in Britain and Ireland*, pp. 172–4; D.F. McMillan, 'Mission accomplished? The Catholic underground', *Eighteenth Century Scotland: New Perspectives*, ed. T.M. Devine and J.R. Young, East Linton 1999, pp. 94, 102–4.

[7] C.G. Brown, *Religion and Society*, p. 31. Brown states the Roman Catholic population of Scotland in 1755 as 16,490, or just over 1 per cent of the total population of Scotland.

[8] See Appendix A/42 (Barra) and 46 (South Uist).

[9] Dillworth, 'Roman Catholic worship', p. 140.

[10] Ian McCraw, *Victorian Dundee at Worship*, Dundee 2002, p. 95; Drummond and Bulloch, *Church in Victorian Scotland*, p. 181; James Inglis, 'The Scottish churches and the organ in the nineteenth century', Glasgow PhD 1987, pp. 80–1.

SCOTTISH EPISCOPALIAN CHURCH INTERIORS 1690–1860

Plate 11 The late-eighteenth-century interior of St Ninian's Roman Catholic Chapel, Tynet, as refurbished by Ian Lindsay in 1951

In the last quarter of the eighteenth century and the first quarter of the nineteenth, the demography of Scottish Roman Catholicism began to change, largely through the move of the population away from the highlands and islands to the expanding lowland cities and towns and as a result of immigration from Ireland. In 1780, there had been only 6,600 Roman Catholics in Scotland below the highland line. There were still only 20 Roman Catholics in Glasgow in 1778, rising to 60 by 1791 and 2,300 by 1808. Thereafter expansion was rapid: there were 20,000 Roman Catholics thereby 1820 and 27,000 by 1831, representing at that stage 13 per cent of the city's population. The Roman Catholic population of Edinburgh increased from less than a thousand in the 1790s to 14,000 by 1829. At the 1841 census several cities, towns and counties recorded high levels of Irish immigrants, mostly Roman Catholics, in their populations, as shown in Table 9. It is notable that all of these areas of high immigration were below the highland line and, therefore, not in those of traditional Roman Catholic strength before 1780. As in England, the expansion of the numbers of Roman Catholics through Irish immigration was to cause major tensions

Table 9 Scottish counties, cities and towns recording high levels of inhabitants born in Ireland in the census of 1841

Counties	%	Cities/Towns	%
Ayrshire	7.3	Airdrie	10.1
Dunbartonshire	11.0	Dundee	9.0
Lanark	13.1	Glasgow	16.2
Renfrew	13.2	Greenock	11.7
Stirlingshire	5.2	Kilmarnock	8.1
Wigtownshire	14.7	Paisley	10.8

between the immigrants and the native Scottish Roman Catholics, both clergy and laity.[11] However, even in some of the traditional areas of Roman Catholic strength, there was continued expansion throughout the eighteenth century. In the highland parish of Braemar a total of 776 Roman Catholic baptisms were recorded between 1703 and 1736 and a total Roman Catholic population of 900 in 1764. By 1800 Roman Catholics had become the majority religious group in Braemar parish, and in the neighbouring parishes about a third of the population was Roman Catholic. As Roman Catholic communities expanded new places of worship were built. The first Roman Catholic church was opened in Edinburgh in 1786. Glasgow got its first resident priest in 1792 and the subscription list for a permanent place of worship was begun in 1797. At Dundee the size of the Roman Catholic community had grown from 14 communicants in 1782 to a congregation of a hundred by the end of the decade.[12]

The church-building programme for this expanding Roman Catholic community had begun in 1773 with a place of worship and house for a priest at Aberdeen. It was followed by simple buildings at Tynet (1779, enlarged 1787), noted earlier, and at Sherval (1780), Kempcairn (1785), Tombae (1786), Huntly (1787), Tomintoul (1788) and Auchindoun (1793). The churches at Kempcairn and Auchindoun were both single-storied and thatched. The church built at Presholme in 1790 was described as 'the first ... which was recognizably a church building'. The early place of worship at Aberdeen was replaced by one more ecclesiastical in style in 1803–1804.[13] This chapel was opened with what was claimed to be the first High Mass celebrated in Scotland since the Reformation.[14] New churches followed at Paisley (1808), Dumfries (1813), Dalbeattie (1814) and Greenock (1816). Between 1820 and 1850 Roman Catholic churches

---

[11] Brown, *Religion and Society*, pp. 32–3; Steve Bruce, *No Pope of Rome: Anti-Catholicism in Modern Scotland*, Edinburgh 1985, pp. 25–7.
[12] Mullett, *Catholics in Britain and Ireland*, pp. 106, 108, 116–17, 177–80.
[13] Johnson, *Developments in the Roman Catholic Church*, p. 153.
[14] P.F. Anson, 'Catholic church building in Scotland from the Reformation to the outbreak of the First World War', *Innes Review*, v (1954), p. 127.

were being built in Scotland at the rate of about two each year.[15] Two of the most impressive new churches were those in Edinburgh (1814) and Glasgow (1816), both of which became cathedrals when the Roman Catholic hierarchy was restored in Scotland in 1878. The Edinburgh church was regarded as the first example of the Gothic Revival in Scotland but has been much altered over the years. At Glasgow the future cathedral has been much less altered and one can get a good impression of the excitement it must have occasioned when it was opened. It cost £20,000 and was the largest church in the city apart from St Mungo's Cathedral, then divided into two churches. Its exceptionally broad nave and aisles are still covered by their original plaster vaults, though the original furnishings were entirely replaced in a remodelling of the interior between 1889 and 1904.[16]

The vast majority of Roman Catholic Church building was in what might be termed a pre-ecclesiological Gothic style and this was to continue until well into the second half of the nineteenth century. Two of the more interesting buildings of the earlier period were the distinctly non-Gothic churches at Keith (1831) and Huntly (1834). Both were designed by priest-architects, Fr Walter Lovi at Keith and Bishop James Kyle at Huntly. St Thomas's, Keith, was designed in the form of a Greek cross, to which a copper dome and sanctuary extension were added in 1916. It retains its original altar reredos, a painting of *The Incredulity of St Thomas* by François Dubois, presented by the former King Charles X of France, but has been otherwise re-furnished. St Margaret's, Huntly, is an octagonal building with a tower over the entrance at one end and a shallow projection for the sanctuary at the other. Although the sanctuary has been re-furnished and a new pulpit installed, the original benches, curved in a semi-circle, the organ gallery and the original paintings decorating the walls have survived. An even more complete survival, in which only the sanctuary has been altered, is St Mary's, Eskdale (Appendix C/35), built at the cost of Lord Lovat in 1826.[17] An interesting surviving plan is that of the combined church of St Mary and priest's house at New Abbey (Dumfries and Galloway), designed by local architect Walter Newell and built in 1824. The church was a simple rectangle with the altar in a raised sanctuary at one end with a box pew on each side. The remaining box pews were placed either side of a central passageway between the sanctuary and the entrance porch. There was no pulpit so sermons were presumably delivered from the altar steps. The priest's house was a two-storey T-plan arrangement behind the church, which had the

---

[15] *Ibid.*, pp. 130–2.
[16] Johnson, *Developments in the Roman Catholic Church*, p. 155; Drummond and Bulloch, *Scottish Church*, p. 141; *BS Glasgow*, p. 193; *SPC*, p. 157.
[17] *SPC*, pp. 157–8.

effect of giving the whole building a cruciform arrangement externally.[18] Although the building remains in use for Roman Catholic worship the interior of the church was completely re-furnished in 1890. An illustration of St Mary's Roman Catholic chapel in Edinburgh, dated as late as 1851 [Plate 12], still shows a very similar arrangement to that at New Abbey. Box pews were placed either side of an exceptionally wide central passageway, but at Edinburgh a canopied pulpit was placed at the eastern end of the northern pew block. Against the east wall was the altar with a tripartite reredos incorporating paintings. On the north and south sides of the altar, set within a railed sanctuary, were doors to the sacristy behind. This illustration confirms the view of Peter Anson that

> the furnishings and decorations of Roman Catholic places of worship in Scotland . . . would have provided little to interest the ecclesiologists until after 1850. . . . Fear of arousing Presbyterian prejudice restrained priests from adorning their chapels with statues. Unlike English Catholics those in Scotland were hardly influenced by the ecclesiological movement of the 'forties and 'fifties. Augustus Welby Pugin

Plate 12 The furnishings of St Mary's Roman Catholic Chapel, Edinburgh, as designed by James Gillespie Graham in 1814

---

[18] DGA, GGD 313/N7/27.

never built a church north of the border. Unlike the Episcopalians, the Catholic body in Scotland . . . did not feel any urge to improve the tone of its services or to introduce a more correct ritual. It was sufficient to provide enough chapels for the laity to fulfil their spiritual obligations. . . . Thus the majority of chapels erected before 1850 were purely utilitarian.[19]

A good example was St Mary's, Arisaig, opened in 1849, which employed the Gothic style but with none of the attention to detail or correct liturgical arrangement to make it acceptable to the ecclesiologists.

2. *Scottish episcopalians*

Those Episcopalians in eighteenth-century Scotland who enjoyed the most secure existence were those attached to what were known as 'qualified chapels'. In 1709, James Greenshields, a clergyman who had been deprived as bishop of Ross, opened a chapel in Edinburgh at which he read the services according to the *Book of Common Prayer*. Attempts by the Presbytery of Edinburgh to force the closure of the chapel and to terminate Greenshields's ministry in the city resulted in the passing of the Toleration Act in 1712. This Act permitted episcopally ordained clergy willing to take the oaths to Queen Anne and her successors to conduct services in Scotland using the *Book of Common Prayer*.[20] As a result a number of 'qualified chapels' were established, mostly in southern Scotland and the larger towns, in which prayer book services were used and in which the ministers were in communion with the Church of England. Those Episcopalians who were not prepared to take the necessary oaths to, in their eyes, an illegitimate ruler, maintained their own independent episcopal church. In 1705, the surviving Scottish bishops took deliberate steps to maintain the episcopal succession in Scotland by consecrating bishops without territorial jurisdiction and began to open up contacts between themselves and the English non-jurors. In 1711 James Gadderar was consecrated by two of the surviving Scottish bishops and the leader of the English non-jurors, Bishop George Hickes. Contact with the English non-jurors meant that the Scottish Episcopal Church was drawn into the conflicts among the English non-jurors over liturgical matters, particularly such innovations as the mixing of water with wine in the chalice, prayers for the departed and alterations in the eucharistic

---

[19] Peter Anson, *Fashions in Church Furnishings 1840–1940*, 2nd edn, London 1965, pp. 105–6.
[20] Henry Sefton, 'Revolution to disruption', Forrester and Murray (eds), *Studies in the History of Worship*, pp. 73–4.

prayers.[21] One of the leading Scottish bishops, Thomas Rattray, eventually produced his own revision of the liturgy, strongly influenced by early Christian and eastern orthodox practice, and this was reflected in the Scottish Communion office of 1764.[22]

Initially there was much variation in the liturgical practices of the non-juring Scottish Episcopalians. They had inherited a situation in which it was normal for churches not to have a fixed communion table or liturgy, or for the minister to wear a surplice, and such arrangements were maintained in some congregations for many years. By the second quarter of the eighteenth century, however, most congregations were using either the *Book of Common Prayer* or the 1637 Scottish prayer book, which had been reprinted in 1712. The English prayer book was introduced at St Andrew's, Aberdeen, in 1735. There was Morning and Evening Prayer, both with a sermon, every Sunday. Morning Prayer was also said on Holy Days, every Wednesday and Friday throughout the year, and on Saturdays and Mondays before and after Sunday celebrations of Holy Communion. Celebrations took place seven times a year, on Christmas Day, the first Sunday in Lent, Good Friday, Easter Day, Whit Sunday 'and twice in the Trinity Season'.[23] When the Scottish Communion Office was published in 1764, based on the 1637 communion rite but incorporating elements from English non-juring liturgies and Thomas Rattray's liturgy, published posthumously in 1744, the bishops of the Episcopal Church, who had by that date re-adopted territorial titles and jurisdictions, strongly encouraged all congregations to use it. In 1788, with the death of Prince Charles Edward Stuart, the 'Young Pretender', the Scottish bishops agreed that they would renounce Jacobitism and pray for King George III at their services. In 1792, the Episcopal Church was granted toleration but its clergy were still, until the 1840s, legally prevented from conducting services or preaching, and until the 1860s from holding benefices, in the United Church of England and Ireland. Anglican clergy from outside Scotland were not prevented from serving in the Scottish Episcopal Church and the time was, therefore, ripe for a union to take place between that church and the clergy and congregations of the 'qualified chapels'. However, the process was a slow one. It was assisted by the decision of the Scottish bishops to require acceptance of the Thirty-Nine Articles of Religion and to permit the use of either the *Book of Common Prayer* or the Scottish Communion Office for celebrations of Holy Communion. In 1792 Daniel Sandford, curate at Hanworth in Surrey, had accepted 'the

---

[21] Rowan Strong, *Episcopalianism in Nineteenth-Century Scotland: Religious Responses to a Modernising Society*, Oxford 2002, pp. 13–14.
[22] For text and commentary see Grisbrooke, *Anglican Liturgies*, pp. 150–9, 333–48.
[23] McMillan, 'Anglican Book of Common Prayer', p. 149; Allan Maclean, 'Episcopal worship', Forrester and Murray (eds), *Studies in the History of Worship*, p. 110.

invitation of certain English churchmen', to establish a new congregation in Edinburgh which worshipped in the Charlotte Chapel, the predecessor of St John's in Princes Street, from 1796. In 1806, Sandford was consecrated bishop of Edinburgh by the Scottish bishops and was instrumental in persuading the 'qualified chapels' in his diocese to join the Scottish Episcopal Church. By 1850 all the former 'qualified chapels' throughout Scotland, with the exception of St Peter's, Montrose, had joined the Episcopal Church.[24]

Episcopal chapels, whether 'qualified' or in communion with the Scottish bishops, were the first in Scotland to introduce organs as accompaniments to singing. Ones were noted in the 1790s at both the English and Scottish episcopal chapels in Peterhead (Appendix A/5) and in the chapel at Kelso (Appendix A/72). By the early years of the nineteenth century there were also organs in episcopal chapels at Aberdeen, Banff, Dundee, Edinburgh, Glasgow, Leith and Montrose.[25] Hymns were also in use in several chapels, which compiled their own hymnals, though the first official church hymnal was not published until 1857.[26] The gradual union of the 'qualified' and former non-juring strands of Episcopalianism required a decision about vesture. In the 'qualified chapels', the surplice had been worn for services, except for preaching when the black gown was used, but in other churches the black gown had been worn for all ministrations. In 1811, the Synod of Aberdeen permitted the use of either the *Book of Common Prayer* or the Scottish Communion Office on sacrament days, and recommended that the surplice should be introduced, except for preaching, 'with prudence and discretion'. The recommendation was, however, widely disregarded and in 1823 Bishop Skinner of Aberdeen issued an injunction to the clergy of his diocese requiring the wearing of the surplice.[27] At St John's, Edinburgh, the surplice and black gown seem to have been used indiscriminately until the death of Bishop Sandford in 1830,[28] and in other parts of Scotland use of the surplice was not adopted until late in the nineteenth century.[29]

From the 1790s, with the lifting of penal legislation, Scottish Episcopalianism began to expand. In 1800, it was estimated that there were about 15,000 Episcopalians in Scotland, of which about two-thirds were in communion

---

[24] Sefton, 'Revolution to disruption', pp. 74–5; Strong, *Episcopalianism*, pp. 15, 19–21; G.F. Terry, *Memorials of the Church of St John the Evangelist, Princes Street*, Edinburgh 1911, pp. 26–7.

[25] Inglis, 'Scottish churches and the organ', pp. 80–1.

[26] Maclean, 'Episcopal worship', p. 121.

[27] *Ibid.*, pp. 114, 120; William Walker, *The Life and Times of John Skinner*, Aberdeen 1887, pp. 276–7.

[28] Terry, *Memorials*, p. 35.

[29] Drummond and Bulloch, *Church in Victorian Scotland*, p. 203.

with the Scottish bishops and a third worshipped in 'qualified chapels'. Fifty clergy acknowledged the authority of the Scottish bishops and 23 served the 'qualified chapels'. However, the former group of clergy and their congregations were based mainly in the Aberdeenshire, Angus and Kincardine area with scattered groups in Argyll, Fife, Moray, Perthshire and Ross and Cromarty. There were only seven clergy in the south of Scotland maintaining communion with the Scottish bishops: four in Edinburgh and one each in Glasgow, Leith and Stirling. In these areas, most Episcopalians worshipped in 'qualified chapels'.[30] The situation was much improved by the consecration of Daniel Sandford as bishop of Edinburgh in 1806. Under his influence the two 'qualified chapels' in Edinburgh, together with those in Haddington, Kelso, Leith and Musselburgh joined the Scottish Episcopal Church between 1805 and 1826. Two new churches were established in Edinburgh and, in 1828, one at Peebles.[31] In 1816–1818, the Charlotte Street Chapel in Edinburgh was replaced with the ambitious new church of St John the Evangelist in Princes Street. This cost £18,013 and the old chapel was sold to a congregation of Baptists for £1550. A contemporary illustration of the interior [Plate 13] shows the pulpit and reading desk placed either side of a vested altar, with an episcopal throne behind the reading desk and painted glass in the window above the altar. The church was built with an organ and the canticles were sung at Morning Prayer and there was an anthem at Evening Prayer. There was also Morning Prayer on all Holy days, Wednesdays and Fridays in Lent and everyday in Holy Week. Before the building of St Mary's Cathedral, towards the end of the nineteenth century, St John's was effectively treated as the bishop of Edinburgh's pro-cathedral.[32]

The change in the fortune of the Scottish Episcopal Church can be illustrated in the developments at Keith (Moray). Here the first episcopal place of worship was a simple cottage at which services were begun in 1791. In 1807, a proper church was built; even though it 'was accounted the first Episcopal Church in the North' of Scotland it still only cost £200 and was replaced in 1882–1883 with a new church costing £2600. In 1815, the old Keith chapel acquired an organ. A contemporary account of a confirmation in the episcopal chapel at Inverness in 1820 noted that there was an organ and 'a choir of singing boys' and that the clergy wore surplices.[33] At Fort William (Highland) an episcopal chapel was

---

[30] Strong, *Episcopalianism*, pp. 19–20.
[31] R. Foskett, 'The episcopate of Daniel Sandford, 1806–1830', *RSCHS*, xv (1965), pp. 146, 151.
[32] Terry, *Memorials*, pp. 30, 32, 34–5.
[33] John Archibald, *History of the Episcopal Church at Keith in the Diocese of Moray*, Edinburgh 1890, pp. 81, 98, 102–3, 123.

Plate 13 View of the interior of St John's Episcopal Church, Edinburgh, as built in 1816–1818 (Glasgow University Library, Special Collections)

erected in 1817 by voluntary subscription, and cost from £500 to £600. ... Divine service is performed twice every Sunday – in the forenoon in English, in the afternoon in Gaelic. The incumbent has, since 1828, superintended the scattered members of the Church in the remote and mountainous districts of Morven, Sunart, and Moydart.

In 1848, there was still

service in both English and Gaelic throughout the year. In 1847, the Baptisms were 13, Marriages 1, Funerals 5, Catechumens 18,

Communicants at Easter, chiefly Gaelic, 40. The church is in tolerable repair, but is subject to a debt of £40.[34]

As at Keith this modest building was in due course replaced, this time with a remarkably handsome building, still retaining all its original furnishings, designed by Alexander Ross, and built between 1879 and 1884.[35]

Part of the success of the Scottish Episcopal Church in the first half of the nineteenth century was its appeal to the upper levels of Scottish society, who found the services and structure of the established church less attractive. By the 1840s 86 per cent of the Scottish nobility and 'two-thirds of the landowning classes generally' were members of the Scottish Episcopal Church.[36] Among those who rented seats at St John's, Edinburgh, at its opening in 1818, were the Duke of Buccleuch, the Earl of Rosebery and the Marquis of Lothian.[37] In 1834, the new episcopal chapel at Fochabers (Moray) was built, complete with organ, at the sole cost of the Duke and Duchess of Gordon.[38] None of these pre-1840 churches survive with their furnishings intact and there are no surviving plans or illustrations of any chapels, other than those, such as St John's in Edinburgh, which were clearly replicating arrangements of Anglican churches in other parts of the British Isles at the same time. Although many episcopal congregations were still worshipping in a similar manner to those in the established Church of Scotland until the middle years of the eighteenth century, the almost universal adoption of a formal liturgy in the latter part of that century had led to various modifications, not just the introduction of organs but also of fixed communion tables. The rector of Ballachulish and Glencoe recorded in the late nineteenth century that

> before the erection of the present church in 1842, the Church people ... met for worship in the Old Church ... which I now use as a barn. This building was originally a storehouse or barn, and was afterwards fitted up as a Church, with a gallery. I believe the Altar used to stand in the side of the Church, same as originally at Portnacrois.[39]

Here the Church of the Holy Cross, consecrated in 1815, still remains in use. It was a simple rectangle of three bays. Until 1887, when the church

---

[34] J.B. Craven, *Records of the Dioceses of Argyll and the Isles 1560–1860*, Kirkwall 1907, pp. 312–13.
[35] *BS Highland and Islands*, pp. 240–1.
[36] Brown, *Religion and Society*, p. 34.
[37] Terry, *Memorials*, p. 33.
[38] Archibald, *Episcopal Church at Keith*, p. 109.
[39] Craven, *Records*, p. 293.

was re-orientated with the altar at the east end, the altar was placed in the middle of the south wall with a three-decker pulpit in the middle of the north wall and lofts across both the east and west walls. The original arrangement was partially restored in 1974 when the church was enlarged by the incorporation into it of a former schoolroom to form a north transept. A T-plan interior, though without lofts, was created by restoring the altar to its pre-1887 location in the middle of the south wall with pews facing it from three different directions. The position occupied by the three-decker pulpit before 1887 is now occupied by a modern font.[40] An eighteenth-century three-decker pulpit survives in the chapel at Fort George, near Inverness, where services were conducted in accordance with the provisions of the *Book of Common Prayer*, but it is not in its original location and most of the other contemporary furnishings have been destroyed.[41]

By the end of the eighteenth century it would appear that most Episcopalian places of worship in Scotland, certainly in the towns, were arranged in much the same manner as their Anglican counterparts in other parts of the British Isles. The chapel at Inverness, visited by Boswell and Johnson in 1773, and in which the altar was described as

> A bare fir table with a coarse stool for kneeling on, covered with a piece of coarse sack-cloth doubled by way of cushion,

was probably a T-plan as it was noted as having 'lofts at each end and one before the pulpit'.[42] The chapel at Dundee, erected in 1812, was described as 'a large room filled with green baize pews'. The altar was covered by a red velvet carpet and railed in, with the pulpit and reading desk, a two-decker, standing in front of it. At Peterhead (1814) and Monymusk (early nineteenth century) the altar appears to have been placed in front of the pulpit and reading desk, as it still is in the Irish churches of Clonguish and Timogue. At Ellon (1816) the more typical Anglican arrangement of placing the pulpit, in this case a three-decker, in front of the altar, was adopted, and the organ and choir placed in a west gallery. At St Andrews (1825) the new chapel was furnished with a pulpit and reading desk standing either side of the entrance to a shallow chancel, a similar arrangement to that which had been adopted at St John's, Edinburgh, and one that was being adopted by many other Anglican churches in the British Isles.[43] Even the unusual liturgical arrangement noted earlier at Portnacrois had equivalent examples

---

[40] *BS Argyll and Bute*, p. 433.
[41] *BS Highland and Islands*, p. 179
[42] *SPC*, p. 145.
[43] *Ibid.*, pp. 148–51.

elsewhere in the British Isles, in this case the Church of King Charles the Martyr at Tunbridge Wells, where an illustration of the interior before its restoration in 1882, shows the pulpit and desks in the middle of the west, and the altar in the middle of the east, wall in a church that was almost square. A similar arrangement survives in the T-plan church of c.1820 at Dromard (co. Sligo).[44]

The prevailing high churchmanship of the Scottish Episcopal Church in the 1840s made it fertile ground for the Tractarians and ecclesiologists, and the five remaining pre-1860 fully ecclesiological churches in Scotland are all episcopal ones. They are those at Poltalloch (Appendix C/11), Dalkeith (Appendix C/22), Dalmahoy (Appendix C/23) and Jedburgh (Appendix C/55), and the chapel at Glenalmond (Appendix C/49). All were Tractarian foundations and at Glenalmond the staff and pupils had worn surplices to chapel services since the college was founded in 1845.[45] St Mary's, Dalmahoy, consecrated on 24 September 1850, was built and endowed at the sole cost of Lord and Lady Aberdour, with the support of Lord Aberdour's father, the seventeenth Earl of Morton. The architect, John Henderson, had previously designed Trinity College, Glenalmond, and its chapel. The church was built together with a parsonage, schoolroom, schoolmaster's house and choir house. At the consecration the music was provided by the choir of St Columba's, Edinburgh, one of the earliest Tractarian churches in Scotland, completed in 1848 and furnished with a rood screen, surmounted by a cross, and a stone altar vested with a frontal and adorned with candlesticks. This church had daily services and a weekly celebration of Holy Communion.[46] St John's, Jedburgh, was built in 1843–1844 at the expense of the Marchioness of Lothian, whose brother, John Talbot, and brother-in-law, Lord Henry Kerr, had been scholars at Oxford during the height of the Tractarian movement in the 1830s. The architect chosen was John Haywood, a member of the Cambridge Camden Society, and a close friend of the leading Tractarian architect, William Butterfield. Several leading Tractarians or Tractarian sympathizers – William Dodsworth, W. F. Hook, John Keble and Robert Wilberforce – attended the consecration, and Wilberforce preached the sermon at Evensong, during which the Revd W. S. White was instituted to the charge. Sermons were preached on the Sunday after the consecration by Dodsworth and Keble, and at the consecration service itself by Hook. The services were fully choral, chanted by the clergy and a robed choir. Inevitably, as Peter Nockles has noted, such 'a

---

[44] *BFW*, pp. 82–3, 228.
[45] Drummond and Bulloch, *Church in Victorian Scotland*, p. 206.
[46] Diana Towsey and Nancy Adams, *St Mary's Dalmahoy 1970–2000*, Edinburgh 2000, pp. 25–6; Nigel Yates, *Anglican Ritualism in Victorian Britain 1830–1910*, Oxford 1999, pp. 125–6.

rally of Tractarian support for the Episcopal church ... drew immediate hostile notice'.[47]

Debates over ritual, eucharistic theology and the use of the Scottish Communion Office were to dominate the small Scottish Episcopal Church in the 1850s. Most of the bishops were pre-Tractarian high churchmen though Torry of St Andrews, Dunkeld and Dunblane and Terrot of Edinburgh were sympathetic to Tractarianism. In 1847, an archetypal Tractarian, A. P. Forbes, was consecrated bishop of Brechin, and a second Tractarian appointment might have been made had William Dodsworth been offered the bishopric of Glasgow and Galloway for which he was seriously considered. Bishop Forbes was also incumbent of Dundee (Scottish bishops also holding parochial appointments at that time) and replaced the former chapel there with a new church, designed by George Gilbert Scott and opened in 1855. Although Bishop Forbes was very cautious about permitting ritual innovations in his new church, in which there were no candles on the altar and the black gown was still used for preaching, there were by 1853 twelve episcopal churches which were clearly moving in a ritualistic direction: St John's, Aberdeen; St Mary's, Dalkeith; St Mary's, Dalmahoy; St Columba's, Edinburgh; St Mary's, Montrose; St Mary's, Dumfries; St John's, Jedburgh; St Serf's, Burntisland; St Michael's, Crieff and St Ninian's, Perth. Even at Glenalmond, where the old-fashioned pre-Tractarian Charles Wordsworth was the warden, there were daily services and weekly communion. In 1852, Wordsworth succeeded Patrick Torry as bishop of St Andrew's, Dunkeld and Dunblane, and was almost immediately involved in a long-running battle with the clergy of St Ninian's, Perth, which had been consecrated by Torry in 1850 to serve as the cathedral of the diocese, the first attempt to provide any Scottish Episcopal diocese with a cathedral. Torry had invited the leading Tractarian, J. M. Neale, to be the first dean. When Neale declined, the post was offered to and accepted by another Tractarian, E. B. K. Fortescue. The first residentiary canons, J. C. Chambers, Henry Humble and Joseph Haskoll were also advanced Tractarians. Possibly from the beginning, but certainly within a few years, vestments, lighted candles, wafer bread and incense were all in use, much to Bishop Wordsworth's consternation. The Church of the Holy Spirit at Millport on Cumbrae [Plate 14] had been designed by the Tractarian architect, William Butterfield, for the Hon G. F. Boyle, was completed in 1851, and was served by a college of three clergy, a provost and two canons, who were expected to be unmarried and to live a communal life. Holy Communion was celebrated on Sundays, Tuesdays, Thursdays and Holy Days; the altar was vested with

---

[47] A.C. Ryrie, *A Vision Pursued: St John's Church, Jedburgh, 1844–1994*, Kelso 1994, pp. 4–6; P.B. Nockles, 'Our Brethren in the north: The Scottish episcopal church and the Oxford Movement', *Journal of Ecclesiastical History*, xlvii (1996), p. 672.

Plate 14 The Episcopal Cathedral of the Isles at Millport, designed by William Butterfield in 1851

coloured frontals, an altar cross and lighted candles and there was a stone credence table.[48]

The Oxford Movement was to have an enormous impact on the Scottish Episcopal Church, to such an extent that its few Evangelical clergy and congregations found it impossible to accept the authority of bishops that they accused of having deliberately tolerated, and even encouraged, what they regarded as 'popery'. After a clash with Bishop Terrot, the Evangelical

---

[48] Yates, *Anglican Ritualism*, pp. 126–34; Strong, *Episcopalianism*, pp. 249–58.

incumbent of Holy Trinity, Edinburgh, left in 1842 to establish the new congregation of St Thomas, which refused to accept the bishop's authority. In 1847, an alliance of 'Church of England Chapels in Scotland' was formed comprising St Paul's in Aberdeen, St Thomas's in Edinburgh, St Jude's in Glasgow and congregations in Dunoon, Gask, Huntly, Nairn and Perth which refused to accept the authority of the relevant Scottish bishop and demanded to be placed under the care of an English one. There were still ten such congregations in 1870: St Thomas's and St Vincent's, Edinburgh; St Jude's and St Silas's, Glasgow; St James's, Aberdeen; St Peter's, Montrose; St John's, Dundee; and chapels in Gatehouse of Fleet, Nairn and Wemyss Bay. High church English bishops such as Denison of Salisbury, Phillpotts of Exeter and Wilberforce of Oxford, denounced these Evangelical clergy as schismatics, but they elicited support from other Anglican bishops including the Evangelical archbishop of Canterbury, J. B. Sumner, the Evangelical bishop of Cashel and Waterford (Robert Daly) and the broad church bishops Stanley of Norwich and Pepys of Worcester. Such action helped to marginalize support for Evangelicalism within the Scottish Episcopal Church even further. It is, however, important to emphasize that, despite the growth in the number of episcopal churches to adopt ritualistic practices, as in England many churches in Scotland maintained the traditional, non-ritualistic, attitudes of pre-Tractarian high churchmen until well into the nineteenth century. In the 1870s, the congregation at Dumfries successfully resisted such attempted innovations as the introduction of a surpliced choir, *Hymns Ancient and Modern*, facing east at the creed and the decoration of the church at Christmas. At St Andrews, the episcopal church was extended in 1853, but still retained its box pews, the use of the black gown for preaching and an altar covered with the traditional carpet of crimson velvet. The clergy still sang the responses alone until the 1860s. When the church was offered a jewelled altar cross and candlesticks by a lay person in the diocese they were refused by the vestry. Seasonal liturgical colours were not introduced until 1893.[49] However, at the other end of the scale, six Scottish Episcopal churches were by 1874 served by incumbents who were members of the extreme ritualist clerical society, *Societas Sanctae Crucis*: St Margaret's, Aberdeen; Cove; Dalmahoy; Dumbarton; All Saints, Edinburgh and St Ninian's, Perth. The first edition of the *Tourist's Church Guide*, published in that year, recorded the use of eucharistic vestments and of lighted candles on the altar at Aberdeen, Cove, Edinburgh and Perth. Three of these churches also had a daily communion services as did that at Dalmahoy; all except the church at Dumbarton also used Gregorian chant.[50]

[49] Ibid., pp. 216–24, 258–9. See also Gavin White, *The Scottish Episcopal Church: A New History*, Edinburgh 1998, pp. 75–81.
[50] Yates, *Anglican Ritualism*, p. 414.

It is very clear that by 1860 the fortunes of the Scottish Episcopal Church had changed dramatically from its state a century earlier in which Episcopalians had formed two very small, and completely separate, groups in Scotland: the non-jurors, primarily in the north-east and the western highlands, and the qualified chapels in the larger towns. The two groups had not only merged but had considerably strengthened their position in Scotland through attracting the support of landed families and a significant section of the professional middle class, as well as immigrants from England and those attracted by the Oxford Movement. By 1860 Scottish Episcopalianism was part of the Anglican mainstream within the British Isles, whereas a century earlier it had been virtually unrecognized in England except by a small group of the more advanced Anglican high churchmen. Although Roman Catholicism in Scotland had also greatly expanded through the same period, largely as a result of immigration from Ireland, it had been slower in achieving a position of religious leadership within Scottish society. It had emerged, especially in terms of its worship and buildings, much more slowly from the constraints of the penal era than Episcopalianism had done. In 1860, Roman Catholics in Scotland were on the verge of establishing their presence more firmly in the religious landscape but that was a position that they did not fully achieve until the last quarter of the nineteenth century.

6

LITURGICAL AND ARCHITECTURAL DEVELOPMENTS SINCE 1860

1860 is a convenient watershed date from which to mark a significant change in liturgical and architectural developments in Scotland. The greatest impact was on the Presbyterian churches, but they were, to some extent, influenced by developments among the non-Presbyterians, especially the Scottish Episcopal Church. In this chapter, we will begin by looking at developments in the Roman Catholic and Scottish Episcopal churches before moving on to consider liturgical and architectural change in the Presbyterian churches. We will conclude with an overview of the religious situation in Scotland in the last 80 years and the impact that the collapse of religious observance in the last 40 years has had on the Scottish architectural heritage. By far the greatest impact on the Scottish liturgical scene in the last four decades of the nineteenth century was ecclesiology. This movement, which had begun south of the border in the 1830s, had aimed to restore British churches to something like their pre-Reformation appearance and to build new churches in the neo-Gothic style. As a movement, it was not confined to the British Isles. Neo-Gothic churches were eventually built throughout Europe, America and Australasia. As well as attention to Gothic detail in their fabrics, these churches were expected to observe certain principles in their furnishing and liturgical arrangement: choirs, preferably vested in surplices or some other quasi-clerical clothing, located between the congregation and the altar or communion table, rather than in galleries; open benches rather than box pews for the congregation, preferably not assigned or rented but 'free and open' to all-comers; the creation of separate liturgical 'stations' in a church through the careful positioning of pulpits, lecterns, baptismal fonts, desks for the clergy, communion tables and organs. As we have seen in the previous chapter, Scottish Episcopalians were the first religious group in Scotland to experiment with ecclesiological design, with churches of this type being opened in the 1840s and 1850s. Roman Catholics, who had been attracted at a very early stage to ecclesiological ideas in both England and Ireland, had not been so attracted in Scotland before the 1860s. Presbyterians did not begin to jump on the ecclesiological bandwagon until the 1870s and 1880s. Once, however, they had done so, the Scoto-Catholic movement in the Church of Scotland and some of the non-established Presbyterian churches became extremely influential and many Presbyterian churches built in Scotland from the 1890s manifest a peculiarly Scottish form of ecclesiology that remained popular for much of the succeeding century.

1. Roman Catholics and Scottish episcopalians

We have already noted that Roman Catholics in Scotland were slow to adopt an ecclesiological approach to church design. After 1860, churches began to be designed along ecclesiological lines but there were still few such buildings of any note and others continued to be designed in a wholly non-ecclesiological manner. The Jesuit churches in Edinburgh (Sacred Heart 1860) and Glasgow (St Aloysius 1908–1910) were handsome Classical buildings. The Classical church of St Margaret at Airdrie, built in 1836–1839, was reordered with furnishings in the high Gothic style while retaining its original elaborate plasterwork. By far the finest ecclesiological building designed for Roman Catholic worship in Scotland was the chapel of 1896–1911 designed by R. R. Anderson for the Marquess of Bute at Mount Stuart, near Rothesay. In 1878, Pope Leo XIII regularized the administrative structure of the Roman Catholic Church in Scotland by replacing the vicariates with a proper hierarchy. This was done 28 years later, and rather less controversially, than it had been in England and Wales. The new diocesan structure comprised two archdioceses, Glasgow, and St Andrews and Edinburgh, and four dioceses: Aberdeen, Argyll and the Isles, Dunkeld and Galloway. The substantial increase of the Roman Catholic population in the Glasgow region in the late nineteenth and early twentieth centuries necessitated the erection of new dioceses at Motherwell and Paisley. In all cases except one, existing churches were used as the cathedrals of the new dioceses. The exception was the diocese of Argyll and the Isles where the handsome new cathedral of St Columba at Oban, designed by Sir Giles Gilbert Scott, was opened in 1932.

Scottish Episcopalians, by contrast, had adopted ecclesiological principles very early. After 1860, they continued to build churches in the high Gothic style with good examples at Challoch (1871–1872), Fort William (1876–1880) and Kelso (1869). Earlier, pre-1840, Episcopal churches also tended to be given the high Gothic treatment after 1860. In 1867, St John's, Edinburgh, was 're-pewed in oak after the style of the old fifteenth-century Norfolk churches, the bench ends being carved with poppy heads'. A new apsidal chancel, with choir stalls, was added in 1881–1882 and consecrated by

LITURGICAL AND ARCHITECTURAL DEVELOPMENTS SINCE 1860

Plate 15 Photograph of the interior of St John's Episcopal Church, Edinburgh, after extension in 1881–1882

Bishop Cotterill of Edinburgh [Plate 15].[1] As happened in the Church of England, the Scottish Episcopal Church was much dominated by controversies over ritual from the 1850s onwards. By 1874, there were four churches in Scotland in which eucharistic vestments had been introduced and which could clearly be classed as 'ritualist'. One of these was the cathedral at Perth, where there was a running battle over ritual between Bishop Charles Wordsworth and the cathedral clergy between the 1850s and 1870s.[2] Part of the debate over ceremonial and eucharistic doctrine revolved around whether the English *Book of Common Prayer* or the Scottish Communion Office, generally regarded as the more Catholic rite, should be used at communion services. By 1878, it looked as if the English lobby would emerge victorious. That year's church directory revealed that only 42 congregations in Scotland used the Scottish rite, of which half were in the diocese of Aberdeen and Orkney where the traditional rite had always been preferred. St John's, Jedburgh, 'with its particular Tractarian tradition', was the only parish in the diocese of Glasgow and Galloway to use the Scottish Communion Office. This situation began to be reversed after

---

[1] Terry, *Memorials*, pp. 40, 43–4.
[2] Yates, *Anglican Ritualism*, pp. 124–37; Strong, *Episcopalianism*, pp. 235–63; White, *Scottish Episcopal Church*, pp. 42–50.

1883 when the Scottish rite was strongly promoted by Bishop Dowden of Edinburgh.[3]

Unlike the Roman Catholics, the Scottish Episcopalians did build new cathedrals in the second half of the nineteenth century. The full complement of the present seven dioceses was achieved by the 1850s: Aberdeen and Orkney; Argyll and the Isles; Brechin; Edinburgh; Glasgow and Galloway; Moray, Ross and Caithness; and St Andrews, Dunkeld and Dunblane. It was in this last diocese that the first Episcopal cathedral in Scotland was established at Perth by Bishop Patrick Torry, shortly before his death in 1852. New cathedrals were begun, in somewhat less controversial circumstances, at Inverness for the diocese of Moray, Ross and Caithness, in 1866 and at Edinburgh in 1874. St Mary's Cathedral, Edinburgh, had fully choral services from its opening in 1879. In 1891, there was Holy Communion at 8 a.m. and 12 noon on Sundays, with Morning Prayer at 11 a.m. and Evening Prayer at 3:30 p.m. and 7 p.m. On weekdays, there was Holy Communion at 8 a.m., Morning Prayer at 11 a.m. and Evening Prayer at 5 p.m. The other Scottish dioceses did not build new cathedrals but designated existing churches as cathedrals: St Andrew's at Aberdeen; Holy Spirit at Millport for the diocese of Argyll and the Isles; St Paul's at Dundee for the diocese of Brechin; and St Mary's at Glasgow. The last two were not officially designated as cathedrals until 1905 and 1907, respectively.[4]

2. *Presbyterian ecclesiology and Scoto-Catholicism*

The pioneer of liturgical reform in the Church of Scotland was Robert Lee of Old Greyfriars, Edinburgh. In 1864, he published his views on the topic, having already made liturgical innovations in his own church. He made it clear that one of the reasons that the Church of Scotland had to contemplate liturgical change was because 'of late years a great number of persons have forsaken the Church of Scotland and Presbytery, to join the Scotch Episcopal Church'. In his view, the main reason for this was 'the character of the worship, especially the manner of praying, and the general want' in the Church of Scotland 'of solemnity, decoration and refinement in the services'.[5] Elsewhere in the book he criticized extempore prayer and postures in public worship, and argued in favour of both instrumental music in church and the use of a wide variety of psalms and hymns in worship. He compared the *Directory* with the *Book of Common Order* and the *Book of Common*

---

[3] Maclean, 'Episcopal Worship', p. 115.
[4] *Ibid.*, p. 112; Drummond and Bulloch, *Church in Victorian Scotland*, p. 209.
[5] Robert Lee, *The Reform of the Church of Scotland: Part I Worship*, Edinburgh 1864, pp. 50, 57.

Prayer, and came down firmly in favour of the last of these as the best liturgy available. He concluded that

> upon the whole it seems now time for the Church of Scotland to consider whether some great reform in her public worship has not become necessary; and particularly whether she should not resume the use of a Liturgy – to some extent at least.[6]

Lee was much criticized, both by members of his own congregation,[7] and by others in the Church of Scotland. James Begg noted that

> in carrying forward the recent innovations in worship, there are very different classes engaged. There are the ignorant and thoughtless. But the most dangerous class are those who know perfectly well what they are doing and aiming at. They are seeking ... virtually to upset the Revolution Settlement by bringing the Scottish Church into as near a resemblance as possible to the Church of England ... all ministers and elders are solemnly and specially bound not only not to introduce innovations in the worship of God, but firmly to resist them if attempted by others.[8]

There is no doubt that Begg regarded Lee as being in the 'dangerous class', but Lee had some powerful supporters. Principal Tulloch of St Andrews noted in 1872 that

> there were two kinds of ritualism. There was a ritualism which lay on a sacerdotal basis, with which on no account could he sympathise. ... But there was another ritualism, and it appeared to him the only one at which it was right to aim – that of promoting order, decorum, seemliness, and beauty of devotional expression.[9]

By 1863–1864, even the General Assembly of the Church of Scotland, initially hostile to some of Lee's innovations at Old Greyfriars, was beginning to relax its opposition to the use of printed forms of prayer.[10]

---

[6] *Ibid.*, p. 186.
[7] A.C. Cheyne, *The Transforming of the Kirk: Victorian Scotland's Religious Revolution.* Edinburgh 1983, p. 93.
[8] James Begg, *Purity of Worship in the Presbyterian Church*, Edinburgh 1876, pp. iii, 72.
[9] John Kerr, *The Renascence of Worship: The Origin, Aims and Achievements of the Church Service Society*, Edinburgh 1909, p. 126.
[10] Bryce, *History of Old Greyfriars*, p. 149.

A major catalyst for liturgical change in the Church of Scotland was the establishment of the Church Service Society in 1865. Its original membership comprised 55 Church of Scotland ministers, though it was notable that not a single one came from the deeply conservative western highlands and islands. Between its foundation and 1907 it attracted some distinguished ministers to the respective offices of President and Vice-President: Principals Barclay and Story of Glasgow, Principal Campbell of Aberdeen, Principal Tulloch of St Andrews, Professor Lee of Edinburgh, Professors Caird and Cooper of Glasgow and Professor Menzies of St Andrews.[11] At St Clement's, Dundee, reopened after redecoration on 31 July 1870, 'the congregation adopted for the first time the standing position for singing and kneeling to pray'. In a series of accounts of church services published in the local magazine, *The Piper o' Dundee*, in 1887, it was noted that at St Mary's a communion table and lectern had been introduced and that the anthems sung included the *Magnificat* and Handel's Hallelujah Chorus. None of the places of worship of the Free Church of Scotland had yet introduced organs. The most elaborate worship in the city was not that of either the Roman Catholic or Scottish Episcopal churches but that of the Catholic Apostolic Church, 'with its glorious nave, beautiful sanctuary, patriarchal minister and attendant white-robed clergy . . . the whole solemn and impressive'.[12]

One of the leading figures in the 'high church' movement within the Church of Scotland was James Cooper (1846–1922), minister at Broughty Ferry 1873–1881 and St Nicholas East, Aberdeen, 1881–1898, when he became Professor of Ecclesiastical History at Glasgow. In 1892, he became the first secretary of the Scottish Church Society, established 'to defend and advance Catholic doctrine' but denounced by its opponents for 'Romanism, Episcopacy and Ritualism'. At Broughty Ferry, Cooper introduced Christmas services in 1874 and Holy Week services in 1878; at Aberdeen he introduced daily services in 1881 and founded the Aberdeen Ecclesiological Society in 1886. He presented the church at Broughty Ferry with a communion set 'of solid silver, Gothic in design and jewelled' and a brass lectern. He regularly attended services in Scottish Episcopal churches and doubted the validity of his own Presbyterian ordination. There were complaints against him at Aberdeen, signed by 11 of the 27 elders, in 1882.[13] His reordering of the St Nicholas East church [Plate 16] reflected his liturgical views. In 1883–1884 both a printed service book and daily services were introduced at St Giles,

---

[11] Kerr, *Renascence of Worship*, pp. 188, 191–2.
[12] McGraw, *Victorian Dundee*, pp. 93, 97–100.
[13] D.M. Murray, 'The Scottish Church Society 1892–1914: A Study of the High Church Movement in the Church of Scotland', Cambridge PhD 1976, pp. 234, 239–40, 245–9, 312–43; B.A. Rees, 'James Cooper and the Scoto-Catholic Party: Tractarian Reform in the Church of Scotland, 1882–1918', St Andrews PhD 1981, pp. 173–82, 184–220, 238.

Plate 16 The interior of St Nicholas East Church, Aberdeen, refurnished in 1882 and 1937

Edinburgh.[14] In 1887, the traditional fast days were abolished by the presbytery of Edinburgh. Christmas services were introduced at the Canongate Church in 1904, 40 years after the congregation had adopted the practices of standing to sing and kneeling to pray, and 30 years after the introduction of an organ.[15]

One of the major liturgical changes in the Church of Scotland from the 1860s was that in communion practice. Fencing of the tables was generally abandoned, followed by the abolition of the traditional communion seasons with their preparatory and thanksgiving services. These were generally regarded as both too demanding in respect of time and too penitential in character. By the late nineteenth century, the majority of congregations had abandoned use of long tables in favour of communicating people in their pews. The use of shortbread or oatcakes was also abandoned for the use of ordinary bread and communion tokens were generally replaced with cards. The movement for abstinence from alcohol, which had an impact on most Protestant churches in the nineteenth century, resulted in disputes over whether the communion wine should be fermented or unfermented, and an increasing number of churches adopted the latter practice. By the early

---

[14] Cheyne, *Transforming the Kirk*, p. 99.
[15] R.S. Wright, *The Kirk in the Canongate*, Edinburgh 1956, pp. 117–18, 131, 136.

years of the twentieth century, concerns about public hygiene and the spread of disease led to the use of the communion cup being replaced with that of individual glasses. From about 1900 communion services in most lowland parishes became more frequent, but in the highland parishes 'twice or even once a year remained the norm'. Here the traditional communion seasons with fasting, preparation and thanksgiving were maintained much longer, as they are to this day in many parts of the western highlands and islands.[16]

As well as James Cooper, three other leading figures of the Scoto-Catholic movement in the Church of Scotland were John Macleod of Duns and Govan, John Charleson of Thornliebank and T. N. Adamson of Barnhill. By 1871 at Duns, Macleod had introduced weekday services, the observance of festivals and monthly communion. A petition against him was presented by 116 members of the 570-strong congregation and in 1875, the presbytery of Duns declared that the use of a cross on the font cover, of a communion table cloth inscribed IHS and the observance of festivals was illegal, and that the congregation should revert to the practice of half-yearly, or at least no more than quarterly, communion. By that date, Macleod had departed to Govan where he introduced similar changes: quarterly communion from 1875 and monthly from 1882, Holy Week services from 1884. Two complaints against Macleod were dismissed by the presbytery of Glasgow when it became clear that the vast majority of his congregation supported him. By 1893, the *Te Deum* was being sung at the morning service on non-communion Sundays, the *Gloria*, Creed, *Sanctus* and *Agnus Dei* at communion services, and the *Magnificat* and *Nunc Dimittis* on Sunday evenings. At Thornliebank, John Charleson, the minister from 1890, introduced a service book with congregational responses, the Three-Hours Devotion on Good Friday and a vigil service at 11.30 p.m. on Holy Saturday. A petition against him was signed by 207 members out of a congregation of 383, alleging that 113 members of the congregation had already resigned because of the changes, in 1896. Five years later, Charleson resigned the charge and became a Roman Catholic.[17]

T. N. Adamson went even further. Formerly assistant minister to James Cooper at Aberdeen, Adamson was appointed minister of Barnhill in 1884. He immediately introduced daily services and quarterly communion, increasing the latter to monthly in 1894. In 1896, allegations of 'popery' were made against Adamson by some ministers in the presbytery of Dundee and by James Primmer, minister of Townhill Church, Dunfermline. Primmer sent a

---

[16] Burnet, *Holy Communion*, pp. 278–9, 287–8, 290–1, 302; Douglas Murray, 'Disruption to Union', and Duncan Forrester, 'Worship since 1929', in Forrester and Murray (eds), *Studies in the History of Worship*, pp. 101–2, 181.

[17] Murray, 'Scottish Church Society', pp. 283–311, 371–96.

letter to all the presbyteries and synods of the Church of Scotland drawing attention to the 'irregularities' at Barnhill

> Adamson had prayed and had celebrated communion with his back to the people, and had 'genuflected' before the altar. The people had gone forward to receive communion and had knelt at the altar ... There was a 'popish' altar in the church, with a large metal cross, vases with flowers, and two candles, and everything ready for the offering of the sacrifice of the mass.[18]

The presbytery eventually took action in 1901 but only requested that Adamson should bring his services more into line with general practice in the Church of Scotland. However, Adamson's opponents appealed to the General Assembly, which ordered the presbytery to review the case. In 1902, the presbytery requested the removal of the altar cross, candlesticks and frontal, but not the vases of flowers or the sanctuary lamp. The font was to be moved from near the entrance to near the pulpit but the eagle lectern was allowed to remain. Adamson initially obeyed the judgement but by 1905 both frontals and an altar cross had been reintroduced. The presbytery also required Adamson not to celebrate eastwards or to communicate his congregation kneeling. He was to omit the elevation and the mixing of water with wine in the chalice, but he was allowed to rinse the chalice after use. He was also obliged to discontinue the use of a communion liturgy based on the English prayer book of 1549.[19]

No other Church of Scotland minister was as advanced as Adamson in his liturgical innovations but several others followed the more moderate pioneering experiments of James Cooper and John Macleod. At North Berwick, G. W. Sprott introduced, with the unanimous support of the kirk session, quarterly communion in 1875, Christmas services in 1879 and Holy Week ones in 1898. H. J. Wotherspoon introduced quarterly communion at Burnbank in 1887; as minister of St Oswald's, Edinburgh, he had a service on Good Friday from 1897, on Christmas Day from 1906, daily in Holy Week from 1908, and on Ascension Day from 1908. At Coatdyke, Cromarty Smith had Holy Week services from 1906 and a Sunday morning service based on Mattins from the *Book of Common Prayer*. His, also from 1906, was the first Church of Scotland church to have a weekly communion service, at 8.30 a.m. on Sundays in a side chapel.[20]

---

[18] *Ibid.*, p. 404.
[19] *Ibid.*, pp. 397–428; Rees, 'James Cooper', pp. 266–310; Douglas Murray, 'The Barnhill Case 1901–4: The Limits of Ritual in the Kirk', *RSCHS*, xxii (1986), pp. 259–76.
[20] Murray, 'Scottish Church Society', pp. 429–40.

3. Reforms in church music

In 1863, the parish church of Rutherglen advertised for a precentor. Candidates for the office,

> Having conducted the psalmody in the church a day each, were invited to attend tonight to be examined as to their knowledge of music ... The Kirk Session unanimously agreed to appoint, and do hereby appoint, Mr James Hossack to be Precentor in the Parish Church of Rutherglen during the pleasure of the Kirk Session at the rate of fifteen pounds stg. a year on condition that he acts as musical director on all necessary occasions, have a practice for church Psalmody at least twice a year, and in general to conform to the instruction of the Kirk Session in musical matters; and especially that his moral and religious character be consistant [sic] and becoming the office he holds.[21]

In the same year that Rutherglen was appointing a new precentor, Old Greyfriars in Edinburgh was installing an organ to accompany the singing. A similar attempt was made by the minister of Inch, near Stranraer, but it was resisted by both the kirk session and the presbytery. Two years later organs were officially permitted by the General Assembly when it passed a deliverance, which did not condemn organs as unscriptural, but vested the power of whether or not to install them in the Presbyteries rather than the kirk sessions.

> From the start ... the general view of Presbyteries was that a congregation which was unanimous in desiring an organ or harmonium should be allowed to have one.

In 1865, organs or harmoniums were installed at Dundonald, Paisley South, Pollockshaws and Skelmorlie. By 1866, no fewer than 18 churches had introduced organs or harmoniums, and by 1867, the number had risen to 31. They included eight churches in Glasgow and some in small market towns, such as Cupar and Duns, as well as the occasional village church, such as Abernyte. By 1871, the number of churches with organs had increased to 58 and by 1874, to over 100. The first organs were introduced in Shetland in 1871 and in Orkney in 1875. By the early twentieth century 1106 out of 1249 Church of Scotland churches had either organs or harmoniums. A small but vociferous minority within the Church of Scotland

---

[21] MLGA, CH2/315/7, 16 February 1863.

continued to oppose them, with the last attempt to ban them completely being made, unsuccessfully, at the General Assembly in 1883.[22] In 1865, the first organ north of the Clyde/Forth Valleys was installed at St Mary's, Dundee. One was installed at Paisley Abbey in 1874 at a cost of £2000. In 1876, the General Assembly rejected the complaints of the parishioners of Elgin against the introduction of an organ 2 years earlier. Organs were introduced at St Michael's, Linlithgow, in 1878, in the western gallery of the nave, and at St Mungo's Cathedral, Glasgow, following the demolition of the choir galleries, in 1879.[23]

The other Presbyterian churches in Scotland were not slow to follow the example of the established church. The United Presbyterian Church, which had set up a Psalmody Committee in 1855, lifted its ban on organs in 1872. The Free Church of Scotland was initially unwilling to do so but its opposition began to crumble in the face of the clear demand for them from some ministers and congregations. At Leith, in 1878, the Free Church was the only one in the town not to have any form of musical accompaniment to the singing. Attempts were made at the Free Church Assembly in 1882 and 1883 to remove the ban on organs. Supporters of organs claimed that the Free Church was losing members, especially younger ones, because of its stance on music. St Luke's, Broughty Ferry, had acquired a harmonium in 1880 but its use was forbidden by the presbytery of Dundee in 1881. An appeal to the Free Church Assembly resulted in the decision of the presbytery being upheld. However, in 1883, the Assembly agreed by 390 votes to 259 that

> there is nothing in the Word of God . . . to preclude the use of instrumental music in public worship as an aid to vocal praise

and that individual congregations should be permitted to introduce organs or harmoniums if they so wished. Three Free Church of Scotland churches in Glasgow acquired organs in 1884–1885; they were installed at Elgin South in 1884 and Corstorphine in 1886. By 1890, there were also organs in churches at Aberdeen, Edinburgh, Greenock and Paisley. However, the split in the Free Church in 1900, which resulted in a small minority refusing to unite with the United Presbyterians in the United Free Church and the setting up a Continuing Free Church (the 'Wee Frees'), led to a decision by the Continuing Free Church in 1905 to repeal the 1883 Assembly Act.

---

[22] Murray, 'Disruption to Union', p. 99; Inglis 'Scottish Churches and the Organ', pp. 157, 160, 162, 165, 169, 171, 187–90.

[23] McGraw, *Victorian Dundee*, p. 96; Howell, *Paisley Abbey*, p. 46; Drummond and Bulloch, *Church in Victorian Scotland*, p. 189; Ferguson, *Ecclesia Antiqua*, p. 261 and photograph opposite p. 110.

Attempts to force the Free Church in Leith to dispose of its organ in 1909 resulted in that congregation seceding to join the Church of Scotland.[24]

Organs were not the only innovation in church music. Their introduction encouraged ministers and congregations to increase the number of psalm tunes. By 1866 Dundee South Church was using 86 tunes in common metre plus 26 others and nine chants. The General Assembly of the Church of Scotland reluctantly agreed to the publication of an official hymn book in 1861, resulting in the publication of *The Scottish Hymnal* in 1870. The Free Church was initially opposed to hymns but its Assembly narrowly agreed to their use in 1866. By 1881, an official hymn book was sanctioned for use in public worship. By the late 1870s, all the Scottish Presbyterian churches had been much influenced by the type of church music promoted by D. L. Moody and Ira Sankey who toured Britain, including Scotland, in 1873–1875.[25]

4. Church building and restoration

The Scottish Presbyterian churches, unlike some of their Free Church counterparts in England, had been largely impervious to the Gothic Revival in architecture before the 1870s. Thereafter the liturgical experiments of the high church ministers in the Church of Scotland were to lead to the building of ecclesiological churches by the last quarter of the nineteenth century. The second half of the nineteenth century was a major period of new church building for the three largest Presbyterian churches in Scotland as Table 10 shows.

There was fierce competition between the three churches in the building of

Table 10 Building of new Presbyterian Churches in Scotland 1850–1899

Decade	Church of Scotland	Free church	United presbyterians
1850–1859	27	25	25
1860–1869	47	49	32
1870–1879	94	76	41
1880–1889	57	36	28
1890–1899	46	29	35
Total	271	215	161

Source: Drummond, A.L. and Bulloch, J. (1978), *The Church in Late Victorian Scotland 1874–1900*. Edinburgh, p. 164.

---

[24] Drummond and Bulloch, *Church in Victorian Scotland*, p. 188; Inglis, 'Scottish Churches and the Organ', pp. 209–11, 214–16, 229–30.

[25] McGraw, *Victorian Dundee*, p. 97; Drummond and Bulloch, *Church in Victorian Scotland*, pp. 184, 186; Ansdell, *People of the Great Faith*, p. 168.

new churches. Both the Church of Scotland and the Free Church built churches for the new community of railway workers at Stromeferry, but when the railway was extended both churches were left without congregations. Churches were also built by wealthy families in estate villages, for example by the Ballantyne family at Walkerburn, where a *quoad sacra* parish was established in 1876.[26] One of the earliest and most extensive church restoration programmes was begun at Paisley Abbey in 1859. It took place in three phases. In the first phase (1859–1862),

> the unsightly galleries were taken down ... the body of the church re-seated ... the pulpit was shifted from the centre of the north side to the east end. A new gallery in the west end was erected.

The second phase, supervised by Rowand Anderson, between 1898 and 1907, largely involved repairs to the fabric, but the floor of the choir was laid with 'stone and encaustic tiles'. The third and final phase, supervised between 1912 and 1928, first by P.M. Chalmers and then Sir Robert Lorimer, resulted in the building one sees today (Appendix E/12). Chalmers was responsible for the new stone vault and Lorimer for the new furnishings. A photograph shows the interior before 1898 with the organ in a gallery behind the pulpit against the west side of the crossing, before the complete restoration of the chancel and transepts. By this date stained glass had been installed in most of the windows of the nave and its aisles. Two further photographs show the temporary arrangement in 1907 with the crossing now in use. The organ was against the east wall of the crossing with a communion table in front and a canopied pulpit placed against the southwest pier of the crossing. There was still a gallery across the west end of the nave, but there were choir stalls and a lectern in the temporary sanctuary. By 1928, a photograph of the completed chancel shows it vaulted and with canopied choir stalls, the organ on the south side, and the new stone communion table at the east end.[27]

In 1882, one of the Scoto-Catholic ministers, G.W. Sprott, produced the first guide to the new church architecture as required by the liturgical reforms of the period. Sprott commented:

> The wretched state of many Parish Churches has affected most unfavourably the character of our worship ... In some parts of the Country, within living memory, umbrellas had to be raised in churches in rainy

---

[26] Drummond and Bulloch, *Church in Late Victorian Scotland*, p. 164.
[27] Howell, *Paisley Abbey*, pp. 46–7, 49 and photographs opposite pp. 79, 82, 85, 92 and 100.

weather... In our own day a new and better spirit has arisen. Many old churches have been restored... and many new ones of a better type have been built. The plans adopted have not, always been satisfactory... The interior of some of these churches resembles a circus, class-room, or music-hall. In the last, on entering you see a strange platform, with a reading desk and sofa in place of an ecclesiastical pulpit, while behind there is a huge organ – the principal object of the building... Strange devices, too, one sometimes hears of for the administration of the sacraments, such as a font at the top of which a board is screwed to do duty as a Table at times of Communion... The parallelogram or simple nave is capable of being treated in a clumsy way by devoting the East end to the pulpit, Communion Table, choir seats, organ and vestry... The seats should all, as far as possible, face the clergyman. Nothing could be worse, for purposes of worship, than the old-fashioned square pews, which obliged half the people to sit with their backs to the pulpit. The pews should be light, and come as near the open bench as possible... The pews should be uniform, for a distinction betwixt the accommodation for the rich and poor in God's House is not merely objectionable, but anti-Christian... if the posture of kneeling during prayers is to be introduced, the seats should be roomy enough to admit of it. Sitting is, in the highest degree irreverent... The rusty iron hoop stuck in the side of the high pulpit to hold the battered pewter basin, to which the parent has to ascend, with his child in his arms, by a staircase used for no other purpose, is an appalling and even perilous arrangement for Baptism. How mean, too, are the cups which we sometimes see on the Lord's Table! While patens and flagons are such as would not be tolerated in a respectable kitchen. Indeed some parishes have not yet got the length of the pewter flagon, and the black bottle may still be seen, and the popping of corks may be heard, at the Holy Table.[28]

Sprott was, in effect, giving advice to his fellow ministers which replicated, 40 years later, the sort of advice given by the Cambridge Camden Society to Anglican clergy in the 1840s.

Most of the major church restorations endeavoured to follow, at least in part, the advice given by Sprott and other Scoto-Catholics. At Haddington, where an extensive programme of restoration began in 1891, new galleries were erected across the east and west end of the nave, the former for an organ and choir. Box pews were replaced with open benches. The east end of the nave, in front of the organ gallery, was reordered with a new marble

[28] G.W. Sprott, *The Worship and Office of the Church of Scotland*, Edinburgh 1882, pp. 228, 231, 233–6, 239.

pulpit and communion table, a font and a lectern, the last incorporating a brass eagle. Between 1892 and 1945, a complete series of stained glass windows was installed in the church.[29] A similar restoration programme took place at St Michael's, Linlithgow, between 1890 and 1905. All the galleries and pews were removed. The nave was brought back into use. Contemporary photographs show the interior facing both east and west. There were open benches in the nave and a pulpit and lectern on opposite sides of the chancel arch. The chancel was fitted with choir stalls, with the organ in the north choir aisle, and a communion table in the apse. From 1896, a series of stained glass windows were placed in the church.[30] By the 1890s a photograph of the interior of Glasgow Cathedral shows that all but the last two bays in the choir had been fitted with open benches with poppy heads. The two easternmost bays formed the sanctuary with choir stalls against the north and south walls and a pulpit at the west end of the north stall block and a Gothic reredos behind the communion table. An eagle lectern was placed in the middle of the sanctuary [Plate 17].[31] The minister of St Vigean's, commenting on these and other restoration programmes in 1896, expressed the view that

> We have, happily, emerged from the barn age of church architecture in Scotland, but even in the case of many of our new churches, which have a tolerably fair exterior, the internal arrangements are lacking in that grace and dignity which, in the experience of many, are to be found to be true aids to devotion ... Surely the Communion Table should always form the central object in a Christian church, and I do not mean to detract in the least degree from the importance of the pulpit ... when I say it should be so placed as neither to interrupt the view of the Communion Table nor to overshadow it.[32]

Whatever, however, is clear from Dr Duke's remarks, is that the critics of Scoto-Catholicism were correct when they alleged that the main thrust of the campaign was to make the buildings of the Church of Scotland resemble more closely those of the mainstream, post-ecclesiological but not ritualist, buildings of the Church of England.

Two of the finest examples of Scoto-Catholic church buildings in Scotland were the new church of St Constantine in the Glasgow suburb of Govan and the Thomas Coats Memorial Baptist Church in Paisley. The surviving plan of the Govan church, dated 1888, is in two sections, one showing the ground

---

[29] Marshall, *Ruin and Restoration*, pp. 33–4.
[30] Ferguson, *Ecclesia Antiqua*, pp. 121–9.
[31] Todd, *Book of Glasgow Cathedral*, p. 260.
[32] Kerr, *Renascence of Worship*, p. 152.

Plate 17 Photograph of the interior of the Choir of Glasgow Cathedral in the 1890s (Glasgow University Library, Special Collections)

floor and the other the galleries. The ground floor plan showed a broad nave with narrow aisles serving only as passageways. There was uniform seating in the nave, facing the chancel, with a central passageway. On the ritual north side of the church was a transept with seating facing south. The pulpit was placed in the ritual south side of the chancel and with a clergy desk on each side of the entrance to the chancel and west of the choir stalls. The communion table was raised on three steps at the ritual east end of the chancel. The gallery plan showed a gallery across the ritual west end of the nave and also across the north transept and the north side of the chancel. The organ case was placed on the south side of the chancel. The west gallery was approached by staircases at the west end of the nave, and the two north galleries by staircases at the west end of the north transept and the east end of the chancel. There was also a matching staircase opposite the latter, which provided access to the organ loft. The area between the north transept and the north chancel gallery, which in an Anglican church would have been occupied by a side chapel, was occupied by the church hall, though this was later incorporated into the church as a chapel for smaller services (Appendix E/10).[33] The Thomas Coats Memorial Baptist Church in Paisley was opened in 1894, and commemorated the Paisley sewing-thread manufacturer who had died in 1883. Nine architects were invited to compete for the winning design and the competition was won by Hippolyte Blanc of Edinburgh. The cost of the building was fixed at £20,000 and the building was to be in the Gothic style with a tower and spire. In fact the completed building cost £110,000 and was one of the most lavish ever built in Scotland, as well as adhering firmly to ecclesiological principles (Appendix E/13).[34] Other churches built by the Church of Scotland in the last two decades of the nineteenth century which adhered firmly to ecclesiological principles included Crathie of 1893–1895 (Appendix E/1), Connel of 1887–1888 (Appendix E/2), the Crichton Memorial Church at Dumfries of 1890–1897 (Appendix E/6) and St Cuthbert's at Edinburgh of 1892–1895 (Plate 18; Appendix E/8), also by Hippolyte Blanc. Slightly later was the church at Forres designed by John Robertson and built in 1904–1906 (Appendix E/14). Between 1889 and 1914 R.R. Anderson and Sir Robert Lorimer carried out the fully ecclesiological restoration of Dunblane Cathedral (Plate 19; Appendix E/15).

One of the Scottish architects who did most to contribute to the ecclesiological movement in the Church of Scotland was P.M. Chalmers. In 1907–1909, he carried out the restoration of Holy Trinity, St Andrews, a church described in 1799 as 'a rotunda of pews and galleries around a central pulpit'.[35] Photographs of the interior before and after restoration show the dramatic difference achieved by Chalmers. Before restoration, the church had a gallery around all four sides of its aisled interior with a canopied pulpit being placed in the middle of one of the arcades. After restoration there was a stalled chancel, a much simpler pulpit in the Gothic style placed to one side of the entrance to the chancel, and a screen separating the chancel from the nave (Appendix E/9).[36] Unlike some ecclesiological architects who were wedded to Gothic, Chalmers

> developed a distinctive style . . . he was not following a tradition, he was seeking to create one. He was following a theory . . . that the

---

[33] MLGA, CH2/1277/104.
[34] Clyde Binfield, 'A Working Memorial? The Encasing of Paisley's Baptists', *Crown and Mitre: Religion and Society in Northern Europe since the Reformation*, ed. W.M. Jacob and Nigel Yates, Woodbridge 1993, pp. 185–202.
[35] Drummond and Bulloch, *Church in late Victorian Scotland*, p. 170.
[36] Drummond, *Church Architecture of Protestantism*, Plate II.

Plate 18 The sanctuary of St Cuthbert's, Edinburgh, showing the marble pulpit, font and communion table, 1892–1895

Norman style and the apse were peculiarly suited to Presbyterian worship.[37]

Good examples of the implementation of Chalmer's theories are his churches at Ardwell (Appendix E/4) and Colvend (Appendix E/5). When D.W. Galloway was working on the restoration of Careston parish church in 1906 he recalled that

---

[37] Whyte, 'Setting of Worship', p. 150.

Plate 19 The Choir of Dunblane Cathedral as refurnished by Sir Robert Lorimer in 1914

two schemes occurred to me. Either the pulpit could be placed on the south wall, facing the aisle, as in the original arrangement [of 1636]; or the east portion of the chancel might be formed into a chancel and the pulpit placed therein. I chose the latter, as not any more in keeping with the general principles of ecclesiastical architecture, but as better fitted to express the ideas which underlie the worship of the Christian Church.[38]

Similar considerations clearly impacted on the design of Blair Drummond church in 1906–1907. The communion table was placed against one of the short walls with the pulpit on one side and the font on the other, and seats for the minister and elders behind the table. All the seating was arranged to face this combined liturgical focus.[39] Although it was largely Church of Scotland churches that responded to the Scoto-Catholic movement in terms of church design, others, in addition to Paisley's Baptists, occasionally did so

[38] *Ibid.*, p. 149.
[39] SA, CH2/1455/20.

as well. In 1896–1899 Charles Rennie Mackintosh's design for the Free Church of Scotland's Queen's Cross Church in Glasgow largely adopted ecclesiological principles of church design (Appendix E/11; Figure 6).

5. *Liturgy and architecture since 1920*

Ecclesiological principles continued to have an enormous impact on the Church of Scotland throughout the interwar period. Their ultimate reflection can be seen in the extraordinary church of St Conan's, Loch Awe, completed in 1930 (Appendix E/3), where the font is in the form of an angel bearing a Breton fishing boat [Plate 20]. From the last decade of the nineteenth century, both Roman Catholics and Scottish Episcopalians made a particular contribution to the ecclesiological movement by rescuing medieval buildings and bringing them back into use. The Roman Catholics did this with the fifteenth-century Grey Friars Church in Elgin in 1891–1898 and the nearby Pluscarden Abbey in 1948, where the chancel, central tower and transepts of the thirteenth-century church were restored for use by a community of Benedictine monks. The Scottish Episcopalians brought back into use the twelfth- or thirteenth-century church at Eoropie on Lewis in 1912 [Plate 21] and the sixteenth-century Grey Friars Church at Kirkcudbright in 1919, with an interior designed by P. M. Chalmers. While liturgical revision was delayed in the Roman Catholic Church until the Second Vatican Council in the 1960s dramatically altered the form of the mass, it was very much on the agenda of both the Scottish Episcopal Church and the Church of Scotland from the 1920s. In 1929, the former produced a new liturgy, which was quickly adopted by most congregations, and this was followed by even more

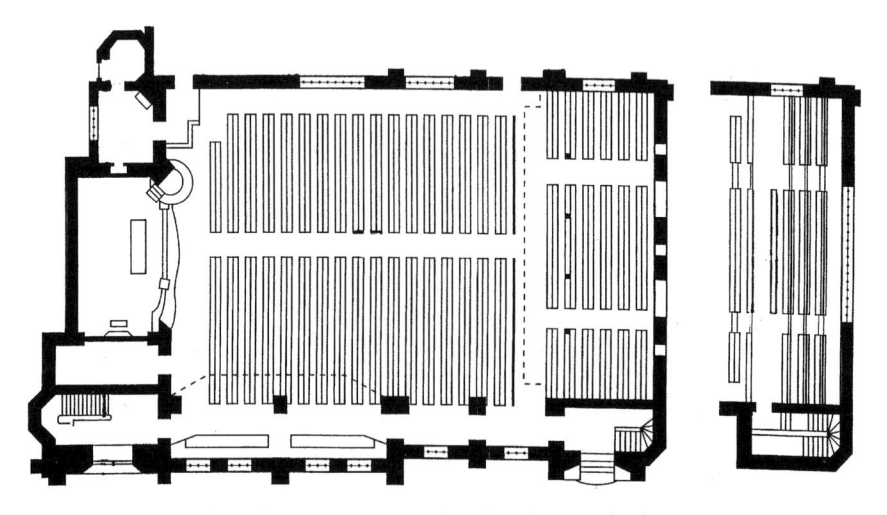

Figure 6 Seating plan of Queen's Cross Church, Glasgow, built in 1896–1899

LITURGICAL AND ARCHITECTURAL DEVELOPMENTS SINCE 1860

extensive revisions in 1966, 1970 and 1982.[40] Liturgical matters were also on the agenda in the pre-war discussions of the Church of Scotland and the United Free Church. In 1928 it was agreed that

> the ministry of the Word, the conduct of Public Worship, and the dispensing of the sacraments belong to the Minister, subject to the control and direction of the Presbytery.

This limited the power of the elders, through the kirk session, to interfere in matters relating to worship. The United Free Church thus adopted a position

Plate 20 The font in the form of an angel supporting a Breton fishing boat at St Conan's Church, Loch Awe, completed in 1930

---

[40] Maclean, 'Episcopal Worship', pp. 109, 123–4.

Plate 21 The Medieval Church of St Moluag at Eoropie, Lewis, restored to ecclesiastical use in 1912

'more in line with previous Church of Scotland than with United Free Church practice'. It resulted from the exercise of strong pressure by the Scottish Church Society, which represented the views of high church Presbyterians, and marked a 'notable success' by the Society 'and one which would have far-reaching effects in the united Church'.[41] Indeed the first action of

---

[41] D.M. Murray, *Rebuilding the Kirk: Presbyterian Reunion in Scotland 1909–1929*, Edinburgh 2000, pp. 186–7, 262.

the General Assembly of the Church of Scotland, following the union with the United Free Church in 1929, was the setting up of a Committee on Public Worship and Aids to Devotion. The committee produced an *Ordinal and Service Book* in 1931, *Prayers for the Christian Year* in 1935, and a new *Book of Common Order* in 1940. Many ministers used material from these books to provide a framework for their services. A revised version of the *Book of Common Order* was published in 1979, and a further revision in 1994. A new *Church Hymnary* was produced in 1928 with further revisions in 1973 and 2005.[42]

From the 1940s, partly as a result of the influence of the worship of the Iona Community founded in 1938, but rather more as a result of increasing ecumenical contacts, Holy Communion became more frequent in many Church of Scotland parishes. However, even by 1956 the vast majority of Church of Scotland parishes still did not have more than a quarterly celebration. Only 27 churches still had just one celebration a year; 1104 had two, 457 had three and 648 had four. By comparison the number of churches with more frequent celebrations did not exceed 53, or 2.3 per cent of the total number of Church of Scotland churches. Only the High Kirk of St Giles in Edinburgh had a celebration of Holy Communion every Sunday. Only 191 Church of Scotland churches (8.3%) had a communion service on Easter Sunday, only 79 (3.5%) had one on Christmas Day and only 24 (1%) had one on Whit Sunday.[43] A similarly conservative approach could be seen in the liturgical arrangement of some churches. The plan of the church at Balquhidder in 1930 shows a very traditional Church of Scotland arrangement still with assigned pews. At one end of the church the seating was arranged to face inwards, presumably either side of a central pulpit. The other seating was placed sideways on to the long walls of a rectangular building; two rows of seats were assigned to the manse and one to the schoolhouse.[44]

The Church of Scotland was late in responding to the experimental ideas of church arrangement that were being developed in Europe, and occasionally even in England, in the interwar period. An interesting experiment was the reordering of the Canongate Church in Edinburgh in 1947–1950. Between 1830 and 1894, there had been a pulpit with a domed

---

[42] Maxwell, *History of Worship*, p. 183; Forrester, 'Worship since 1929', pp. 179–80, 185–6, 188. It is interesting to note that the 1979 revision of the *Book of Common Order* was not a success as the committee of high church Presbyterians who produced it had, rather strangely, assumed that service with communion was normal practice in most Church of Scotland churches when it clearly was not. Pressure for a new revision began almost immediately. I am grateful to the Revd Dr Paul Middleton for pointing this out to me.

[43] *Ibid.*, p. 183; Burnet, *Holy Communion*, p. 297.

[44] SA, CH2/469/20.

canopy against the short wall opposite the entrance. In 1894, a new pulpit platform was installed, incorporating the communion table in front and the organ case behind. The reordering, supervised by George Hay and Ian Lindsay, involved the conversion of the previous session house behind the pulpit into an apsidal chancel. The side galleries were removed, the nave reseated, a new canopied pulpit placed on one side of the chancel arch and a lectern on the other, canopied clergy desks placed in the chancel and a communion table with a 'Laudian drape' frontal in the apse.[45] This was a deliberate attempt to provide the church with a late seventeenth-century type of Anglican interior in order to complement its late seventeenth-century Dutch-style fabric. The first example of a Church of Scotland church influenced by the post-war liturgical movement was St Columba's, Glenrothes, in 1962.

> Wheeler and Sproson's church ... was the first where the architect gave independent thought to the requirements of Reformed worship and the contemporary church. The church at Burntisland was the inspiration for this centrally-planned church, though the lightness of its structure is as contrasting as could be to the solidity of Burntisland.[46]

The seating was placed on three sides of a central communion table with the pulpit, choir stalls and organ placed on the fourth side. The subsequent reordering of some other Church of Scotland churches also borrows from the liturgical movement in Anglican and Roman Catholic churches, notably the new central communion table in the crossings of St John's, Perth, St Giles's, Edinburgh and St Mary's, Haddington. At Haddington, after much discussion and a donation of £20,000, it was agreed to restore the church to its original size and shape by reroofing the ruined chancel, but the decision was rescinded in 1968 because of rising costs. The decision to rebuild the chancel was taken again after much external pressure and offers of £37,000 to add to the original £20,000. An appeal to raise additional funds was launched in 1969. The new chancel was completed in 1977 after which repairs were carried out to the nave. One of the main features of the church is its central communion table placed under the crossing [Plate 22]. As an additional scheme, the Lauderdale Aisle was restored by the Anglo-Catholic Earl of Lauderdale, a Guardian of the Shrine of Our Lady of Walsingham, and consecrated by the Scottish Episcopal Bishop Haggart of Edinburgh in 1978. The altar in this chapel has been used both for Anglican

---

[45] Wright, *Kirk in the Canongate*, pp.141–3, Plates 16 and 17.
[46] Whyte, 'Setting of Worship', p. 150.

Plate 22 The reordered sanctuary at St Mary's, Haddington, 1977

eucharists and the Roman Catholic mass, as a deliberate ecumenical gesture by the church authorities.[47]

The very late development of modern church architecture, influenced by the ecumenical liturgical movement, in Scotland is in stark contrast to much earlier experiments in some other parts of Calvinist Europe. A new Reformed church in Basel, designed by Otto Senn in 1954, has a central pulpit with a communion table in front, and seating around them in five angled blocks.[48] Even earlier, the Reformed church at Zürich-Altstetten had the pulpit and communion table 'placed side by side, so as to give equal prominence to word and sacrament', in a raised sanctuary with the font below them, and a free-standing cross placed between them. Peter Hammond noted, in 1960, that 'the Dutch Reformed Church is making sustained

---

[47] *Ibid.*, p. 151; Marshall, *Ruin and Restoration*, pp. 36–41, 45–6, 6, 66–7.
[48] Reymond, *L'Architecture Religieuse*, p. 79.

efforts to create an architecture genuinely informed by contemporary theological insights', such as the octagonal Maranathakerk in Amsterdam, designed by J.H. Groenervegen and H. Mieras.[49] Compared with the Reformed churches in the Netherlands and Switzerland, the Presbyterian churches in Scotland were distinctly old-fashioned in their attitude to both the liturgical movement and modern church design. St Columba's, Glenrothes, was followed by the tent-like St Mungo's, Cumbernauld, in 1966 and Craigsbank Church of Scotland in Edinburgh in 1964–1967. Slightly more progress was made by the Roman Catholics in Scotland from the 1960s. Good examples are St Bride's at East Kilbride (1963–1964), St Patrick's at Kilsyth (1965), Our Lady of Sorrows on South Uist (1965) and St Andrew's at Livingston (1970).[50] Scottish Episcopalians, like Presbyterians, remained rather more wedded to traditional concepts of church design.

6. Preserving the Scottish architectural heritage

The union between the Church of Scotland and the United Free Church created problems for the united church, which are still in the process of being resolved. The chief one has been a serious over-provision of church accommodation, especially since the beginnings of a rapid decline in church-going in Scotland from about 1960. This situation is not unique to Scotland but to date the measures that have been taken for the preservation of the ecclesiastical dimension of Scotland's architectural heritage have been far from adequate. None of the Scottish churches, and particularly the established Church of Scotland where the problem has been most acute, have developed satisfactory mechanisms to ensure that buildings with important furnishings are not closed, demolished, secularized or insensitively reordered. The various conservation bodies in Scotland have done little to preserve important ecclesiastical interiors. Compared with the National Trust (which covers England, Wales and Northern Ireland), English Heritage or Cadw, all of which have some ecclesiastical buildings in their care; neither Historic Scotland nor the National Trust for Scotland exercise an equivalent role. The latter has the care of the Scottish Episcopal chapel at Falkland Palace and the non-denominational one Haddo House. None of the ecclesiastical buildings in the care of the former are still fitted up for worship, even when, like St Clement's, Rodel, in Harris, they are still roofed. Whereas in England large numbers of churches have been vested in the Churches Conservation Trust, jointly funded by the Treasury and the Church of England, and

---

[49] Peter Hammond, *Liturgy and Architecture*, London 1960, pp. 39, 65, 80, 90, Plate 6.
[50] John Hume, *Scotland's Best Churches*, Edinburgh 2005, pp. 135–40.

somewhat smaller numbers in the Historic Chapels Trust or the Friends of Friendless Churches (the latter also operating in Wales), the Scottish Historic Churches Trust, with very limited funds at its disposal, has only been able to take on responsibility for a miniscule number of redundant buildings. A few others have been preserved by local trusts, or, in the case of the former parish church at Ullapool (Appendix C/43), converted into museums without compromising the significant nature of their largely unaltered furnishings.

Unfortunately, as the evidence in Appendix B shows only too clearly, the loss of significant buildings, either through abandonment, demolition, secularization or insensitive reordering, has been considerable. It is likely that the number of surviving interiors listed in Appendix C, only 70 altogether, represents virtually the complete total of surviving pre-1860 interiors in Scotland, and some of these, such as the rapidly deteriorating interior at Quaff (Appendix C/63), are already at serious risk of loss in the near future. Within the last year (2007), the church at Ascog in the Isle of Bute has been sold, complete with its original furnishings, to a private developer for use as a dwelling.[51] It is a building of exceptional quality, consisting of a highly unusual Italianate design with a broad nave, a campanile and a vestry behind the pulpit with a bell cote over its gable end. Internally the fittings were still intact, when viewed through the windows, with the pulpit against one of the short walls and open benches facing it. At the time of writing the important ecclesiological interior of St Constantine's, Govan (Appendix E/10), is under threat of closure as a result of its proposed merger with a neighbouring church. No serious consideration appears to have been given to its future in the light of the recommendation that the other church, a far inferior building, should be used for worship by the merging congregations.

These are serious matters about which anyone concerned with the ecclesiastical heritage of Scotland needs to be greatly concerned. It appears to the present writer that, despite some activity in this area, especially that connected with the Scotland's Churches Scheme to make religious buildings more accessible to both visitors and the local community, appreciation of church buildings in Scotland, especially those of the post-Reformation period, is far less developed than it is in England, or even in Wales. The recent administrative changes within the Church of Scotland, which have seen the amalgamation of committees, have resulted in the newly formed Committee on Church Art and Architecture, which has replaced the former Committee on Artistic Matters, having a very lowly position in the structure of the church. The committee is responsible to the church's Mission and Discipleship Council, the primary concerns of which are not in this area of church policy and indeed are, in respect of part of its remit, actually at variance with the objectives of the Committee on Church Art and

---

[51] Information from the Revd Ian Currie, 15 June 2007.

Architecture. Even within the committee's own remit, 'the conservation of the nation's heritage as expressed in its Church buildings' is somewhat downplayed.[52] It will of course be argued that buildings being used for worship have to meet the needs of those who worship in them and cannot be treated as ecclesiastical museums. This is an absolutely fair point but there are plenty of examples, in Scotland as elsewhere, of where they have been adapted or reordered without compromising the historical integrity of the building. What is needed is a greater commitment to this balanced approach, relevant publications to support it and appropriate opportunities to provide such guidance through seminars or training sessions. There also has to be a recognition that sometimes the only alternative for a building that cannot be adapted for modern worship without compromising its historical integrity, or one of historical importance that is no longer required for worship, is for it to be preserved as part of the nation's architectural heritage. There seems to be a deep reluctance on the part of both ecclesiastical and non-ecclesiastical bodies, for slightly different reasons, to provide the necessary financial resources for the preservation of religious buildings. In the case of the non-ecclesiastical bodies the reluctance to spend public money on the preservation of religious buildings can be contrasted with a much greater willingness to spend public money on secular buildings. This strange and indefensible prejudice needs to be challenged. It is, of course, not just confined to Scotland but will be found just as strongly in other parts of the British Isles. It is, however, not replicated in many other parts of Europe, both Catholic and Protestant, where there appears to be far less reluctance, and sometimes even positive enthusiasm, for spending public money on religious buildings, whether no longer or still in use for worship. In Scotland both the churches themselves, and especially the Church of Scotland which has the largest number of churches of historic interest, and the conservation bodies, local authorities and national government need to commit themselves much more firmly to the preservation of those buildings that demonstrate the development of church architecture and liturgical arrangement over the centuries. Without such a commitment, more churches of historic interest will be so transformed that the ecclesiastical heritage of the nation, in terms of surviving buildings, will be weakened forever.

---

[52] *Church of Scotland Year Book 2005–6*, Edinburgh 2005, pp. 9, 23–4.

Appendix A

EXTRACTS FROM THE FIRST STATISTICAL ACCOUNT OF SCOTLAND (1791–1799) RELATING TO THE CONDITION OF CHURCHES

Aberdeenshire

1. Vol 15, p. 60 Clatt: 'The fabric of the church had a thorough repair in 1779; with regular seats, it would be a decent place of worship; but the old clumsy seats still being retained, disfigures the look of it, and affords less convenient accommodation'.
2. Vol 15, p. 186 Fyvie: 'The church ... was repainted in 1776, at which time the session gave L.20 for liberty to erect a loft or gallery in the west end, the seats of which they let at a moderate rent, for the benefit of the poor, for which they draw about 10 per cent of their money'.
3. Vol 15, p. 202 Huntly: 'The church, when first erected, might have been perhaps large enough to contain more than, at that time, attended the Established worship, but it cannot now hold above 3 fourths of the parish, though 3 galleries of late have been erected. One of these is directly fronting the pulpit, which, from the narrowness of the church, proves a great encumbrance to the speaker's voice, and equally so to many of the hearers. The other 2 galleries were erected at the expence of the session, and the rest of the seats annually paid for the use of the poor. If there had been a church erected here, equal to the number of the inhabitants, and suited to the high rank of the patron [Earl of Gordon], it would have prevented many dissenters and sectaries, and, what is of greater consequence, would have contributed to a more religious observance of the Sabbath; as many, who cannot find room in the church, either go to other places of worship, stay at home, or stroll in the fields'.
4. Vol 14, p. 535 Kemnay: 'The church ... was new roofed, plastered, and adorned on the inside, with great taste and elegance, by the late Mr Burnett of Kemnay; but the walls are not likely to stand long'.

5. Vol 15, pp. 412–13 Peterhead: 'The church was built in 1771 . . . and is an elegant building 78 feet long, and 39 feet broad over the walls, which are of a proper height to admit of the galleries being sufficiently raised. From the position of the pulpit, and the arrangement of the seats, both in the galleries and on the ground-floor, it is the most convenient place of worship with which I am acquainted. The plan was sent by one of the heritors residing at Edinburgh, and was got from an eminent architect there. There has been a great alteration in the style of building churches in the Synod of Aberdeen since its erection, but without attending to the strict proportion and simplicity of this plan, which might serve as a model for any church, the pulpit being placed at an equal distance from the east and west end of the north wall, and every person both seeing and hearing the minister. The whole expence of the building was only L.520 Sterling; and a small fund being obtained, by the rent of a few seats, which were fixed after the plan was completed, at present under the management of the kirk-session, the heritors have paid nothing for repairs since the church was built. The Scotch and English Episcopals and Seceders have each a very convenient place of worship in the town of Peterhead. There is an organ in each of the Episcopal chapels'.

Angus

6. Vol 13, p. 499 Maryton: 'A new church was built last year, which is both elegant and commodious, and to the praise of the heritors be it spoken, not a farthing demanded for seat-rents; a practice by no means common in Scotland, but highly worthy of imitation'.
7. Vol 13, pp. 545–6 Montrose: 'The old church of Montrose was a Gothic structure, rendered very gloomy and irregular, by large additions to the galleries and to the building itself. It was originally, however, venerable and well proportioned. Having fallen into decay, the heritors, town-council, kirk-session, trades, and proprietors of seats, agreed unanimously to build another in its stead. . . . The plan has been formed with deliberation; it has been submitted to the inspection of skilful architects; and, it is to be hoped, will be executed in such a manner as to merit public approbation. . . . The town-council and session, lately petitioned the managers of the Episcopal and Anti-burgher churches, that the members of the established church might have the liberty of enjoying divine service in their meeting-houses, till the parish-church was rebuilt. They, and their congregations, not only granted this petition, but declared, in the handsomest manner, their willingness to submit to considerable inconveniences, in order to accommodate their fellow Christians to their wishes. . . . The Episcopal chapel . . . was founded in 1722. It is an ornament to the town, and was even praised by

the author of the Rambler,[1] in his Tour Through Scotland, as a neat and cleanly place of worship'.
8. Vol 13, p. 646 Stracathro: 'The church is little better than a heap of ruins'.

Argyll

9. Vol 8, p. 126 Glenorchy: 'The church ... outwardly, appears a decent building. Within, though far from elegant, it is neither uncomfortable nor incommodious. ... It is to be regretted, that places appointed to the public worship of God, should not be rendered suitable to a service so sacred and so important. The magnificent temples of the heathen world indicated a becoming reverence for the objects of their worship. The church of Rome, the church of England, and the several separatists from our own establishment, are careful to have such places, as are constructed to the service of the Universal Parent, made decent and comfortable: whilst, with us the church of Scotland, many of our Country Kirks, are such dark, damp, and dirty hovels, as chill and repress every sentiment of devotion. They, besides, endanger the health of every class of worshippers, and encourage the indifferent and the indolent, in their neglect of institutions'.
10. Vol 8, p. 152 Inveraray: 'Since the demolition of the old town, there have been only temporary places of worship. Two new churches, under one roof, are to be built next season. The design, by Mr Milne of London, is partly Gothic; it is ornamented by a handsome spire of 107 feet in height, rising from the centre of the building, and the whole is calculated to unite elegance with utility and convenience'.
11. Vol 20, pp. 381–2 Jura and Colonsay: 'The church and manse are in Jura. The church has stood for twelve years at least, has no place for a bell, and was never seated'.
12. Vol 8, pp. 223–4 Kilfinan: 'The church was repaired, or almost rebuilt, in 1759, and is now little more than half-seated. ... The church stands in need of a second repair, which it is to be hoped it will soon have'.
13. Vol 20, p. 318 Kilfinichen and Kilvickeon: 'There are 4 places of worship in the parish ... but there has been no church in any of them since the Reformation, except in Ross. In every other district, divine worship is at the side of a hill. The Church of Ross is also ruinous, and has been condemned by the presbytery of Mull, who passed a decree for

---

[1] *Boswell's Journal of a Tour to the Hebrides with Samuel Johnson, LLD*, 1773, ed. F.A. Pottle and C.H. Bennett, Melbourne 1963, pp. 50–1: 'the English chapel ... is really an elegant building, both within and without. The organ is adorned with green and gold'.

re-building it, and another church in Kilfinichen in Airdmeanach; but none is as yet built'.
14. Vol 8, p. 263 Kilmartin: 'The church was built in 1601 . . . and has had no reparation or improvement since it was built, except giving it a new roof'.
15. Vol 8, pp. 277, 282 Kilmore and Kilbride: 'The walls of Kilmore church are very sufficient. The roof and windows have received repairs at different times. It is poorly seated; but there is reason to think, that the heritors will soon make up this defect. The kirk of Kilbride is not so sufficient in the walls, as that of Kilmore; and the seats are equally bad. It stands greatly in need of repairs. . . . It is intended to build a chapel of ease in Oban, as the number of inhabitants are rapidly increasing, insomuch, that none of the parish churches can contain them. The building will be begun, as soon as proper funds are collected for that purpose, and for affording a competent salary to the preacher'.
16. Vol 8, p. 370 Morvern: 'There are 2 churches so called from their outward appearance, but with respect to decency of accommodation, they might as properly be called shades. In these the minister alternately officiates'.
17. Vol 8, pp. 321–2 South Knapdale: 'The present incumbent, when he came to the parish, found neither a church, or proper place of worship, in the whole bounds. . . . In the year 1772, he was under the necessity of suing the heritors at law before he could prevail upon them to build a kirk.[2] He was forced, for the space of six years, to preach in the fields'.

Ayrshire

18. Vol 6, p. 248 Irvine: 'The church was rebuilt in 1774. . . . The lofts form an octagon inside, and, gradually ascending, place every hearer in full view of the preacher. . . . The area below is neatly fitted up with pews, all of them facing the pulpit. Three-fourths of the church were built by the magistrates, and one fourth by the other heritors. The communion tables consist of two rows of table seats, extending from the pulpit, on the north-west, to the south-east door, the partitions of which form the ends of the said seats, and are movable at pleasure. These seats are the property of the session, and yield from 8l to 9l annually. The magistrates, reserving one loft for themselves, disposed of the rest of their property to the inhabitants, who fitted up their own seats, according to a plan previously agreed upon. The money which they raised in this manner defrayed their share of the expence of the building, and left

---

[2] The church was built, at Achahoish, in 1775, see *BS Argyll and Bute*, p. 99.

them with an overplus of near 300l. This sum they laid out, with an addition of near 500l more, in building a very elegant steeple adjoining to the church on the north-west side'.
19. Vol 6, p. 363 Kilwinning: 'The church is a very beautiful structure, built partly in the ancient Gothic taste, to correspond to the venerable ruins of the monastery. But though it be almost 20 years since it was built, it has never been seated. This has been owing to an unhappy difference of opinion among the heritors about the division of the area of the church, and which is still unsettled'.
20. Vol 6, p. 387 Kirkoswald: 'In 1777 a new church was built . . . fit to hold 800 hearers, from a plan, and under the direction, of David Earl of Cassilis, who is resident proprietor of above two-thirds of the parish; and it is considered as one of the neatest churches in this country . . . having a gallery at each end, and an aisle, with a fire room, furnished at the expence of the Earl of Cassilis, and which he is obliged to keep up'.
21. Vol 6, p. 522 St Quivox: 'The church was repaired in 1767, uniformly seated, and plaistered by the heritors; and a new aisle built by the patron, Mr Oswald of Auchencruive'.
22. Vol 6, pp. 566–7 Sorn: 'The parish church could not nearly accommodate the inhabitants; therefore, in the year 1792, a subscription for building a Chapel of Ease here [at Catrine] was set on foot. Its promising appearance at first, induced Mr Alexander [the proprietor] to feu out ground for the site of the chapel; and he himself subscribed for the masonry of it. The building was accordingly begun in the spring of that year, and finished in the spring following. . . . Many of the subscribers failed to pay the amount of their subscriptions. There was not more than L.80 Sterling of the whole collected. Mr Alexander, therefore, advanced above L.750 Sterling on the security of the seat-rents, but has not, as yet, received a single farthing of either benefit or interest. . . . The seats erected in the area of the chapel, have never yet been completely filled. When the galleries are put up, the chapel will contain above 1500 sitters. . . . It is esteemed a great ornament to the place'.
23. Vol 6, p. 641 Symington 'The church is old. . . . About 40 years ago it received a thorough repair, being furnished with new pews, all painted, and the roof was plaistered. It has received partial repairs since that period . . . but the ceiling begins to fail'.

Banffshire

24. Vol 16, p. 30 Banff: 'The parish church was built in the years 1789 and 1790 after the model of the new church at Dundee. . . . Four Ionic columns support the galleries, which form five sides of an octagon, and are high and spacious. The church is elegantly finished within, and,

exclusive of roomy passages, will contain 1500 persons. The pulpit is perhaps raised to an incommodious height, being an ascent of 21 steps. Some of my brethren, accustomed to a more humble rostrum, decline officiating in so elevated situation. ... The spire still remains in an unfinished state. ... It is intended, however, to resume the work next season. The church has already cost L.2400'.

25. Vol 16, pp. 336–7 Mortlach: 'The church is indeed venerable, but it is only because it is old ... the roof, which it got about 80 years ago, is ruinous. ... And as its shape, that of an oblong square of about 90 feet to 28, is a very incommodious one, as a place of public worship, both for the spectator and the hearers, it will probably be found advisable to get over the veneration for its antiquity, and new model it into a more convenient form'.

26. Vol 16, pp. 380–1 Ruthven: 'As the heritors have entered into a contract with an undertaker to build a new church, on an approved plan, to contain 1000 persons, it is not necessary to say much respecting the present one. ... Next year it is to be taken down, and the materials employed in building the new church'.

Berwickshire

27. Vol 3, p. 213 Hutton: 'has lately been ceiled, plastered, and flagged, and is now a very handsome country place of worship'.

Caithness

28. Vol 18, pp. 92–3 Halkirk: 'The manse and church ... have always been in a bad state of repair ... though repaired four times, and at considerable expence during that period, *viz.* 23 years. The last of these repairs is going on just now, at an estimated sum of L.154 Sterling; and as soon as the undertaker puts them off his hands, they will call for another immediate repair, whether the minister calls for it or not. It is to be regretted, that heritors, from a mistaken notion of saving their purses, should so unaccountably injure their own interest, and incommode the minister, when both might have been avoided with little expence'.

Dumfriesshire

29. Vol 4, p. 10 Applegarth: 'It [the church] is large and well built and sufficient, at present, to contain the whole inhabitants of the parish. It has a large *jam*, very commodious for dispensing the Sacrament of the

Lord's Supper, which in some of the neighbouring parishes, from want of room in the churches, is dispensed in the fields'.
30. Vol 4, p. 261 Keir: 'The church was repaired about 30 years ago but has never properly been seated, and the number of inhabitants having increased considerably of late years, it is rather too small for their accommodation'.
31. Vol 4, p. 303 Kirkmichael: 'The church ... was partly rebuilt and somewhat enlarged, in 1729, and covered with slates in place of heath, with which it had been formerly thatched'.
32. Vol 4, p. 462 St Mungo: 'The present church was built in 1754, but seems never to have been properly finished. It has no bell; and the seats are in a ruinous condition'.
33. Vol 4, p. 515 Tynron: 'The church was built near of the beginning of the century, and the half of it, by the roof giving way, obliged to be rebuilt about 40 years ago. A slight repair has been made upon both walls and roof in 1787, and is now pretty comfortable, except upon a fall of snow, which penetrates through several crevices in the roof'.

Dunbartonshire

34. Vol 9, p. 110 Luss: 'The church is uncommonly good. It was built in 1771, by the late Sir James Colquhoun of Luss, without laying any part of the burden upon the other heritors'.

East Lothian

35. Vol 2, p. 473 Dunbar: 'The church, till lately, was in the inside especially, one of the worst, and most inconvenient, perhaps in Scotland. . . . It was repaired by the heritors in 1779, floored with deal, and ceiled in the roof . . . it was regularly seated; so that it now looks clean and neat, the quire only remaining unaltered'.

Fife

36. Vol 10, pp. 111–12 Carnbee: 'The church ... has undergone many expensive repairs within these 40 years, and from the faulty state of parts of it, the heritors it is probable will find it more for their interest to build a new one,[3] than to keep in repair the old fabric'.
37. Vol 10, pp. 294–5 Dunfermline: 'The church is of great antiquity. . . . It

---

[3] A new church was built in 1793–1794, see *BS Fife*, p. 120.

is very capacious, and ... susceptible of much improvement, and of being made, if not neat and comfortable, at least a dignified looking place of worship. It is much to be regretted, that far from any attempts being made to beautify so venerable a structure, very little attention has been paid to have it seated, and fitted up with becoming decency; the whole is cold and dirty, and wears rather a gloomy appearance. A stranger may well be surprised, to find the church of a town so prosperous and thriving, and which externally has so grand an appearance, so miserably fitted up within. This may be accounted for, from the church having never been legally divided among the heritors, ... from the inattention of the town-council, and from the disposition very prevalent among heritors, to be at as little expence as possible, in what regards either churches, or those who officiate in them. To these causes may be added the want of the interference of some spirited and generous individual, from whose exertions, improvements in general are often found to originate'.

38. Vol 10, p. 486 Kingshorn: 'The church was rebuilt in 1774. The shell of the house is respectable enough; but within, it has rather an awkward and paltry appearance, from its not being as yet completely seated, and from the mixture of new, and of old pews and forms'.

39. Vol 10, p. 508 Kirkcaldy: 'The church ... is a large, unshapely pile, that seems to have been regarded at different times, to suit the growing population of the parish, and in the construction of which convenience has been more consulted than unity of design or beauty. ... The choir is fitted up in common with the nave for the reception of parishioners; and a large wing has been added for their farther accommodation'.

40. Vol 10, pp. 747–8 St Monans: 'What is at present used for the church of the parish is part of an old convent. ... The burden of upholding this fabric, was laid by the proprietor of the lands of Newark upon the feuars of St Monance, when he let off the ground on which the town stands. ... But the building seems to have been totally neglected by them. In 1772 it was in such a ruinous state, that the incumbent raised a process for reparation before the presbytery, and obtained a decree for that end against the heritors. But the feuars were reluctant, pretending they were not obliged to uphold it. This brought on a process between the heritors and them, before the lords of Session, in which they were cast, and found liable to uphold the fabric. During the process, it received a partial reparation, but nothing equal to what was granted by the presbytery; and nothing more has yet been done, either by the heritors, to enforce the decree of the Lords upon the feuars, or by them, to testify their compliance with it; and if they continue long so to do, this venerable pile must sink into ruins. What a pity it is, that such a beautiful monument of antiquity ... should be suffered to go to desolation!'

41. Vol 10, p. 756 Saline: 'The church is ... in a bad state, having got no

material repairs for a long period; it will scarcely admit of repairs now, and probably must soon be rebuilt'.[4]

Inverness-shire

42. Vol 20, pp. 146–7 Barra: 'The number of Protestants has always been so small [80 out of a population of 1604, see p. 140], that it was thought unnecessary to put the heritor [Roderick Macneil] to the expence of building a church. . . . The minister preaches two Sundays at Borve . . . the third Sunday at Kilbar . . . and the fourth at Watersay'.

43. Vol 17, p. 32 Boleskine and Abertarff: 'The present incumbent has a commodious manse, and a large church . . . built and slated about 30 years ago. These underwent a late reparation, at a considerable expence to the heritors; but, from the exposure of both these edifices to the violence of the storm, they will almost require an annual repair, for which there was a fund established at the last presbytery visitation, which, if wisely applied, may in future relieve the heritors from a great expenditure, similar to what they were already put to'.

44. Vol 17, p. 57 Daviot and Dunlichity: 'The church of Dunlichty [sic] was rebuilt in 1759, and has had but one repair since, of 25l, about 4 years ago. The church and manse of Daviot, in 1763 and 1764, but not so substantially, having had two repairs since, to the extent of between 80l and 90l each time, and now much in need of a third, at the distance only of 7 years from the last repair given them. It has happened to these buildings, what is often the fate of public works of this kind, when given to tradesmen who exhibit the lowest estimates, without enquiring sufficiently into their character and ability . . . to the great loss of the heritors, and daily inconvenience and prejudice of the minister'.

45. Vol 17, pp. 103–4 Inverness: 'The church for the English congregation was built in the year 1772, by the magistrates, in consequence of a compromise with the heritors, who were to have preference of seats at an equitable yearly rent. The church is an elegant structure. . . . A new church is now building for the Gaelic congregation, and will be completed next summer,[5] at the joint and equal expense of the heritors on the one hand, and the Magistrates and six incorporations on the other'.

46. Vol 20, p. 132 South Uist: 'There has been no church built in the parish since the Reformation. The Protestants assemble in the school-houses, which are now in good order and repair, and the Roman Catholics have three mass-houses in the parish'.

---

[4] The church was rebuilt, 1808–1810, see *BS Fife*, p. 408.
[5] The church was built in 1792–1794, see *BS Highland and Islands*, p. 186.

Kincardineshire

47. Vol 14, p. 112 Fetteresso: 'The church is old, inconvenient, and unfit to contain the congregation, when fully assembled together. ... Opposite to the pulpit, there is an aisle, which is of service to the preacher, by enabling him to speak with greater ease. The aisle was built in 1720. ... Neither walls nor roof are plastered; and as the floor is from 3 to 4 feet lower than the surface of the ground on the outside of the walls, pools of water stand in the area several days after a heavy rain'.

Lanarkshire

48. Vol 7, p. 278 Glasford: 'The church was built in 1633. It never was elegant or convenient. Its present uncouth appearance fixes the attention of every beholder; and scarce a stranger passes by without making it a compliment. It is not in good repair. The heritors, unlike the ancient Jews, love not to decorate the temple; though it would be doing them injustice not to observe, that they love to attend it'.

Midlothian

49. Vol 2, p. 119 Carrington: 'As the roof is much decayed, as the windows are shattered, the walls rough from the hand of the mason, the seats crazy and irregular, its internal appearance is the very reverse of that simple elegance which befits a place of public worship'.
50. Vol 2, p. 214 Dalkeith: 'The church, though old, is in good repair, and in winter is rendered comfortable, by being warmed with stoves'.
51. Vol 2, p. 242 Duddingston: 'The seats in the lower part of the church are in a tottering and ruinous state, though the pews in the galleries wear a respectable aspect. It would not require much expence to render the whole both commodious and elegant'.
52. Vol 2, p. 271 Heriot: 'The church is an old and infirm building. It is scarcely safe to perform public duty in it. It is neither dry above, nor decently seated. It is, perhaps, the most shabby and miserable place of accommodation for divine service in Scotland'.
53. Vol 2, p. 302 Inveresk: 'The whole [church] is now in a ruinous condition, and is truly a disgrace to the parish. Several attempts have lately been made to have it rebuilt[6] ... which have failed'.

---

[6] The church was rebuilt in 1805, see *BS Lothian*, p. 263.

54. Vol 2, p. 435 Temple: 'ill seated, and very cold in winter, from having bad doors, and no ceiling'.

Moray

55. Vol 16, pp. 479–80 Drainy: 'The church ... looks tolerably decent without, but is very naked and ill furnished within. Our churches are, in general, exceedingly cold and dirty, and there is little hope of this evil being soon remedied'.
56. Vol 16, pp. 549–50 Dyke and Moy: 'A new and commodious church ... was built in 1781, at the expence of the heritors, for the sum of L.525, beside the carriages performed by the parish. It is neatly plastered and ceiled, well lighted, paved in the areas, and regularly seated. It has a geometrical stair in each end, with galleries quite round; and none are allowed to bury in it. The plan has been adopted by other parishes'.

Orkney

57. Vol 19, pp. 82–3 Evie and Rendall: 'The kirk of Evie was situated near the manse, and near the middle of that parish ... And the kirk of Rendall lies almost in the south extremity of that parish. They were both, originally, poor small houses, thatched annually with straw. As far back as 1769, when the present incumbent came to Orkney, they were both in a very ruinous situation; but as the late incumbent ... was very old and infirm ... no steps were taken by him to get them any ways repaired; and the present incumbent officiated in them, without a pane of glass, or even a window-frame, as assistant and successor, from the year 1772. Upon the death of his predecessor, in the year 1781, he applied to the principal heritors, and afterwards at their desire, to his presbytery, when, after a legal visitation, where the principal heritors assisted, they were both judicially condemned as ruinous and irreparable; and upon a petition from the principal heritors ... the presbytery ordained a new centrical church to be built for the whole charge, in place of the two ruinous ones;[7] fixed the dimensions, and gave a general decree for the expence of building the new church, of L.156 Sterling; against which no objections were offered. The minister continued, as usual, to officiate alternately in these condemned kirks, till in the year 1788, when the danger became so

---

[7] This new church was built, at Evie, in 1799, see *BS Highland and Islands*, p. 299.

conspicuous, that he fortunately deserted that of Evie, as the walls soon afterwards tumbled down on a Sunday, and the materials were set up for auction. The minister then travelled every Sunday to Rendall, and officiated in that ruinous house . . . till October 1794, when, having lost his health by officiating there, and that house also becoming very hazardous, he was obliged, by the injunction of his physician, to desert it; so that, since that period, there has been no public worship in this charge, except in the open air, in the church-yard. He has repeatedly applied to the heritors, or their factors, and the very hard case of this charge has been often and warmly recommended by this presbytery and synod to the General Assembly, but no address has been obtained; and these matters continue in this deplorable position at the present moment'.

58. Vol 19, p. 109 Hoy and Graemsay: 'The whole of the church about nine years ago fell down of itself before the heritors would offer to make any reparation of it, and at last they rebuilt it, and that in a very slight manner, so that it is not above half finished'.
59. Vol 19, pp. 115–16 Kirkwall: 'The Cathedral of St Magnus . . . is certainly the most entire one in Scotland . . . in which state it has been preserved by the judicious management of the kirk-session, out of the seat rents, and other trifling funds, without any the least expence to either the town or the country heritors'.
60. Vol 19, p. 209 St Andrews and Deerness: 'The church of St Andrews was rebuilt about 40 years ago, but is now in a dangerous and ruinous state; and though the present incumbent has repeatedly applied to the heritors to get it repaired, and both his presbytery and synod have, year after year, stated their grievance to the General Assembly, nothing has yet been done to lessen the danger.[8] St Peter's Church, in Deerness, is now roofless. In 1789, it was declared by tradesmen, on oath, too small, ruinous, and irreparable; a decreat was passed by the presbytery for a new one: and this year, the heritors, after a long and unaccountable delay, have at last paid a part of their proportions for erecting it; so that, it is hoped, it will be built and finished next year'.
61. Vol 19, pp. 332–3 Stronsay and Eday: 'The kirks were in a ruinous state in 1779. The kirk of Stronsay, which was built in 1726, got new slates put on its roof in 1785, but it still needs great repairs. The kirk of Eday, which was built about the year 1730, is in a ruinous state; it had not a pane of glass in any of its windows in the memory of any man living. As it is . . . in so bad a state, the minister will not be able to officiate there at all if the heritors do not rebuild it or repair it'.[9]

---

[8] A new church was built in 1801, see BS *Highland and Islands*, p. 374.
[9] No new church on Eday was erected until 1815–1816, see BS *Highland and Islands*, p. 296.

THE FIRST STATISTICAL ACCOUNT OF SCOTLAND (1791–1799)

Perthshire

62. Vol 12, p. 69 Bendothy: 'A chapel of ease was built about eleven years ago at North Persy.... It cost L.150 Sterling, raised by contributions in the Country. It is slated, seated, and contains 400 people. The seat-rents and collection amount to about L.30, which maintains the preacher. Application was made for and from the Royal Bounty, and from the Society for Propagating Christian Knowledge, without effect. In this last case, the failure was partly owing to the want of concurrence on the part of landed gentlemen, to comply with the rules of the Society, which require half of the preacher's salary to be made good by them'.

63. Vol 12, p. 127 Blairgowrie: 'The church ... was built in 1767, and is a plain substantial edifice, at present in good repair, but cold in winter. It would be much improved with being ceiled, and having porches at the doors'.

64. Vol 12, p. 244 Clunie: 'It would be a credit to this Country, if all the old crazy kirks ... in it were razed to the foundations, and new ones built in a workmanlike manner, on a decent and convenient plan, and of the most substantial and permanent materials. This would occasion some expense to the present proprietors of the Country, which in general are opulent and liberal; but what it would take out of their pockets, it would put into those of their posterity and successors.... The kirk of Clunie, though one of the best in the neighbourhood, has neither comeliness nor proportion ... has been repeatedly patched, and was last repaired in 1788'.

65. Vol 12, pp. 322, 325–6 Dunkeld: 'The quire of the cathedral is now converted into the parish church, and forms a decent, and not incommodious place of worship, though, from the height of the walls, and the want of ceiling, it is not only bare and meagre to the eye, but is liable to be uncomfortably cold to the congregation during the winter. In 1762, James, Duke of Atholl, finding the roof had gone to decay, obtained from Government L.300 Sterling for rendering it, and accomplishing such other repairs as were necessary. This sum, together with the price of the old materials, and about L.80 paid by different persons for purchasing space on the ground of the area for seats, was employed in putting on the present roof, and in completely new seating the body of the church. Two galleries have since been erected, at the expence of two lodges of Free Masons belonging to the town, who draw the rents paid for them. In front of the pulpit, there is a spacious and handsome seat fitted up for the family of Atholl; and it should be known to their honour, that while they are at Dunkeld-House, the seat is seldom empty during Divine service.... The area of [the nave] is employed as a burial-ground by the inhabitants. On the day on which the Sacrament is dispensed in the church, a tent is erected within it, and sermons

delivered. . . . One cannot cease looking at the nave and aisles of the cathedral, without lamenting as he sees them stand roofless and in desolation. While he muses, he mourns with regret over the blind and hasty zeal, which in the ardour of changing a creed, demolished a building, not spared, in its hatred at the rites of the worshipper, the temple where he worshipped'.

66. Vol 12, p. 701 Lethendy: 'Notwithstanding the small size of this parish, it is provided with three churches; one belonging to the Establishment, one to the Antiburgher Seceders, and one to the English Episcopals. Of them, the Established church is by far the worst in point of structure and accommodation. None of the heritors reside in the parish and consequently less attention is paid to keep it in a state of any decent repair. The other two are more in the stile of modern buildings, and much better fitted up for the accommodation of the hearers'.

67. Vol 11, p. 624 Tulliallan: 'The present church . . . was built in 1675; and, were it not for its Gothic windows, would be taken for a modern edifice. It appears, from the parish records, that though the heritors built the church, they did not seat it. This the kirk-session, in order to accommodate the people, did, out of the poor's funds; and afterwards, to reimburse those funds, sold them to the parishioners; which they, their heirs, and assignees, possess to this day. A seat, holding 5 persons, that was then sold for 4s, now sells for 5l.'

Renfrewshire

68. Vol 7, p. 738 Inchinnan: 'The only repairs it [the church] seems to have got for these many years, is upon the roof, which is plastered; yet a stranger, upon entering into it, would hardly believe that public worship had been performed in it for a century past'.

Ross and Cromarty

69. Vol 17, p. 662 Urquhart: 'The present church has been recently condemned, as unworthy of reparation, and a new one is begun to be built in a different and more eligible situation; for which, and a wall to enclose it, a sum of L.580 Sterling is allotted'.

Roxburghshire

70. Vol 3, p. 348 Bedrule: 'The whole fabric is much decayed, and has been, for a considerable time, in a ruinous state. . . . We are extremely sorry we have to regret the bad state of many of our public churches.

... We are the more particular on this head, for the information of *strangers*, many of whom, we understand, form an unfavourable opinion of the religion, people and clergy of this Country on that account'.

71. Vol 3, p. 391 Castletown: 'The church was built in 1777. The rain penetrates through the walls, and part of the timber is already rotten'.
72. Vol 3, p. 512 Kelso: 'The Parochial Church and Episcopal chapel are both new; the former a spacious octagon, with a handsome dome, and constructed to accommodate three thousand hearers; the latter a small neat gothic building, and has lately been ornamented with an organ'.
73. Vol 3, p. 534 St Boswells: 'The church, between 3 and 4 years ago, was ruinous, unpleasant, extremely cold, and injurious to health; but, by thorough repair, has been made one of the best in the Country. The expense incurred was 100l Sterling'.
74. Vol 3, pp. 620–1 Roxburgh: 'The church was built in the year 1752 ... it is in good repair, neat and commodiously fitted up for holding the people. Though plain and simple in its construction, the present church forms a striking contrast to the old one here, and shows how differently men in ancient and modern times think of places fittest for devotional exercises. Agreeably, as it would seem, to the old idea, that the spirit of devotion likes best to dwell in gloomy retreats, the kirk at Roxburgh was almost wholly underground, roofed with a strong arch, and totally overgrown with grass'.

Stirlingshire

75. Vol 9, p. 154 Alva: 'Although the fabric of the church is still good and sound, yet it appears to have never been completely finished within; the walls and roof are not plaistered, and the seats are in a very ruinous condition. The windows are too small and ill-placed. As the structure is sufficient, it might be repaired at a moderate expence; and, without any enlargement of the area, might be rendered a very commodious and elegant church'.
76. Vol 9, p. 605 Slamannan: 'The walls of the church were rebuilt about the year 1753; but the old seating was still continued, which indeed is very old; many seats being marked with the year 1632, and some of them even so far back as 1556. It stands, therefore, in much need of being renewed'.
77. Vol 9, pp. 644–5 Strathblane: 'The church is a mean building, erected in the beginning of the present century; and having never been lathed or plaistered, the bare walls and roof without ceiling, present a very sorry appearance for a place of worship'.

Sutherland

78. Vol 18, pp. 311–12 Assynt: 'The church . . . had a slight repair seven or eight years ago; so slight, indeed, that owing to the very high winds, which occasionally prevail here, many of the slates . . . are driven or fallen off, and the rain gets in . . . and the glass windows . . . are greatly injured'.

Appendix B

CHURCHES WITH SUBSTANTIALLY COMPLETE PRE-1843 FURNISHINGS LISTED BY GEORGE HAY: AN UPDATE

Aberdeenshire

1. p. 241, Aberdeen, St Nicholas West, 1755. 'original pulpit, galleries, magistrates' pew and chandeliers'. Interior substantially intact, see Appendix C/1.
2. p. 242, Bourtie, 1806. 'original pulpit and fittings'. Interior substantially intact, see Appendix C/2.
3. p. 243, Glenbuchat, '18th-cent pulpit and pews, 1828 east loft'. Interior completely intact, see Appendix C/3.

Angus

4. p. 246 Logie Pert, 1840. 'original furniture complete'. The charge has been dissolved and the building was sold in the 1980s to a private individual for conversion to living accommodation.[1]

Berwickshire

5. p. 251, Channelkirk, 1817. 'original pulpit and fittings'. Interior substantially intact, see Appendix C/52.

Dunbartonshire

6. p. 255, Kirkintilloch, Old Parish Church, 1644. '18th-cent pulpit and fittings'. Converted for use as a local authority museum in 1961 and

---

[1] Information from Rev'd Linda Broadley, Minister of Dun and Hillside, 18 April 2007.

most furnishings removed. Only two of the former four lofts remain, one with tiered seating of 1788, together with the pulpit of 1782, which has a backboard and shallow shell-type canopy, now barely visible amid the museum exhibits.

Fife

7. p. 256, Collessie, 1839. 'original pulpit and fittings'. Interior substantially intact, see Appendix C/25.
8. p. 258, Strathmiglo, 1787. 'original pulpit and fittings'. Hay's description was inaccurate. The original pulpit was relocated in 1848–1849 when the church was completely reseated with box pews. Although the pews remain intact, the pulpit itself was found to be rotten and was replaced in the 1890s. The gallery seating also remains intact.[2]

Inverness-shire

9. p. 259, Bracadale, 1831. 'original pulpit and fittings'. Sold to Free Presbyterian Church and all the furnishings removed in 1970s, to be replaced with recycled late nineteenth-century furnishings from other churches.
10. p. 259, Duirinish, 1832. 'original pulpit and fittings'. The church has been reseated on the ground floor but the other furnishings remain intact. These include the canopied pulpit with its precentor's desk on the short wall opposite the entrance, penitent's platform, box pews on each side of the pulpit, former long communion tables (now placed against the entrance wall) and the galleries around three sides of the interior with tiered seating.
11. p. 259, Scarista, 1840. 'original pulpit and fittings'. Completely refurnished in 1994, largely with late nineteenth-century furnishings from other churches.

Peebleshire

12. p. 268, Newlands, 1838. 'original pulpit and fittings'. Interior substantially intact, see Appendix C/57.

---

[2] *BS Fife*, p. 413.

Perthshire

13. p. 270, St Martins, 1843. 'original pulpit and fittings'. Interior substantially intact, see Appendix C/51.

Ross and Cromarty

14. p. 272, Edderton, 1842. 'original pulpit and fittings'. Disused from 1948 but later reinstated and furnishings altered. Original pulpit has been replaced though the 'ogee-domed' sounding board, 'decorated with Adamish *stucco duro* work on the frieze, survives'.[3]
15. p. 272, Lochbroom, 1817. 'repaired 1835; original pulpit and fittings'. Church in fact completely rebuilt in 1844–1845;[4] interior substantially intact, despite insertion of a false ceiling at gallery level, see Appendix C/40.
16. p. 273, Plockton, c.1825. 'original fittings'. The original pulpit and precentor's desk and the gallery, painted a delicate blue, survive intact. However, there are new pews and a new long communion table, placed in front of the precentor's desk, in the body of the church.
17. p. 273 Rosskeen, 1832. 'original pulpit and fittings'. Disused already by the time Hay wrote, the church was acquired by Highland Council which has tried, and so far failed, to find an alternative use for it. To prevent further vandalism the windows have been boarded and the doors bolted. The pulpit has been removed and placed in storage. Most of the pews are intact though some have been removed at both ground floor and gallery levels.[5] Conversion to some type of heritage use, based on the successful model of Ullapool (see Appendix C/43), with reinstatement of as many furnishings as possible, could be the best long-term solution for this building.

Roxburghshire

18. p. 274, Makerstoun, 1808. 'original pulpit and fittings'. The handsome canopied pulpit and balustraded precentor's desk survive, as does the seating in the gallery. The seating in the body of the church was significantly reordered in the 1960s.[6]

---

[3] *BS Highland and Islands*, p. 410.
[4] *Ibid.*, p. 433.
[5] Information from the Council's conservation architect, John Duncan, 17 January 2007.
[6] *BS Borders*, pp. 511–12.

Selkirkshire

19. p. 274 Ettrick and Buccleuch, 1824. 'original pulpit and fittings'. Interior substantially intact, see Appendix C/53.
20. p. 274, Galashiels, Old Parish Church, 1813. 'original pulpit and fittings'. The church had been closed in 1931 but was completely demolished in 1960.[7]

West Lothian

21. p. 276, Livingston, 1732. 'renovated and refurnished 1837'. The original pulpit of 1732 survives as does the pulpit canopy and tiered seating in the lofts of 1837. Seating on the ground floor replaced with late Victorian pews from another church in the 1970s.

Zetland

22. p. 277, Quarff, 1829. 'original fittings'. Interior substantially intact though no longer used for worship, see Appendix C/63.

Note also the following churches recorded by Hay which are also no longer intact.

23. p. 252, St Colmac's, North Bute, 1836. 'original long communion table and seating', now 'abandoned and roofless'.[8]
24. p. 258, Newburn, Fife, 1815. 'original pulpit and table pews'. Converted to a house in 1970; canopied pulpit installed in Largo parish church as part of a reordering by L. A. L. Rolland in 1965.[9]
25. p. 278, South Yell, Shetland, 1841. 'original pulpit and long communion table', subsequently converted for use as a private house, and furnishings not preserved.[10]

---

[7] *Ibid.*, p. 296.
[8] *BS Argyll and Bute*, p. 614.
[9] *BS Fife*, pp. 334, 421.
[10] *BS Highland and Islands*, p. 472.

Appendix C

EXAMPLES OF SUBSTANTIALLY UNALTERED INTERIORS OF SCOTTISH CHURCHES BUILT BEFORE 1860

Churches are listed by modern unitary authority, though grouped in two cases, rather than the old counties. Each church has been placed in one of the following categories of liturgical arrangement:

Type A: pulpit on the long wall
Type B: T-plan with central pulpit
Type C: pulpit, or liturgical focus, on the short wall
Type D: ecclesiological arrangement

Aberdeen and Aberdeenshire

1. Aberdeen (St Nicholas West) Church of Scotland: Type A. The nave of the former parish church of St Nicholas, divided into three churches after the Reformation, was rebuilt in 1752–1755 to an elaborate design by the English architect, James Gibbs. The interior has been slightly altered by the introduction of a fixed communion table and an organ in the late nineteenth century but otherwise preserves its original furnishings intact. The canopied pulpit is placed in the middle of the nave opposite a railed pew for the elders. There are box pews facing it in the nave and north aisle and galleries around four sides of the interior, one containing the pew for the Lord Provost and members of the City Council.
2. Bourtie (Parish Church) Church of Scotland: Type A/C. The church retains a virtually unaltered square interior of 1806 with a canopied pulpit to which is attached a bracket for the baptismal bowl, precentor's desk, penitent's platform, manse pew and open benches. There is a gallery across the entrance wall and a number of collecting shoes, the earliest dating from 1671.

3. Glenbuchat (St Peter) former Church of Scotland, now belonging to Aberdeenshire Council: Type A. The earliest surviving unaltered church interior in Scotland, refitted in 1792 and carefully repaired by Aberdeenshire Council in 1948 and 1964. The box pews are placed directly on to the earthen floor. The pulpit and precentor's desk, which preserves its holder for the psalm-tune cards, are placed in the middle of the long entrance wall, and the opposite long wall is lined with table pews with movable partitions. The laird's loft across one of the short walls was added in 1828.
4. Kildrummy (St Brigid) Church of Scotland: Type A. The church was built in 1805. It has a steeply pitched roof and an apsidal projection for the bell-cote and gallery staircase. The interior is largely complete with galleries around three sides of the interior and the pulpit on the long wall, opposite the entrance, with a modern communion table in front. Seating is provided by open benches, which are tiered in the galleries.

Angus

5. Murroes (Parish Church) Church of Scotland: Type B. A substantially unaltered church of 1848 with a spired bell-turret over the entrance. The canopied pulpit stands in an enclosure fitted with a late nineteenth-century communion table, minister's seat and elders' chairs. There are box pews in all three projections and excellent plaster-vaulted ceilings. The laird's loft, now occupied by a mid-nineteenth-century organ, is placed across the end of the transept opposite the pulpit. The rose window at each end of the cross aisle, and the four large windows in its long wall, are filled with rich stained glass of c.1900.

Argyll and Bute

6. Ardchattan (St Modan) Church of Scotland: Type C. The church was built in 1836 and has been slightly altered internally with a later set of benches against one of the long walls. The majority of the original furnishings have, however, been preserved with an, especially handsome canopied pulpit, complete with a bracket for the baptismal bowl, a precentor's desk in the form of a miniature pulpit, box pews for the elders on each side of the pulpit, and a long communion table, with benches on each side, running down the middle of the church from the precentor's desk to the entrance wall. There is a gallery around three sides of the interior with tiered seating.
7. Craignish (Parish Church) Church of Scotland: Type A. The church was built in 1826 and has been only slightly altered inside. The pulpit

and precentor's desk are placed in the middle of one of the long walls with benches on three sides of the central liturgical space and galleries around three sides of the interior with tiered seating.

8. Kilberry (St Berach) Church of Scotland: Type A. The church was built in 1821 and has an arrangement identical to that at Craignish, though some of the benches also have tables for use on communion Sundays.

9. Kilmodan (St Modan) Church of Scotland: Type B. The church was built in 1783 and was refurnished in the middle of the nineteenth century. The pulpit, with its pilastered backboard, is in the middle of the long wall with a long communion table in front. There are open benches in all three projections as well as laird's lofts for the principal heritors: the Campbells of Glendaruel, Ormidale and Southall.

10. Oban (Free High Church) Free Church of Scotland: Type B. The church was designed by David Cousin and built in 1846–1847. It is an early example of ecclesiological influence on Scottish Presbyterianism, having an aisled nave, with a tower at one end of the aisle and the vestry at the other, and steeply pitched roofs. Inside the arrangement is the traditional T-plan with the pulpit in the middle of the long wall, its canopy incorporating a clock on both faces. The area in front of the pulpit has been slightly altered to permit the installation of a modern communion table. In each projection, there are raked sets of open benches with Gothic ends, again emphasizing ecclesiological influences, focused on the pulpit. There are no galleries.

11. Poltalloch (St Columba) Scottish Episcopal Church: Type D. The church was designed by Thomas Cundy and built in 1852–1854 for the Malcolm family of the, now ruined, Poltalloch House. The church comprises nave, chancel, organ chamber north of the chancel and a small south chapel containing memorials to members of the Malcolm family. The complete contemporary furnishings comprise a marble font, simple benches and choir stalls, a wooden pulpit on a stone base and a brass eagle lectern. The altar is raised three steps above the level of the nave and both the chancel and the south chapel are elaborately tiled. The nave has a steeply pitched roof and the chancel a wagon one painted with stars. There is a complete scheme of contemporary stained glass by William Wailes.

12. Portnahaven (Parish Church) Church of Scotland: Type B. This is one of the two parliamentary churches built on Islay, the other, on the Oa, having been allowed to become a ruin. It was built in 1828, to a standard design by William Thomson, and is little altered internally. The pulpit, in the middle of the long entrance wall, has a pilastered backboard and a seat in front for the precentor, though the desk has been replaced with a modern communion table. There is a large table pew between the pulpit and both entrance doors. On the far side of the central passageway open benches face the pulpit. There are galleries in

all three projections, linked together across the internal angles of the cross aisle and transept, with tiered benches. All the woodwork is painted a pale grey.

13. Southend (St Blane) Church of Scotland: Type A. The church was built in 1773–1774 and, although some changes have been made, the reordering of the seating and the relocation of the pulpit alleged to have taken place in 1881 (BS *Argyll and Bute*, p. 462) does not seem to be borne out by the internal evidence and is much more likely to reflect the original internal arrangement. The pulpit is placed in the middle of one of the long walls with a U-shaped gallery around the other three sides of the interior and staircases against the two short walls. All the seating on the ground floor and in the gallery, where it follows the curve of the gallery front, focuses on the pulpit. Two pews with poppyheads were placed either side of the communion enclosure and a communion table in front of the pulpit, at the expense of the Duchess of Argyll, in 1911. There is a handsome mid-nineteenth-century collecting box in the porch, another addition of 1911.

Dumfries and Galloway

14. Crossmichael (St Michael) Church of Scotland: Type B. The church was built in 1749–1751 and partly refitted in 1822–1825. The slightly altered interior has canopied family pews at each end of the cross aisle. The pulpit faces the transept and its backboard incorporates the door to the belfry behind it. There are lofts in all three projections with tiered seating. Some of the box pews on the ground floor are fitted with tables.
15. Dalry (St John Evangelist) Church of Scotland: Type B. The church was designed by William McLandish and built in 1830–1832. The interior is a T-plan with the domed pulpit in the middle of the long wall backing on to the tower. Original seating, mostly with doors, in the three lofts, but the benches on the ground floor have been slightly altered. The organ and communion table date from the twentieth century, and the outer part of the transept opposite the pulpit was glazed to form a porch in 1976.
16. Durisdeer (St Cuthbert) Church of Scotland: Type B. The interior was refitted in 1825 and has been only marginally reordered. The pulpit is placed facing the entrance transept and has a bracket for the baptismal bowl and a sermon-glass attached to it. The seating is provided by a mix of box pews and benches, the former in the entrance transept comprising two rows of table pews. There are lofts in all three projections, the one for the Queensberry family of Drumlanrig leading into a two-storey retiring room and session house. The transept behind the pulpit, which

has a separate entrance, contains the splendid monument by John van Nost to the Second Duke of Queensberry who died in 1711.
17. Kirkcudbright (St Cuthbert) Church of Scotland: Type B. The church was built in 1835–1838 to a design by William Burn and was slightly altered in 1886 when an apsidal vestry and organ chamber was built behind the canopied pulpit and precentor's desk. Open benches face the pulpit in all three projections, which also contain lofts fitted with tiered box pews.
18. Tynron (Parish Church) Church of Scotland: Type B. An ambitious design by William Burn, built between 1835 and 1837, and with a distinctly ecclesiological exterior, its gabled ends supported by carved beasts. Traditional T-plan interior with the canopied pulpit in the middle of the long wall and open benches in all three projections. There are no lofts. The whole interior is covered by a contemporary plaster vault. A modern platform, in front of the pulpit, houses the communion table, font and a small organ.

East Dunbartonshire

19. Baldernock (Parish Church) Church of Scotland: Type A. The church of 1795 preserves complete mid-nineteenth-century furnishings, though the bow-fronted pulpit and the gallery fronts may be original. The galleries have external staircases and the plastered ceiling has an elaborate rose. The pulpit is approached by a curved wrought-iron staircase.

East Lothian

20. Spott (Parish Church) Church of Scotland: Type B. The church was built in 1809 but reused the eighteenth-century pulpit, complete with a bracket for the baptismal font, from its predecessor. There are box pews in all three projections, some with movable partitions to form communion tables, but no lofts or gallery.
21. Yester (St Cuthbert) Church of Scotland: Type B. The church was refitted in 1830, but retaining the seventeenth-century pulpit, its canopy surmounted by a golden dove, complete with a bracket for the baptismal bowl. The pulpit was further embellished in 1895 when it was given carved side panels and a communion enclosure of the type common in Dutch Reformed churches, complete with communion table. There are box pews and lofts in all three projections, one of the latter containing the Tweeddale pew, with a retiring room and a separate external entrance.

Edinburgh and Midlothian

22. Dalkeith (St Mary) Scottish Episcopal Church: Type D. The church was built in 1843–1846, to a design by William Burn and David Bryce, at the cost of the Duke of Buccleuch, and initially as the private chapel for Dalkeith Palace. Despite the addition of a north chapel in 1890 as a memorial to the fifth duke, the original church, comprising nave, chancel and north transept, retains virtually all its contemporary furnishings. The nave is fitted with open benches with poppyheads and an octagonal font in stone and marble. The stone pulpit, in the south-east angle of the nave, is entered by a vaulted staircase through the chancel wall. The choir stalls were designed by William Butterfield, there is a handsome brass eagle lectern and the altar retains its original cross and candlesticks. The floor of both the nave and chancel are laid with Minton tiles and there is contemporary stained glass by Ward and Nixon.

23. Dalmahoy (St Mary) Scottish Episcopal Church: Type D. The church was designed for Lord and Lady Aberdour by John Henderson and consecrated in 1850. The original furnishings are complete and comprise simple bench seating, a small stone pulpit and an octagonal stone font in the nave, and in the chancel an organ, choir stalls and a painted stone altar raised five steps above the level of the nave. There are also three contemporary corona chandeliers, stained glass and elaborate tiling covering the whole floor of both the nave and chancel. The roofs are steeply pitched and that over the chancel has been recently restored to its original colours.

Fife

24. Ceres (Parish Church) Church of Scotland: Type C. The church was built in 1805–1806 to a design by Alexander Leslie. The slightly altered interior has a canopied pulpit on the short wall opposite the entrance. Box pews are angled against the long wall to focus on the pulpit, and between the pulpit and the entrance are two rows of table pews on either side of a central passageway. The U-shaped gallery around three sides of the interior has tiered seating. A rare and valuable survival is the pewter baptismal bowl of 1752 on a later wooden stand.

25. Collessie (Parish Church) Church of Scotland: Type B. The church was built in 1838–1839 to a design by R and R Dickson. The magnificent canopied pulpit is approached by a double staircase and there are galleries in all three projections. In the body of the church, the seating is largely original though the rake against the outside wall was slightly altered in 1911.

EXAMPLES OF SUBSTANTIALLY UNALTERED INTERIORS

26. Cults (Parish Church) Church of Scotland: Type A. The church was refitted in 1835. The pulpit is placed in the middle of one of the long walls and several of the box pews on the ground floor are fitted with tables. The gallery around three sides of the interior has tiered seating and a family pew in the corner adjacent to the belfry. There is an iron stand for the former baptismal bowl.
27. Falkland (Parish Church) Church of Scotland: Type C. The church was built in 1848–1850 to an ambitious ecclesiological design by David Bryce at the expense of Mr and Mrs Onesiphorus Tyndall-Bruce, who are commemorated on wall tablets inside. Over the entrance is an impressive tower and spire, which acts as a local landmark. Inside the pulpit is approached by a double staircase under three tall lancet windows, filled with rich stained glass by Ballantine and Gardiner in 1897. The seating on the ground floor comprises a double set of box pews in the middle of the church with two side blocks of box pews, those at the pulpit end at right-angles to them facing the pulpit. Both pulpit and gallery fronts are decorated with carved and linenfold panels. The gallery, around three sides of the interior, and the elaborate roof are supported by stone pillars with gilded corbels. There are tiered box pews in the side galleries, but those in the gallery over the entrance were removed when an organ and seating for the choir were installed in 1930. More recently the space under this gallery has been partitioned off to form a meeting room.
28. Kilmany (Parish Church) Church of Scotland: Type A. The church was refitted in 1860 but retains its pulpit of 1768, the date of the building, complete with brackets for the baptismal bowl and sermon-glass. The seating is provided by a mix of long box pews, two of which convert into communion tables, and benches. The brass lamps attached to the walls, pulpit and seating also date from 1860. There are lofts across both short walls but one has been partitioned off.
29. Largoward (Parish Church) Church of Scotland: Type A. Built as a chapel-of-ease in 1835, the church is a simple rectangle with a birdcage bellcote. The substantially unaltered interior has the pulpit on one of the long walls and incorporating the minister's seat in the alcove behind it. There are four blocks of open benches facing the pulpit along the opposite long wall and one block each side of the pulpit placed sideways on to that long wall. The communion enclosure has been enlarged to include a modern font and communion table. The five-sided gallery around three sides of the interior has tiered benches and is supported on metal columns. The church has an attractive coved and plastered ceiling painted blue.
30. Monimail (Parish Church) Church of Scotland: Type B. The church was built in 1794–1797 to a design by Thomas Falconer with a tower added in 1811 by Robert Hutchinson. The furnishings are mid-nineteenth

century and comprise a pulpit with a plastered backboard, a five-sided gallery with a laird's loft opposite the pulpit and seating is provided by a mix of benches and box pews.

Highland

31. Altnaharra (Parish Church) Church of Scotland: Type C. The church was built in 1854–1855 as a Free Church. The complete contemporary fittings include a large platform pulpit, rather advanced for its date, with a backboard and double staircase. The seats in front of the pulpit incorporate tables for communion. The oil lamps are also original but have been converted to electricity.
32. Croick (Parish Church) Church of Scotland: Type B. Built in 1825–1827 by James Smith to a design by William Thomson, this is the most perfectly preserved of the surviving churches erected under the parliamentary legislation of 1823. The canopied pulpit, complete with a bracket supporting a ceramic baptismal bowl, and the precentor's desk are placed in the middle of the long entrance wall, with box pews on each side. The rest of the seating is provided by open benches and there is a long communion table across the middle of the cross aisle with benches on each side. There are no lofts or galleries.
33. Edderton (Old Parish Church) former Free Church of Scotland, now vested in a local trust: Type B. The former parish church was acquired by the Free Church and refitted in 1851, but retaining its canopied pulpit of 1794 within a bobbin-headed enclosure incorporating a simple desk for the precentor. There are benches throughout, some converting to form communion tables, and lofts in all three projections.
34. Eriboll (Chapel-of-Ease) former Church of Scotland, now owned by the Eriboll estate: Type C. An unaltered wood-lined church of 1804 carefully restored by the Eriboll estate after a period of disuse. The pulpit incorporates a door to the minister's vestry in its backboard. The seating is provided by straight-backed benches raked towards the entrance.
35. Eskadale (St Mary) Roman Catholic Church: Type C. The church was built in 1825–1826. Although the sanctuary was altered in 1881 the nave preserves its original open benches and tall pulpit. The church contains two brass memorials to the Frasers of Lovat who paid for the building.
36. Golspie (St Andrew) Church of Scotland: Type B. The church was built in 1736–1737 and extended by an additional transept to create a cruciform interior in 1750–1751. The church was carefully repaired in 1953–1954 under the direction of George Hay, when the original box pews were found to be rotten and were replaced with exact replicas, including table pews with movable partitions. In the transept opposite the ori-

ginal canopied pulpit is the Sutherland loft with its retiring room and separate external entrance. Lofts, with tiered seating, were placed across the short walls of the cross aisle in 1849. The arrangement of the transept behind the pulpit has been altered to incorporate a modern organ, seating for the choir and a communion table.

37. Halladale (Free Church) Free Church of Scotland: Type C. This simple building, partitioned off at one end to serve as a Sunday schoolroom, was built in 1852. Its unaltered wood-lined interior has a door to the minister's vestry in the short wall opposite the entrance and, to one side of this, a five-sided pulpit, complete with a bracket for the baptismal bowl and a seat for the minister. Two blocks of open benches are separated by a central passageway with a third block to the side of the vestry door facing the pulpit. The front seats of all three pew blocks convert to form communion tables.

38. Kinlochmoidart (St Finan) Scottish Episcopal Church: Type D. The church was built in 1857–1860 to a design by Alexander Ross. It comprises a simple nave and chancel with a western bell-cote. The substantially original furnishings include the simple benches and pulpit, the stencilled wooden altar and the elaborate encaustic tiles.

39. Laggan (Parish Church) Church of Scotland: Type C. The church was built in 1842–1844 to a design by James Ross. The slightly altered interior has a canopied pulpit in the middle of one short wall opposite the entrance, complete with a bracket for the baptismal bowl, and a semi-circular precentor's desk wrapped around the front of the pulpit. Seating is provided by open benches throughout, and there is a gallery around three sides of the interior, with tiered seating, supported on wooden columns, which also support the original plaster ceiling.

40. Lochbroom (Parish Church) Church of Scotland: Type C. The church was built in 1844–1845 to a design by A and W Reid, though the bell-cote dates from 1878. The furnishings are original and comprise box pews against the side walls, two long communion tables with flanking benches down the middle of the church, and a canopied pulpit with a precentor's desk against the short wall opposite the entrance. The gallery around three sides of the interior also retains its original seating but a false floor has been inserted at gallery level which cuts off the pulpit canopy which can now only be seen from the gallery.

41. Rogart (St Callan) Church of Scotland: Type C. The church was refitted in 1817 and its interior has been little altered. Although the entrance is in one of the long walls the canopied pulpit has been placed in the middle of one of the short walls, with box pews on each side and with, very unusually, the communion pew with its long table being placed towards the pulpit end of one of the long walls. Seating is provided by open benches, which are raked towards the short wall opposite the pulpit. There are no lofts or galleries.

42. Snizort (Paris Church) Church of Scotland: Type B. The cross-aisle was built in 1800–1801 to a design by James Gillespie Graham. The church was made a T-plan in 1839 when the transept opposite the pulpit was added. This has now been converted to meeting rooms leaving the interior of the church in its original shape. The furnishings probably date from 1839. They comprise a canopied pulpit in the middle of the long wall with table pews on either side. There are benches behind the table pews and in the body of the church. The five-sided gallery has the usual arrangement of tiered seating following the line of the gallery fronts.

43. Ullapool (Old Parish Church) former Church of Scotland, now vested in Ullapool Museum Trust: Type B. A small T-plan parliamentary church of 1829 to William Thomson's design. Disused since 1935 the church was acquired by Ullapool Museum Trust in 1988 and has since been very successfully converted into a community museum while preserving the core of its original furnishings. Blocks of seating have been retained in the middle of the ground floor and the part of the gallery facing the pulpit. This, complete with its original canopy and hangings, and a precentor's desk is placed in the middle of the long entrance wall.

Moray

44. Spynie (Holy Trinity) Church of Scotland: Type B. The church was rebuilt in 1735–1736 and retains its original canopied pulpit. The other furnishings, comprising lofts with painted fronts in all three projections, and seating provided by a mix of box pews, many incorporating tables, and open benches are early nineteenth century. Minor alterations took place in 1949, when most of the woodwork was stripped of its paint, and a platform installed in front of the pulpit for a communion table, font and lectern.

45. Tynet (St Ninian) Roman Catholic Church: Type B. The church was converted from a house and byre in 1787 and carefully repaired in 1951 under the direction of Ian Lindsay. The original canopied pulpit is entered from the sanctuary and an eighteenth-century golden dove is suspended over a modern free-standing altar. In addition to the pulpit, the original furnishings include the wooden chancel arch, the baptistery screen, confessional and benches, some of which are incorporated in box pews. The tabernacle from the original altar has been incorporated in the west wall of the baptistery.

Orkney

46. Sandwick (St Peter) Former Church of Scotland, now vested in Scottish Historic Churches Trust: Type A. The church was built in 1835–1836

EXAMPLES OF SUBSTANTIALLY UNALTERED INTERIORS

and reopened in 2003 after expensive repairs. The excellently preserved interior has a canopied pulpit, with the minister's vestry underneath, against one of the long walls, with a precentor's desk in front. The seating is provided by open benches on the ground floor, and is tiered in the five-sided gallery around three sides of the interior, all focused on the pulpit.

47. South Ronaldsay (St Peter) Church of Scotland: Type A. The church was noted as being in ruins in the First Statistical Account of Scotland. It was repaired in 1801 and is little altered. The canopied pulpit, on one of the long walls, retains the bracket for the baptismal bowl. In front of the pulpit is a large square pew, originally fitted with a communion table, and there are narrow communion tables, with benches on each side, between this central pew and the short end walls, both of which have lofts. The seating is provided by a mix of box pews and benches.

Perth and Kinross

48. Clunie (Parish Church) Church of Scotland: Type C. The church was built in 1840 and largely preserves its contemporary furnishings. The pulpit, with its handsome staircase, and communion enclosure with seats for the elders are on the short wall opposite the entrance. There is raked seating facing the pulpit in the body of the church and tiered seating in the U-shaped gallery. The gabled entrance wall incorporates a pinnacled tower.

49. Glenalmond (Holy Trinity) Scottish Episcopal Church: Type D. The chapel was designed to reflect the desire of the school's founders to have a Tractarian form of worship. The design is by William Butterfield, one of the leading Tractarian architects, and the chapel was built between 1846 and 1851. Although some alterations have been made at the east end, with the marble altar and rather pedestrian war memorial reredos by Sir Ninian Comper, the stained glass and other furnishings are largely original. The staff and pupils sat in stalls facing inwards on either side of a central passageway. However, the conservatism of some local Episcopalians was catered for in the ante-chapel, where visitors sat, as this was provided with low box pews facing east, and is separated from the main chapel by a screen.

50. Portmoak (Parish Church) Church of Scotland: Type A. The church was built in 1832. The pulpit, with its domed tester and railed enclosure in front, incorporating a modern communion table, font and lectern, is placed on one of the long walls. The seating is provided by box pews, which are tiered in the five-sided gallery around three sides of the interior.

51. St Martins (Parish Church) Church of Scotland: Type B. The church was built in 1843. The canopied pulpit and precentor's desk are placed in the middle of one of the long walls. The former table pews have, however, been replaced with a modern platform for the communion table. The remaining box pews, tiered in the lofts in all three projections, remain intact.

Scottish Borders

52. Channelkirk (St Cuthbert) Church of Scotland: Type A. The church was built in 1817. The interior has been little altered apart from the placing of a modern communion table, font and lectern in front of the canopied pulpit with its handsome staircase and velvet-lined seat for the minister. There are three blocks of box pews on the ground floor of the church and tiered box pews in the gallery around three sides of the interior. The church has several contemporary collecting shoes on long poles.
53. Ettrick and Buccleuch (Parish Church) Church of Scotland: Type B. The church was built in 1824. Pulpit and precentor's desk are placed in the middle of the long wall and a modern communion table has been inserted in front of these. The seating is provided by open benches and there are lofts in all three projections, one containing the laird's seat and reached by a separate external staircase.
54. Fogo (Parish Church) Church of Scotland: Type B. The church was refitted in 1817. The pulpit, with its domed canopy, is placed in the middle of the long wall. There are box pews in all three projections, those in the transept opposite the pulpit being arranged in tiers, and there are lofts, containing family pews, and reached by external staircases, at each end of the cross aisle. A small organ, communion table and large collecting boxes date from the minimal alterations made in 1905.
55. Jedburgh (St John Evangelist) Scottish Episcopal Church: Type D. The church was built in 1841–1844 and is the earliest example of an Anglican church in Scotland reflecting the ideas of both the Oxford Movement and the Cambridge ecclesiologists. It was financed by the Marchioness of Lothian and designed by John Hayward, an Exeter-based architect who also designed the unaltered early Tractarian church at Sowton in Devon. Although there have been some alterations, notably the rood figures on the top of the screen, the extension of the altar and the modern Stations of the Cross, the core of the church remains that designed by Hayward. The nave is furnished with open benches and has a stone font near the south door and a stone pulpit, entered through the wall from the vestry, in the north-east corner. The chancel is separated from the nave by a wooden screen and has a stone altar, originally

comprising three carved compartments but later extended to five. The stained glass and tiling are contemporary, with each step between the nave and the altar being inscribed with biblical texts. There is elaborate stencilling on the wall behind the altar and also at the back of the piscina and sedilia on the south side of the chancel.

56. Lauder (St Mary) Church of Scotland: Type B. The church was refitted in 1820–1821. Built in 1673, it is a rare example of the cruciform variant of the T-plan arrangement (cf. Golspie earlier), with box pews and lofts, with tiered seating, in all four projections. The canopied pulpit, as at Golspie, is placed against one pier of the crossing but is visible from all parts of the church. The central space in front of the pulpit now houses a modern communion table, font and lectern. The walls of the church are lined with hat pegs.

57. Newlands (Parish Church) Church of Scotland: Type B. The church was built in 1838. The canopied pulpit, approached by a double staircase, and precentor's desk are placed in the middle of the long wall with a modern platform in front for the communion table, font and lectern. The original seating has been retained on the ground floor of all three projections but has been removed from two out of the three lofts.

58. Traquair (House Chapel) Roman Catholic Church: Type C. The original chapel was in the upper part of the house, but it was moved to the service block in c.1820. At the back of the chapel is the family pew with benches for servants in front. The eighteenth-century Italian altarpiece was installed in 1870. Along the walls are two sets (six in each) of sixteenth-century Flemish panels showing scenes from the nativity and passion of Christ; these were formerly in the earlier chapel at Traquair.

Shetland

59. Dunrossness (Parish Church) Church of Scotland: Type A. The church was built in 1787–1790 but the furnishings appear to date from the mid-nineteenth century. The pulpit has a backboard, incorporating a clock, but, unusually for Shetland, no canopy. The enclosure includes a modern communion table, font and lectern. The bench seating incorporates against one of the short walls a canopied family pew. There is a gallery around three sides of the interior with steeply tiered benches. An unusual feature is the two contemporary collecting boxes.

60. Lunna (St Margaret) Church of Scotland: Type A. Built as a chapel-of-ease in Nesting parish in 1753, the church was refurnished in c.1840. There is a canopied pulpit and precentor's desk with a communion enclosure on one side. The bench seating on the ground floor is arranged in five blocks to focus on the pulpit. The gallery around three sides of the interior is approached by an external staircase and is fitted with tiered

benches in the same formation as those on the ground floor. The side galleries have panelled fronts but the front of the gallery across the long wall is balustraded. There are two eighteenth-century memorial tablets to Robert and Thomas Hunter of Lunna House.

61. Mid Yell (St John Evangelist) Church of Scotland: Type B. Built in 1832 and retaining its original furnishings, the tall canopied pulpit has a large balustraded enclosure in front with a modern communion table. There are lofts at each end of the cross aisle, but not in the transept opposite the pulpit, each with tiered seating. There are open benches on the ground floor in all three projections with two square pews in the cross aisle at the corners with the transept.

62. Nesting (Parish Church) Church of Scotland: Type A. The church was built in 1792–1794 but the furnishings appear to date from the mid-nineteenth century. The canopied pulpit has a large enclosure, with a modern communion table, in front of it. The bench seating on the ground floor is in three blocks, facing across the church against the long wall opposite the pulpit. The gallery around three sides of the interior has the same tiered seating arrangement as on the ground floor. The original long communion table is now kept in the vestry and in the gallery are displayed two large pewter patens of 1820.

63. Quarff (Parish Church) Former Church of Scotland, now vested in a local trust: Type B. A parliamentary church built in 1828–1829 by John Davidson and Thomas Macfarlane to William Thomson's design. The ends of the cross aisle have been partitioned off by simple wooden screens but otherwise the original furnishings survive. These comprise a tall canopied pulpit against the long wall, two blocks of benches facing the pulpit and two long communion tables. There are no galleries. The building is in a poor state of repair.

64. Scalloway (Chapel-of-Ease) Church of Scotland: Type C. The chapel, which is in the parish of Tingwall, was built in 1840–1841 and slightly altered in 1871–1872, when a porch was added and the two blocks of original benches placed against the long walls to create a wide central passageway. The canopied pulpit stands in a large communion enclosure which now contains a modern communion table and, to one side, the organ, lowered into the floor beneath the U-shaped gallery which has steeply-tiered box pews, some of which have had their doors removed, following the curve of the gallery. At the back of the gallery is a cupboard, with a seat for the bell-ringer. All the woodwork is attractively painted a pale green and the boarded ceiling is painted blue.

65. Tingwall (St Magnus) Church of Scotland: Type A. The church was built in 1788–1790 but the furnishings appear to date from the mid-nineteenth century. The canopied pulpit is placed in a large enclosure incorporating a modern communion table. One block of bench seating

EXAMPLES OF SUBSTANTIALLY UNALTERED INTERIORS

immediately opposite the pulpit has been replaced with chairs. The gallery around three sides of the interior has tiered box pews, some of which have had their doors removed.

66. Whalsay (Parish Church) Church of Scotland: Type A. The church, built in 1767 and refurnished in c. 1860, is delightfully situated on an islet connected to Whalsay by a short causeway. The jamb, with its separate roof, attached to the long wall opposite the pulpit, and with a separate external staircase, contains the burial vault and retiring room of the Bruce family, the latter now used as a vestry. The canopied pulpit has a modern communion table in front of it and the bench seating on the ground floor, some of which converts to form communion tables, is in the same arrangement as at Nesting. The gallery, around three sides of the interior, is divided in the section along the long wall, half of it forming the family pew of the Bruce family, the other half being fitted with tiered open benches as in the sections across the short walls.

South Ayrshire

67. Auchincruive (St Quivox) Church of Scotland: Type B. The church was much enlarged in 1767 when a transept was added to the late sixteenth-century church. The pulpit, with its handsome canopy, dates from this enlargement but the remainder of the furnishings are early nineteenth century. They include box pews on each side of the pulpit, lofts with family pews in all three projections, all with separate external entrances, and an unusual semi-circular arrangement of benches in the main body of the church. A modern communion table has been placed in front of the pulpit.

West Lothian

68. Torphichen (Parish Church) Church of Scotland: Type B. The church was refitted in 1803, the canopied pulpit being placed in the middle of the long wall. The seating on the ground floor is in the form of low benches with doors, those in the transept opposite the pulpit converting for use as communion tables. There are lofts in all three projections with tiered benches and a family pew in the loft opposite the pulpit. This loft has a small retiring room behind reached by an external staircase. A modern communion table has been placed in front of the pulpit. The church was carefully repaired in 1972 when all the woodwork was painted a pale grey and the loft fronts decorated with armorials.

Western Isles

69. Manish (Parish Church) Church of Scotland: Type A. Built as a Free Church in 1853, this is a simple double-pile building, the two roofs being supported internally by a row of iron columns. The largely original interior has the majority of its simple benches raked against the long entrance wall, with a lavish pulpit and precentor's desk, complete with their fringed velvet hangings, placed in the middle of the opposite long wall, with blocks of seating facing them on each side. There are no galleries. The communion enclosure has been altered to accommodate a modern communion table, font and lectern.
70. Stornoway (Free Church) Free Church of Scotland: Type C. A progressive building for its date, designed by Alexander Mackenzie in 1851, with a narrow tower in the centre of the short entrance wall. The opposite short wall is dominated by a large pulpit, with a canopied seat for the minister, and an enclosure incorporating a precentor's desk and elders' pew. There are three blocks of raked seating facing the pulpit on the ground floor. The elaborate roof and the galleries around three sides of the interior, with their tiered seating, are supported by iron columns.

Appendix D

SELECTED LIST OF SCOTTISH CHURCHES WITH TRADITIONAL PRESBYTERIAN INTERIORS OF A DATE LATER THAN 1860

Aberdeenshire

1. Kinneff (St Anthony), Church of Scotland
   Type B. The church was refitted in 1876 and retains its contemporary furnishings including the pulpit in the middle of the long wall and a contemporary communion table in front, box pews for the manse and the Sunday school and open benches in the three projections and lofts. The pulpit, communion table and the gallery front in the transept opposite the pulpit retain their original velvet coverings.

Argyll and Bute

2. Luss (St Kessog), Church of Scotland
   Type B. Despite its moderately ecclesiological exterior, this church, built at the expense of Sir James Colquhoun in 1875, has a traditional T-plan interior with the pulpit approached by a double staircase in the middle of the long wall with a vestry behind it. The seating is arranged to focus on the pulpit and there is a laird's loft in the transept opposite the pulpit. The area in front of the pulpit has been modernized with a communion table of 1956 and a re-used medieval font from the late fifteenth-century chapel of St Mary at Rossdhu.
3. Torosay (Parish Church), Church of Scotland
   Type A. A small rectangular church of 1783 conservatively refurnished in 1887 with the pulpit in the middle of one of the long walls. The lofts across both short walls, approached by external staircases, are probably original.

Dumfries and Galloway

4. Hutton and Corrie (Parish Church), Church of Scotland
   Type B. The church was built in 1710 and extended in 1764. The interior was refurnished in 1871 in the traditional manner with open benches facing the pulpit, in the middle of the long wall, in the three projections. There are no lofts.
5. Kirkmaiden (St Medan), Church of Scotland
   Type B. The very early T-plan church of 1638 was repaired and conservatively refurnished in 1885. The transept opposite the pulpit, complete with its original brass oil lamps, is raised over a burial vault and approached by an external staircase. The seating at both ends of the cross aisle comprise a mixture of open benches and box pews, two of which have tables. There is a modern communion table in front of the pulpit.

Edinburgh and Midlothian

6. Cranstoun (Parish Church), Church of Scotland
   Type B. The church was built in 1824, but the interior dates from 1861, when it was rebuilt after a fire. There are lofts across each of the cross aisles with the pulpit in the middle of the long wall. Opposite the pulpit is the Dalrymple aisle. The only concession to modernity is the very early, non-representational, stained glass in the windows on each side of the pulpit, which is contemporary with the furnishings.

Highland

7. Canisbay (St Drostan), Church of Scotland
   Type B. The cruciform church incorporates parts of a fifteenth-century building much repaired, in stages, between 1704 (the date of the tower) and 1736, and again in 1831–1832 (the date of the lofts across each end of the cross aisle). The present internal arrangement dates from 1891 when the south transept was turned into a porch and a T-plan interior created by the placing of the pulpit and precentor's desk against the long wall with seating facing them in all three projections.
8. Lochalsh (Parish Church), Church of Scotland
   Type A. The church was built in 1804–1807 and refurnished in 1910 in a wholly traditional manner with a five-sided gallery around three sides of the interior and a pulpit and precentor's desk placed in the middle of one of the long walls. Most of the gallery seating has, unfortunately, been removed.

SELECTED LIST OF SCOTTISH CHURCHES

9. Sleat (St Mary), Church of Scotland
   Type C. The church was built in 1876–1877 and retains a completely unaltered interior with the pulpit and precentor's desk on the short wall opposite the entrance and in front of them a square pew within the central block of seating containing a square communion table. Pulpit and communion table preserve their original brass lamps. Across the entrance wall is a gallery containing the family pew of the MacDonalds of Sleat.
10. Tongue (St Andrew), Church of Scotland
    Type B. The church was built in 1728–1729 and conservatively refurnished in 1861–1862, apart from the Reay loft opposite the pulpit, the canopy of which is now in the Royal Museum of Scotland. This is raised above the level of the transept and has a separate entrance. The pulpit is placed in the middle of the long wall and there are four table pews, one each side of the pulpit and two backing on to the Reay loft.
11. Uig (Chapel-of-Ease), Church of Scotland
    Type C. A delightful building of 1860–1861 with a pulpit and precentor's desk in the middle of the short wall opposite the entrance and three blocks of raked seating facing them. There is a gallery over the entrance wall. All the furniture is attractively painted dove grey.
12. Urquhart (Ferintosh Church), Free Church of Scotland
    Type C. The church was built in 1843 and largely refurnished in 1907 when a small tower was added. The gallery across the entrance wall dates from 1843 and retains its original seating. The furnishings in the body of the church, remarkably conservative for their date, include three blocks of seating facing the canopied pulpit and precentor's desk on the short wall opposite the entrance and additional seats to the side of the pulpit and precentor's desk. The three front pews facing the pulpit convert to form communion tables. The splendid three-stall wrought-iron urinal in the churchyard may be contemporary with the refurnishing.

Scottish Borders

13. Maxton (St Cuthbert), Church of Scotland
    Type B. The medieval church was substantially remodelled in 1812 and then made a T-plan by the addition of a transept in 1866. There are lofts across the two ends of the cross aisle and the pulpit is placed in the middle of the long entrance wall. The seating in the transept opposite the pulpit seems to match that in the other two projections. Some 1812 woodwork may have been reused but it is likely that it all dates from 1866. All the woodwork has been attractively painted dove grey.

Shetland

14. Northmavine (Parish Church), Church of Scotland
    Type C. A very traditional church designed by Roderick Coyne in 1869. The exterior has two rows of windows along the side walls and three over the entrance. Against the short wall opposite the entrance is a magnificent canopied pulpit and precentor's desk in a large communion enclosure. The seating comprises three blocks of open benches on the ground floor facing the enclosure and tiered benches in the gallery, with an upper set of tiered benches under the belfry, where part of the gallery has been converted into a meeting room. The galleries themselves are interestingly formed, tapering towards the outside wall at the pulpit end of the interior.
15. Weisdale (Parish Church), Church of Scotland
    Type C. The church was built as a Free Church in 1863. It has a low balustraded pulpit against the short wall opposite the entrance, as at Altnaharra (see Appendix C/31). The original benches, possibly slightly altered, are placed against the side walls facing the pulpit in a steeply raked interior. There is a balustraded communion enclosure in front of the pulpit containing a modern communion table. There is no gallery.

Appendix E

SELECTED LIST OF SCOTO-CATHOLIC PROTESTANT CHURCH INTERIORS IN SCOTLAND

Aberdeenshire

1. Crathie (Parish Church), Church of Scotland
   Type D. A cruciform church with a central tower and spire and long west porch built in 1893–1895. The apsidal chancel has a marble communion table, seats for the elders against the walls, and a pulpit and font placed on opposite sides of the chancel arch. The royal pew, occupied when the monarch is at Balmoral castle, is placed in the south transept with the organ in the west gallery.

Argyll and Bute

2. Connel (St Oran), Church of Scotland
   Type D. The church was built in 1887–1888 to a design by David Mackintosh of Oban inspired by the buildings on Iona. The nave is separated from the chancel by a squat central tower. The communion table is placed at the east end of the chancel and the pulpit to one side of the chancel arch.
3. Loch Awe (St Conan), Church of Scotland
   Type D. The church was built in 1881–1886 to the designs, and at the expense, of Walter Douglas Campbell. Between 1907 and 1930, the original church was much enlarged to its present shape. It now comprises a nave, with a south aisle leading into the south-west chapels of St Brigid and St Conval, and an apsidal chancel with an ambulatory, on the south side of which is the Bruce chapel. The chancel is lined with canopied stalls, with the communion table placed at the east end, and a font in the form of an angel bearing a Breton fishing boat on a pedestal in the middle of the chancel. A modest pulpit is placed in the north-east

angle of the nave and there is a screen, supporting the organ, across the west end. The three chapels are separated from the main body of the church by elaborate inscribed screens and the Bruce chapel contains a commemorative effigy of Robert the Bruce in alabaster and stained timber. The windows are filled with contemporary stained glass.

Dumfries and Galloway

4. Ardwell (Parish Church), Church of Scotland
   Type D. The church was designed by P. M. Chalmers for Lady McTaggart Stewart and built in 1900–1902. It comprises a broad nave, with shallow transepts and a short raised chancel, together with a handsome tower and spire. Complete contemporary furnishings comprise a communion table carved with figures of St Peter, St Paul, St Andrew and St John in the chancel, a pulpit to one side of the chancel arch, a stone font, an organ in the north transept and a family pew in the south one.
5. Colvend (St Brigid), Church of Scotland
   Type D. The church was designed by P.M. Chalmers and built in 1910–1911. It comprises a short chancel, nave, four-bay north aisle, two-bay south transept and a west tower with a pyramid roof. The contemporary furnishings comprise low benches for the congregation, a communion table with seats for elders on the north and south sides of the chancel, a pulpit on the south side of the chancel arch and a font on the north side. The chancel is raised three steps above the level of the nave. The stained glass in the windows dates from between 1918 and 1930.
6. Dumfries (Crichton Memorial Church), Undenominational
   Type D. This magnificent cathedralesque church of 1890–1897 was designed by Sidney Mitchell as the chapel of the Crichton Royal Hospital. It comprises an aisled nave with tall clerestory, central tower, transepts and a long chancel. The largely contemporary furnishings include the pulpit, communion table, canopied stalls in the chancel and the large organ. The brass angel lectern is slightly later. There are chapels in each transept and the floor throughout is laid with marble.

Edinburgh and Midlothian

7. Edinburgh (Canongate Church), Church of Scotland
   Type D. The church was opened in 1691 and was designed in the shape of a cross (cf. Lauder). Its present arrangement, which is more neo-Laudian than Scoto-Catholic, dates from an extensive restoration of the interior between 1940 and 1954 by Ian Lindsay, in which two of the

three galleries were removed, a canopied pulpit (from the Territorial Free Church of 1847) placed on the ritual south side of the chancel, canopied clergy stalls placed in the chancel with the communion table covered with a Laudian drape in the apse and an organ placed in the gallery over the entrance. The aim was, as far as possible, to recreate an Anglican interior of the early seventeenth century.

8. Edinburgh (St Cuthbert)
Type D. The church was rebuilt in 1892–1895, apart from the former spire of 1789–1790, to a very ambitious neoclassical design by Hippolyte Blanc. The size of the interior has been reduced recently by partitioning off a large section at the west end, but the eastern part of the building remains intact. The floor of the chancel is laid with mosaic and lined with choir stalls, the marble communion table being raised on several steps in an eastern apse. The pulpit, to one side of the entrance to the chancel, is also marble, as is the font. The bronze angel lectern was designed by D.W. Stevenson. In 1906–1908, Blanc added the elaborate frieze, a modified version of Leonardo's *Last Supper*, to the upper walls of the apse. The murals in the apse vault (Christ in Glory) and the chancel vault (four evangelists), together with the angels painted in the spandrels of the chancel arch, were completed in 1931. The stained glass by Ballantyne and Gardner dates from between 1893 and 1904.

Fife

9. St Andrews (St Nicholas), Church of Scotland
Type D. The fifteenth-century town church had been dramatically remodelled in 1798–1800. Under the direction of P.M. Chalmers it was, between 1907 and 1909, remodelled again, this time with the aim of recapturing something of its medieval atmosphere. Both nave and chancel are aisled. Chalmers renewed the arcades to their fifteenth-century appearance and provided benches in the nave, choir stalls in the chancel, wagon roofs to both nave and chancel, a pulpit of alabaster and onyx on the north side of the entrance to the chancel, and a screen behind the communion table across the easternmost bay of the chancel.

Glasgow and Renfrewshire

10. Glasgow (St Constantine, Govan), Church of Scotland
Type D. Designed by R.R. Anderson for the Scoto-Catholic minister, John Macleod, and built in 1883–1888, this is one of the earliest and finest fully ecclesiological churches built for the Church of Scotland. The church comprises an aisled nave, chancel with raised sanctuary, chapels

on either side of the chancel and a galleried west (ritual north) transept. The furnishings, which are contemporary or installed over the next fifteen years, are complete and comprise simple bench seating in the nave with the pulpit on one side of the chancel arch, a stone font, choir and clergy stalls, eagle lectern and free-standing communion table. The church has a particularly splendid series of stained-glass windows, mostly by C.E. Kempe, but also including work by four other leading firms of stained-glass manufacturers: Heaton, Butler and Bayne; Burlison and Grylls; Clayton and Bell; and Shrigley and Hunt. With the merger of this congregation with that of St Mary's, Govan Cross, and the proposal that this rather than St Constantine's should be the parish church, the future of this magnificent building is very much in doubt. With careful design, it could be converted satisfactorily for museum purposes, providing all the major furnishings and some of the seating is retained, especially as the church also contains one of the finest collections of early Christian monuments (the Govan sarcophagus, two cross shafts and five hogback tombstones) in Scotland.

11. Glasgow (Queen's Cross Church), Formerly Free Church of Scotland, now the headquarters of the Charles Rennie Mackintosh Society
    Type D. The church was designed by C.R. Mackintosh in 1896–1899 with a separate shallow chancel raised above the level of the nave containing the communion table and, on one side of the chancel arch, a canopied pulpit and, on the other, a piscina-type niche for the baptismal bowl. Within the chancel arch itself is a non-representational rood beam. The body of the church retains its original pews and there is a cantilevered gallery across part of the nave aisle, and another gallery across the entrance wall, both with tiered seating. This was a particularly advanced quasi-ecclesiological design for a Free Church congregation.

12. Paisley (Abbey Church of St Mary, St James, St Mirin and St Milburga), Church of Scotland
    Type D. The medieval nave was retained after the Reformation to serve as the parish church and the remainder of the former abbey church was unroofed. Between 1890 and 1928, the chancel, central tower and transepts were restored and the whole building completely refurnished. The chancel was lined with canopied stalls and a stone communion table placed at the east end. Pulpit and font are placed on opposite sides of the entrance to the chancel. In the north transept, there are substantial remains of a medieval frieze.

13. Paisley (Thomas Coats Memorial Church), Baptist Church
    Type D. The church was opened in 1894 at the expense of the Coats family and designed by Hippolyte Blanc. The remarkable interior, for a church in this normally deeply Protestant tradition, includes exceptionally elaborate woodwork, ironwork and stained glass. There is a marble

pulpit on one side of the entrance to the chancel in front of which is a marble baptistery. The chancel is stalled, originally for a surpliced choir, and there is an elaborately carved communion table at the ritual east end. Among the contemporary works of art are elaborate panels of the adoration of the Magi, the baptism of Christ and the Last Supper.

Moray

14. Forres (St Lawrence), Church of Scotland
    Type D. The church was designed by John Robertson in 1904–1906. It has a raised chancel with choir stalls and a marble communion table. A stone and marble pulpit, to one side of the chancel arch, a marble font and brass eagle lectern complete the Scoto-Catholic ensemble. The only concession to Presbyterianism is the bulging galleries, resembling those in a theatre, across the nave aisle. There is a fine series of stained glass windows by Douglas Strachan.

Stirling

15. Dunblane (Cathedral of St Laurence and St Blane), Church of Scotland
    Type D. The cathedral nave was abandoned after the Reformation and worship confined to the chancel. The restoration of the cathedral, and the rebuilding of the aisled nave, is one of the most successful cathedral restorations in Scotland, begun in 1889–1893 under the direction of R.R. Anderson and completed in 1912–1914 by Sir Robert Lorimer. The cathedral is now arranged as a quasi-Anglican building. The communion table, at the east end of the chancel, with standing candelabra each side, the choir screen, the canopied pulpit in the north-east angle of the nave, the stone font and the brass lectern are by Anderson. The canopied choir stalls, reredos behind the communion table, elaborate organ case on the north side of the chancel and the nave seating are by Lorimer. The cathedral is fortunate in preserving some of the most important surviving examples of medieval woodwork in Scotland, six canopied and seven uncanopied choir stalls, now placed respectively at the west end of the nave and the east end of the chancel.

BIBLIOGRAPHY

1. *Archives and Manuscripts*
(a) Dumfries and Galloway Archives, Dumfries
   GGd 313/N7/27   Seating plan of the Roman Catholic church at New Abbey and elevation of the church and priest's house, 1824
(b) National Archives of Scotland, General Register House, Edinburgh
   GD 248/85/1   Seating plan of church at Inverallan, c.1700
   GD 259/4/7   Seating plan of church at Kippen, 1779
   GD 172/628   Seating plan of church at Dalgetty, 1830
(c) National Archives of Scotland, West Register House, Edinburgh
   RHP 20589   Seating plan of St Cuthbert's, Edinburgh, 1779
   RHP 45480   Seating plan of church at Ellon, 1828
(d) Glasgow Archives, Mitchell Library, Glasgow
   CH2/216/6   Kirk session minute book for Kilsyth, 1793–1820
   CH2/863/3   Kirk session minute book for Cadder, 1798–1882
   CH2/51/3–4   Kirk session minute books for Campsie, 1811–1870
   CH2/119/3   Kirk session minute book for Eastwood, 1817–1861
   D/TC/13/602   Drawing of proposed pulpit at St David's Ramshorn Church, Glasgow, 1824
   D/TC/13/603   Seating plans of St David's Ramshorn Church, Glasgow, 1824–1826

BIBLIOGRAPHY

    D/TC/13/604   Seating plan of church at Govan, 1830

    CH2/315/7   Kirk session minute book for Rutherglen, 1839–1863

    CH2/1277/104   Seating plans of old and new churches at Govan, 1884–1888

(e) Orkney Archives, Kirkwall

    OCR/14/95   Plan of burials in the nave, aisles and transepts of St Magnus's Cathedral, Kirkwall, 1769

(f) Stirling Archives, Stirling

    MP/5B/257   Seating plan of Barony Church, Paisley, 1789

    MP/5B/262   Proposed plans of pulpit and seating in East Church, Stirling, 1789–1799

    MP/5B/258   Plans of existing and new seating in East Church, Stirling, 1802

    CH2/942/45   Allocation of seats in church at Alloa, 1819

    CH2/1455/20   Seating plan of church at Blair Drummond, 1906–1907

    CH2/469/20   Seating plan of church at Balquhidder, 1930

2. *Primary Printed Sources*

Begg, J. (1876), *Purity of Worship in the Presbyterian Church*. Edinburgh.

Collie, J. (1835), *Plans, Elevations, Sections, Details and Views of the Cathedral at Glasgow*. London.

Hunter, W.G. (1858), *History of the Priory of Coldingham from the Earliest Date to the Present Time*. Edinburgh.

Kerr, J. (1909), *The Renascence of Worship: The Origin, Aims and Achievements of the Church Service Society*. Edinburgh.

Lee, R. (1864), *The Reform of the Church of Scotland: Part I Worship*. Edinburgh.

The Ministers of Respective Parishes (1845), *New Statistical Account of Scotland*. Edinburgh.

Sinclair, J. (ed) (1973–1983), *Statistical Account of Scotland 1791–1799* (reprint edn). East Ardsley.

Sprott, G.W. (1882), *The Worship and Offices of the Church of Scotland*. Edinburgh.

3. *Secondary Sources*

Ansdell, D. (1998), *The People of the Great Faith: The Highland Church 1690–1900*. Stornoway.

Anson, P. (1954), 'Catholic Church Building in Scotland from the Reformation to the Outbreak of the First World War, 1560–1914', *Innes Review*, 5, 125–40.

BIBLIOGRAPHY

Anson, P. (1965), *Fashions in Church Furnishings 1840–1940* (2nd edn). London.
Archibald, J. (1890), *History of the Episcopal Church at Keith in the Diocese of Moray*. Edinburgh.
Bebbington, D. (1989), *Evangelicalism in Modern Britain: A History from the 1730s to the 1980s*. London.
Bradley, I. (1976), *The Call to Seriousness: The Evangelical Impact on the Victorians*. London.
Brown, C.G. (1997), *Religion and Society in Scotland since 1707*. Edinburgh.
Brown, S.J. (1984), *Thomas Chalmers and the Godly Commonwealth in Scotland*, Oxford.
Brown, S.J. (2001), *The National Churches of England, Ireland and Scotland, 1801–1846*. Oxford.
Brown, S.J. and Fry, M. (eds) (1993), *Scotland in the Age of the Disruption*. Edinburgh.
Bruce, S. (1985), *No Pope of Rome: Anti-Catholicism in Modern Scotland*. Edinburgh.
Bryce, W.M. (1912), *History of the Old Greyfriars Church*. Edinburgh.
Burleigh, J.H.S. (1960), *A Church History of Scotland*. London.
Burnet, G.B. (1960), *The Holy Communion in the Reformed Church of Scotland*. Edinburgh and London.
Cant, H.W.M. and Firth, H.N. (eds) (1989), *Light in the North*. Kirkwall.
Caspers, C., Lukken, G. and Rouwhorst, G. (eds) (1995), *Bread of Heaven: Customs and Practices Surrounding Holy Communion*. Kampen.
Chalmers, P.M. (1914), *The Cathedral Church of Glasgow*. London.
Cheyne, A.C. (1983), *The Transforming of the Kirk: Victorian Scotland's Religious Revolution*. Edinburgh.
Cowan, I.B. (1982), *The Scottish Reformation: Church and Society in Sixteenth-Century Scotland*. London.
Cragg, G.R. (1966), *The Church and the Age of Reason 1648–1789* (2nd edn). Harmondsworth.
Craven, J.B. (1907), *Records of the Dioceses of Argyll and the Isles 1560–1860*. Kirkwall.
Cruft, K., Dunbar, J. and Fawcett, R. (2006), *Buildings of Scotland: Borders*. New Haven and London.
Dercsényi, B., Hegyi, G., Marosi, E. and Takács, B. (1992), *Calvinist Churches in Hungary*. Budapest.
Devine, T.M. and Young, J.R. (eds) (1999), *Eighteenth-Century Scotland: New Perspectives*. East Linton.
Donaldson, G. (1960), *The Scottish Reformation*. Cambridge.
—— (1990), *The Faith of the Scots*. London.
Drummond, A.L. (1934), *The Church Architecture of Protestantism*. Edinburgh.
Drummond, A.L. and Bulloch, J. (1973), *The Scottish Church 1688–1843*. Edinburgh.
—— (1975), *The Church in Victorian Scotland 1843–1874*. Edinburgh.
—— (1978), *The Church in Late Victorian Scotland 1874–1900*. Edinburgh.
Ferguson, J. (1905), *Ecclesia Antiqua*. Edinburgh.
Forrester, D. and Murray, D. (eds) (1996), *Studies in the History of Worship in Scotland* (2nd edn). Edinburgh.
Foskett, R. (1965), 'The Episcopate of Daniel Sandford, 1806–30', *RSCHS*, xv, 141–52.

BIBLIOGRAPHY

Foster, W.R. (1975), *The Church Before the Covenants: The Church of Scotland 1596–1638*. Edinburgh.

Foster, W.R. (1958), *Bishops and Presbytery: The Church of Scotland 1661–1688*. London.

Galloway, P. (2000), *The Cathedrals of Scotland*. Edinburgh.

Gifford, J. (1988), *Buildings of Scotland: Fife*. London.

—— (1992), *Buildings of Scotland: Highland and Islands*. London.

—— (1996), *Buildings of Scotland: Dumfries and Galloway*. London.

—— (2007), *Buildings of Scotland: Perth and Kinross*. New Haven and London.

Gifford, J., McWilliam, C. and Walker, D. (1984), *Buildings of Scotland: Edinburgh*. Harmondsworth.

Gifford, J. and Walker, F.A. (2002), *Buildings of Scotland: Stirling and Central Scotland*. New Haven and London.

Graham, M.F. (1996), *The Uses of Reform: 'Godly Discipline' and Popular Behaviour in Scotland and Beyond, 1560–1610*. Leiden.

Grisbrooke, W.J. (1958), *Anglican Liturgies of the Seventeenth and Eighteenth Centuries*. London.

Hammond, P. (1960), *Liturgy and Architecture*. London.

Hay, G. (1957), *The Architecture of Scottish Post-Reformation Churches 1560–1843*. Oxford.

Henderson, G.D. (1937), *Religious Life in Seventeenth-Century Scotland*. Cambridge.

Howell, A.R. (1929), *Paisley Abbey*. Paisley.

Hume, J. (2005), *Scotland's Best Churches*. Edinburgh.

Inglis, J. (1987), 'The Scottish Churches and the Organ in the Nineteenth Century', PhD Thesis. Glasgow.

Jackson, C. (2003), *Restoration Scotland 1660–1690: Royalist Politics, Religion and Ideas*. Woodbridge.

Jacob, W.M. and Yates, N. (eds) (1993), *Crown and Mitre: Religion and Society in Northern Europe since the Reformation*. Woodbridge.

Johnson, C. (1983), *Developments in the Roman Catholic Church in Scotland 1789–1929*. Edinburgh.

Johnson, D. (1972), *Music and Society in Lowland Scotland in the Eighteenth Century*. Oxford.

Kieckhefer, R. (2004), *Theology in Stone: Church Architecture from Byzantium to Berkeley*. Oxford.

Kirk, J. (1989), *Patterns of Reform: Continuity and Change in the Reformation Kirk*. Edinburgh.

Lamb, J.A. (1958), 'The Kalendar of the Book of Common Order: 1564–1644', *RSCHS*, xii, 15–28.

—— (1959), 'Aids to Public Worship in Scotland 1800–1850', *RSCHS*, xiii, 171–85.

Lindsay, I. (1960), *The Scottish Parish Kirk*. Edinburgh.

Lindsay, I. and Cosh, M. (1973), *Inveraray and the Dukes of Argyll*. Edinburgh.

Lindsay, I. and Walker, D. (1973), *Georgian Edinburgh*. Edinburgh.

Lovibond, M. (2005), 'The Use of Spaces for Public Worship in the Early Reformed Tradition', PhD Thesis. Manchester.

MacColl, A.W. (2006), *Land, Faith and the Crofting Community: Christianity and Social Criticism in the Highlands of Scotland, 1843–1893*. Edinburgh.

MacDonald, A.R. (1998), *The Jacobean Kirk, 1567–1625: Sovereignty, Polity and Liturgy*. Aldershot.

BIBLIOGRAPHY

MacGibbon, D. and Ross, T. (1897), *The Ecclesiastical Architecture of Scotland from the Earliest Times to the Seventeenth Century*. Edinburgh.

MacInnes, J. (1951), *The Evangelical Movement in the Highlands of Scotland, 1688 to 1800*. Aberdeen.

Maciver, I.F. (1995), 'Unfinished Business? The Highland Churches Scheme and the Governance of Scotland', *RSCHS*, xxv, 376–99.

MacLaren, A.A. (1974), *Religion and Social Class: The Disruption Years in Aberdeen*. London.

Maclean, L. (ed) (1986), *The Seventeenth-Century Church in the Highlands*. Inverness.

McCraw, I. (2002), *Victorian Dundee at Worship*. Dundee.

McMillan, W. (1932), 'The Anglican Book of Common Prayer in the Church of Scotland', *RSCHS*, iv, 138–49.

McWilliam, C. (1978), *Buildings of Scotland: Lothian*. Harmondsworth.

Marshall, R.K. (2005), *Ruin and Restoration: St Mary's Church, Haddington*. Haddington.

Maxwell, W.D. (1955), *A History of Worship in the Church of Scotland*. London.

Mullett, M. (1998), *Catholicism in Britain and Ireland, 1558–1829*. Basingstoke.

Murray, D.M. (1976), 'The Scottish Church Society 1892–1914: A Study of the High Church Movement in the Church of Scotland', PhD Thesis. Cambridge.

—— (1986), 'The Barnhill Case 1901–4: The Limits of Ritual in the Kirk', *RSCHS*, xxii, 259–76.

—— (2000), *Rebuilding the Kirk: Presbyterian Reunion in Scotland 1909–1929*. Edinburgh.

Nockles, P.B. (1996), 'Our Brethren in the North: The Scottish Episcopal Church and the Oxford Movement', *Journal of Ecclesiastical History*, xlviii, 655–82.

Patrick, M. (1949), *Four Centuries of Scottish Psalmody*. London.

Picken, D.S.B. (1972), *The Soul of an Orkney Parish*. Kirkwall.

Pottle, F.A. and Bennett, C.H. (eds) (1936), *Boswell's Journal of a Tour to the Hebrides with Samuel Johnson, LL.D*. London.

Purser, J. (1992), *Scotland's Music: A History of the Traditional and Classical Music of Scotland from Earliest Times to the Present Day*. Edinburgh.

Rees, B.A. (1981), 'James Cooper and the Scoto-Catholic Party: Tractarian Reform in the Church of Scotland, 1882–1918,' PhD Thesis. St Andrews.

Reymond, B. (1996), *L'Architecture Religieuse des Protestants*. Geneva.

—— (1997), *Temples de Suisse Romande*. Yens and St Gingolph.

Ryrie, A. (2006), *The Origins of the Scottish Reformation*. Manchester.

Ryrie, A.C. (1994), *A Vision Pursued: St John's Church, Jedburgh, 1844–1994*. Kelso.

Sanderson, M.H.B. (1997), *Ayrshire and the Reformation: People and Change 1490–1600*. East Linton.

Spicer, A. (2007), *Calvinist Churches in Early Modern Europe*. Manchester.

Strong, R. (2002), *Episcopalianism in Nineteenth-Century Scotland: Religious Responses to a Modernising Society*. Oxford.

van Swigchem, C.A., Brouwer, T. and van Os, W. (1984), *Een Huis voor het Woord: Het Protestantse Kerkinterieur in Nederland tot 1900*. The Hague.

Terry, G.F. (1911), *Memorials of the Church of St John the Evangelist, Princes Street*. Edinburgh.

Thomas, D.B. (1972), *The Kirk of Brechin in the Seventeenth Century*. Perth.

Todd, G.E. (ed) (1898), *The Book of Glasgow Cathedral: A History and Description*. Glasgow.
Todd, M. (2002), *The Culture of Protestantism in Early Modern Scotland*. New Haven and London.
Towsey, D. and Adams, N. (2000), *St Mary's Dalmahoy 1970–2000*. Edinburgh.
Walker, F.A. (2000), *Buildings of Scotland: Argyll and Bute*. London.
Walker, G and Gallagher, T. (eds) (1990), *Sermons and Battle Hymns: Protestant Popular Culture in Modern Scotland*. Edinburgh.
Walker, W. (1887), *The Life and Times of John Skinner*. Aberdeen.
Ward, W.R. (1992), *The Protestant Evangelical Awakening*. Cambridge.
White, G. (1998), *The Scottish Episcopal Church: A New History*. Edinburgh.
Wigan, B.J. (ed) (1964), *The Liturgy in English*. London.
Williams, G., Jacob, W.M., Yates, N. and Knight, F. (2007), *The Welsh Church from Reformation to Disestablishment, 1603–1920*. Cardiff.
Williamson, E., Riches, A. and Higgs, M. (1990), *Buildings of Scotland: Glasgow*. London.
Withers, C.W.J. (1984), *Gaelic in Scotland 1698–1981*. Edinburgh.
Wright, R.S. (1956), *The Kirk in the Canongate*. Edinburgh.
Yates, N. (1992), 'Church Buildings of the Protestant Establishments in Wales and Scotland: Some Points of Comparison', *Journal of Welsh Ecclesiastical History*, ix, 1–19.
—— (1999), *Anglican Ritualism in Victorian Britain 1830–1910*. Oxford.
—— (2000), *Buildings, Faith and Worship: The Liturgical Arrangement of Anglican Churches 1600–1900* (2nd edn). Oxford.
—— (2006), *The Religious Condition of Ireland 1770–1850*. Oxford.
—— (2008), *Liturgical Space: Christian Worship and Church Buildings in Western Europe 1500–2000*. Aldershot.

INDEX

Abercorn, West Lothian 84
Abercromby, Hon. George 84
Aberdeen 6, 11, 63, 94, 96, 101, 121
   St Andrew (Episcopal) 100, 114
   St James (Episcopal) 109
   St John (Episcopal) 107
   St Machar's Cathedral 21, 29, 39
   St Nicholas East 30, 116, 117
   St Nicholas West 30, 47, 66, 68, 70, 84, 155, 159
Aberdour, Lord 106, 164
Abernyte, Perth and Kinross 120
Abertarff, Highland 147
Adam, John 79
Adam, William 76, 79
Adamson, T. N. 118–19
Airdrie, N. Lanarkshire 96, 112
Akkrum, Netherlands 32
Alford, Aberdeenshire 29
Alloa, Clackmannanshire 83–4
Altnaharra, Highland 75, 166, 178
Alva, Clackmannanshire 153
Amsterdam, Netherlands 32, 35, 37, 136
Anderson, R. R. 112, 123, 127, 181, 183
Andrewes, Bishop Lancelot 15
Anson, Peter 98–9
Anstruther Easter, Fife 36, 38
Anstruther Wester, Fife 48
Anti-Burghers 23, 152
Anwoth, Dumfries and Galloway 38
Appin, Argyll and Bute 61
Appingedam, Netherlands 32
Applecross, Highland 61, 80
Applegarth, Dumfries and Galloway 144–5
Ardchattan, Argyll and Bute 80, 86, 160
Ardclach, Highland 24, 38

Ardnamurchan, Highland 81n
Ardwell, Dumfries and Galloway 128, 180
Argyll, Duchess of 162
Argyll, Duke of 79
Arisaig, Highland 93, 99
Ascog, Argyll and Bute 137
Assynt, Highland 154
Atholl, Duke of 151
Auchterhouse, Argyll and Bute 38
Augsbuur, Netherlands 32
Ayr, S. Ayrshire 40

Balcanqual, Dean 17
Baldernock, E. Dunbartonshire 163
Ballachulish, Highland 104
Ballantine, Bishop 18
Ballinderry, Antrim 36
Balquhidder, Stirling 113
Banchory, Aberdeenshire 20
Bancroft, Archbishop Richard 15
Banff, Aberdeenshire 94, 101, 143–4
Barclay, Principal 116
Barnhill, Angus 118–19
Barra, W. Isles 9, 56, 61, 93, 147
Barvas, W. Isles 49, 50
Basel, Switzerland 32, 135
Bedrule, Borders 152–3
Begg, James 115
Belhaven, E. Lothian 76
Benbecula, W. Isles 93
Bendothy, Perth and Kinross 151
Bergen, Norway 36
Bermuda 43
Björnståhl, Jacob 14
Blair Drummond, Stirling 129
Blairgowrie, Perth and Kinross 151
Blanc, Hippolyte 127, 181, 182
Boleskine, Highland 147
Boswell, James 62, 105, 141

191

INDEX

Bothwell, Bishop Adam 6
Bourtie, Aberdeenshire 41, 70, 80, 89, 155, 159
Bowden, Borders 84
Bowmore, Islay 76
Boyle, Hon. G. F. 107
Bracadale, Skye 156
Braemar, Aberdeenshire 96
Bramhope, Leeds 36
Brechin, Angus 29, 40, 41
Brenchley, Kent 42
Broek-in-Waterland, Netherlands 32
Broughty Ferry, Angus 116, 121
Brown, Callum 92
Bruce, Thomas 47
Brunton, Alexander 48
Bryce, David 164, 165
Buccleuch, Duke of 104, 164
Burghers 23
Burn, William 163, 164
Burnbank, S. Lanarkshire 119
Burnet, Bishop Gilbert 20, 21
Burntisland, Fife 33, 36, 37–8, 107, 134
Burray, Orkney 55
Bute, Marquess of 112
Butterfield, William 106, 107, 108, 164, 169

Cadder, E. Dunbartonshire 46, 49, 57
Caird, Professor 116
Calvin, John 9
Cambuslang, S. Lanarkshire 23
Cameronians 23, 92
Campbell, Principal 116
Campbell, Sir James 83
Campbell, W. D. 179
Campsie, E. Dunbartonshire 57–8, 82, 89, 90
Canisbay, Highland 72, 176
Canna, Highland 9, 61, 93
Canonbie, Dumfries and Galloway 3, 82
Careston, Angus 36, 128–9
Carnbee, Fife 145
Carnock, Fife 23, 51
Carrington, Midlothian 148
Carsphairn, Dumfries and Galloway 86
Carstairs, A. G. 48
Cassalis, Earl of 143
Castletown, Borders 153

Catrine, E. Ayrshire 143
Ceres, Fife 35, 73, 87, 164
Challoch, Dumfries and Galloway 112
Chalmers, P. M. 123, 127–8, 130, 180, 181
Chalmers, Thomas 24, 63
Chambers, J. C. 107
Channelkirk, Borders 70, 155, 170
Charenton, France 34
Charles I, King 17–18
Charles II, King 19–20
Charles X, King of France 97
Charleson, John 118
Chavornay, Switzerland 35
Chêne-Bougeries, Switzerland 76
Chêne-Pâquier, Switzerland 76
Church Service Society 116
Clatt, Aberdeenshire 139
Clonguish, Longford 43, 105
Clunie, Perth and Kinross 151, 169
Cluny, Aberdeenshire 47
Coatdyke, N. Lanarkshire 119
Coldingham, Borders 59, 61
Colintrave, Argyll and Bute 82
Coll, Argyll and Bute 9, 62
Collessie, Fife 156, 164
Collie, James 59
Colonsay, Argyll and Bute 9, 141
Colquhoun, Sir James 84, 145, 175
Colvend, Dumfries and Galloway 128, 180
Comper, Sir Ninian 169
Connel, Argyll and Bute 127, 179
Contin, Highland 20
Convinth, Highland 38
Cooper, James 116, 118
Corstorphine, Edinburgh 121
Cotterill, Bishop Henry 113
Cousin, David 161
Cove, Aberdeenshire 109
Cowan, Ian 5, 6
Cowan, Isobel 89
Cowper, Bishop 17
Coyne, Roderick 178
Craignish, Argyll and Bute 7, 160–1
Cranstoun, Midlothian 176
Crathie, Aberdeenshire 127, 179
Crieff, Perth and Kinross 107
Croick, Highland 63, 71, 80, 86, 166
Cromarty, Highland 3, 70
Crossmichael, Dumfries and Galloway 84, 162

192

INDEX

Crowcombe, Somerset 42
Croy, Highland 24
Culross, Fife 13, 45
Cults, Fife 164–5
Cumbernauld, N. Lanarkshire 136
Cumine, George 21
Cundy, Thomas 161
Cupar, Fife 120

Dairsie, Fife 38, 39
Dalbeattie, Dumfries and Galloway 96
Dalgetty, Fife 74
Dalkeith, Midlothian 106, 107, 148, 164
Dalmahoy, Edinburgh 106, 107, 109, 164
Dalmeny, Edinburgh 51
Dalry, Dumfries and Galloway 162
Daly, Bishop Robert 109
Davidson, John 172
Daviot, Highland 81n, 147
Deerness, Orkney 55, 150
Denison, Bishop Edward 109
Dingwall, Highland 6
Dirleton, E. Lothian 38
Disserth, Powys 36
Dodsworth, William 106, 107
Donaldson, Gordon 28
Dornoch, Highland 30, 38
Dowden, Bishop John 114
Drainy, Moray 149
Dreghorn, Allan 72
Dreghorn, N. Ayrshire 76
Dromard, Sligo 106
Drummond Castle 94
Drumoak, Aberdeenshire 31, 47
Dubois, François 97
Duddingston, Edinburgh 148
Duirinish, Skye 3, 41, 50, 80, 89, 156
Dumbarton, W. Dunbartonshire 25, 109
Dumfries, Dumfries and Galloway 20, 96, 107, 109, 127, 180
Dunbar, E. Lothian 145
Dunblane, Stirling 29, 127, 129, 183
Dundas, Lord 55
Dundee 30, 66, 96, 101, 105, 107, 109, 114, 116, 121, 122, 143
Dundonald, S. Ayrshire 120
Dunfermline, Fife 118, 145–6
Dunkeld, Perth and Kinross 6, 29, 38, 151–2

Dunlichity, Highland 147
Dunlop, E. Ayrshire 36
Dunnet, Highland 3, 82
Dunoon, Argyll and Bute 109
Dunrossness, Shetland 84, 171
Duns, Borders 118, 120
Dunscore, Dumfries and Galloway 81n
Durisdeer, Dumfries and Galloway 80, 84, 87, 162–3
Durness, Highland 25, 39, 50, 61
Duror, Highland 50, 61
Dyke, Moray 80–1, 149

East Kilbride, S. Lanarkshire 136
Eastwood, Glasgow 49, 58
Eckford, Borders 88
Edam, Netherlands 32
Eday, Orkney 55, 150
Edderton, Highland 157, 166
Eddrachillis, Highland 50, 61
Edinburgh 11, 16, 23, 25, 64, 94, 95, 96, 99, 101, 121, 140
  Canongate Church 133–4, 180–1
  Craigsbank Church 136
  Episcopal Cathedral 102, 114
  Holy Trinity (Episcopal) 109
  New Greyfriars 48
  Old Greyfriars 48, 49, 114, 115, 120
  Roman Catholic Cathedral 97, 98
  Roxburgh Place Chapel 51
  Sacred Heart (Roman Catholic) 112
  St Andrew 76
  St Columba (Episcopal) 106, 107
  St Cuthbert 40, 46, 66, 68–9, 127, 128
  St Giles' Cathedral 18, 30, 38, 52, 116–17
  St John (Episcopal) 102, 103, 104, 105, 112–13
  St Oswald 119
  St Stephen 78
  St Thomas (Episcopal) 109
  St Vincent (Episcopal) 109
  Tron Church 48
Edinkillie, Moray 38, 81
Edmonstone, Sir C. 89
Egmond aan den Hoef, Netherlands 32
Eigg, Highland 9, 61, 93
Elgin, Moray 13, 29, 66, 67, 121, 130
Elie, Fife 38
Ellon, Aberdeenshire 70, 105
Emden, Germany 35–6

INDEX

Eoropie, W. Isles 130–132
Eriboll, Highland 73, 166
Erskine, Ebenezer 23
Erskine, John 48
Erskine, Lady Charlotte 84
Erskine of Mar, John Francis 83–4
Eskdale, Highland 97, 166
Eskdalemuir, Dumfries and Galloway 81n
Ettrick, Borders 158, 170
Evie, Orkney 55, 149–50
Exeter, Devon 42

Fairfoul, Archbishop Andrew 20
Falconer, Thomas 65
Falkland, Fife 136, 165
Fenton, Richard 56
Fetteresso, Aberdeenshire 148
Fintray, Aberdeenshire 47, 80
First Book of Discipline 28
Fleming, Donald 90
Fochabers, Moray 94, 104
Fogo, Borders 71, 170
Forbes, Bishop A. P. 107
Forres, Moray 127, 183
Fort George, Highland 80–1, 105
Fort William, Highland 102–4, 112
Fortescue, E. B. K. 107
Fortrose, Highland 6, 29
Foss, Perth and Kinross 81n
Fowlis Wester, Perth and Kinross 31
Frazer, Andrew 76
Free Church of Scotland 24–6, 50, 51, 63–4, 121, 122
Free Presbyterian Church of Scotland 25, 156
Fyvie, Aberdeenshire 139

Gadderar, Bishop James 99
Galashiels, Borders 158
Galloway, D. W. 128–9
Galloway, Patrick 16
Garvald, E. Lothian 88
Gask, Perth and Kinross 109
Gatehouse of Fleet, Dumfries and Galloway 109
Geneva, Switzerland 14, 35, 76
George III, King 100
Gibbs, James 72, 159
Gigha, Argyll and Bute 56, 61
Gillespie, Thomas 23
Gladsmuir, E. Lothian 51

Gladstanes, Archbishop 39
Glasford, S. Lanarkshire 148
Glasgow 11, 23, 25, 64, 94, 95, 96, 101, 116, 120, 121
  Barony Church 59
  Episcopal Cathedral 114
  Queen's Cross Church 130, 182
  Roman Catholic Cathedral 97
  St Aloysius (Roman Catholic) 112
  St Andrew 13, 50–1, 72–3
  St John 49
  St Jude (Episcopal) 109
  St Mungo's Cathedral 21, 30, 52, 59, 60, 121, 125, 126
  St Paul 59
  St Silas (Episcopal) 109
  Wellington Church 76
Glenalmond, Perth and Kinross 106, 107, 169
Glenbuchat, Aberdeenshire 47, 70, 84, 87, 155, 160
Glencoe, Highland 61, 104
Glengarry, Highland 93
Glenmoriston, Highland 38
Glenorchy, Argyll and Bute 78, 141
Glenrothes, Fife 134, 136
Glenshiel, Highland 61
Glenurquhart, Highland 21
Golspie, Highland 3, 70, 84, 85, 166–7, 171
Gordon, Bishop Alexander 6
Gordon, Duke of 104
Gordon, Earl of 139
Gouda, Netherlands 32
Govan, Glasgow 74–5, 118, 125–7, 137, 181–2
Graham, J. G. 98, 168
Grant, Sir Archibald 47
Greenock, Inverclyde 26, 38, 90, 94, 96, 121
Greenshields, Bishop James 99
Groenervegen, J. H. 136
Guild, Principal William 39

Haccombe, Devon 42
Haddington, E. Lothian 58, 102, 124–5, 134–5
Haddo House 136
Haggart, Bishop 134
Halkirk, Highland 144
Hall, E. H. 56
Halladale, Highland 75, 87, 167

INDEX

Hamilton, Bishop James 20
Hamilton, Duke of 76
Hamilton, S. Lanarkshire 76, 77, 79
Hammond, Peter 135–6
Hanworth, Surrey 100
Haskoll, Joseph 107
Hay, Bishop 94
Hay, George 1, 36, 73, 134, 155–8, 166
Haywood, John 106, 170
Henderson, G. D. 38–9
Henderson, John 106, 164
Heriot, Borders 47, 148
Hickes, Bishop George 99
Holyrood, Edinburgh 17, 20, 39
Honeyman, Charles 84
Hook, W. F. 106
Hoorn, Netherlands 35
Horgen, Switzerland 76
Hossack, James 120
Howmore, S. Uist 86
Hoy, Orkney 55, 150
Humble, Henry 107
Hunter, Robert 172
Hunter, Thomas 172
Huntly, Aberdeenshire 96, 97, 109, 139
Hutchinson, Robert 165
Hutton, Borders 144
Hutton, Dumfries and Galloway 176

Inch, Dumfries and Galloway 120
Inchinnan, Renfrewshire 152
Inverallan, Highland 66, 68
Inveraray, Argyll and Bute 79, 141
Inveresk, E. Lothian 148
Inverkeithing, Fife 23
Inverkeithney, Aberdeenshire 80
Inverness, Highland 102, 105, 114, 147
Iona, Argyll and Bute 30, 179
Irvine, N. Ayrshire 142–3

James VI and I, King 7, 15–17, 39
James VII and II, King 22
Jedburgh, Borders 51, 106, 107, 113, 170–1
Jewel, Bishop John 11
Johnson, Samuel 62, 105, 141
Jones, Theophilus 56–7
Jura, Argyll and Bute 141

Keble, John 106
Keir, Dumfries and Galloway 145
Keith, Moray 97, 102, 104
Kelso, Borders 101, 102, 112, 153
Kemback, Fife 37
Kemnay, Aberdeenshire 47, 139
Kempe, C. E. 182
Kennethmont, Aberdeenshire 47
Kerr, Lord Henry 106
Kilarrow, Islay 50, 61
Kilberry, Argyll and Bute 161
Kilbirnie, N. Ayrshire 84
Kilbrandon, Argyll and Bute 24, 50
Kilbride, Argyll and Bute 142
Kilchattan, Argyll and Bute 24
Kilchoman, Islay 50, 61
Kildalton, Islay 50
Kildrummy, Aberdeenshire 70, 160
Kilfinan, Argyll and Bute 141
Kilfinichen, Mull 141–2
Killean, Argyll and Bute 61
Kilmany, Fife 80, 165
Kilmarnock, E. Ayrshire 96
Kilmartin, Argyll and Bute 142
Kilmaveonaig, Perth and Kinross 37
Kilmodan, Argyll and Bute 86, 161
Kilmore, Argyll and Bute 7, 142
Kilmuir, Skye 50
Kilsyth, N. Lanarkshire 57, 89, 136
Kiltarlity, Highland 38
Kiltearn, Highland 6, 48
Kilvickeon, Mull 141–2
Kilwinning, N. Ayrshire 143
Kincardine, Fife 31, 38
Kingsbarns, Fife 38
Kingshorn, Fife 146
Kinlochmoidart, Highland 167
Kinneff, Aberdeenshire 72, 87, 175
Kinross, Perth and Kinross 23
Kintore, Aberdeenshire 47
Kippen, Stirling 70–1, 83
Kirk, James 6, 7, 9, 38
Kirkcaldy, Fife 146
Kirkcowan, Dumfries and Galloway 81n
Kirkcudbright, Dumfries and Galloway 130, 163
Kirkintilloch, E. Dunbartonshire 81, 155–6
Kirkmaiden, Dumfries and Galloway 36, 72, 82, 176

INDEX

Kirkmichael, Dumfries and Galloway 145
Kirkoswald, S. Ayrshire 143
Kirkwall, Orkney 24, 30, 38, 54–5, 150
Knox, Bishop Thomas 9
Knox, John 7, 10, 11, 14, 44
Knoydart, Highland 93
Kyle, Bishop James 97

La Chaux-des-Fonds, Switzerland 76
La Rochelle, France 34
Laggan, Highland 80, 167
Langholm, Dumfries and Galloway 81n
Largo, Fife 158
Largoward, Fife 165
Laud, Archbishop William 17–18
Lauder, Borders 72, 73, 171, 180
Lauderdale, Earl of 134
Lausanne, Switzerland 32
Lee, Robert 50, 114–15, 116
Leiden, Netherlands 35, 36
Leighton, Bishop Robert 20
Leith, Edinburgh 101, 102, 121, 122
Lemon, William 84
Leo XIII, Pope 112
Leslie, Alexander 164
Lethendy, Perth and Kinross 152
Lindsay, Ian 95, 134, 168, 180
Linlithgow, Earl of 42
Linlithgow, W. Lothian 42, 58–9, 121, 125
Lismore, Argyll and Bute 30, 61, 93
Liston, William 48
Little Hadham, Hertfordshire 36
Livingston, W. Lothian 3, 81, 136, 158
Loch Awe, Argyll and Bute 130, 131, 179–80
Lochalsh, Highland 70, 90, 176
Lochbroom, Highland 41, 75, 86, 87, 157, 167
Lochs, W. Isles 25, 50, 61
Lockerbie, Dumfries and Galloway 76
Logie Pert, Angus 155
London 72
Lorimer, Sir Robert 123, 127, 183
Lothian, Marchioness of 106, 170
Lothian, Marquis of 104
Lovat, Lord 97
Lovi, Fr Walter 97
Lundie, Archibald 22

Lunna, Shetland 171–2
Luss, Argyll and Bute 72, 84, 145, 175
Luther, Martin 9
Lyne, Borders 40

Macdonald, Bishop Hugh 93
Macfarlane, Thomas 172
Mackay of Clashfern, Lord 26
Mackenzie, Alexander 174
Mackintosh, C. R. 130, 182
Mackintosh, David 179
McLandish, William 162
Macleod, John 118, 119, 181
Macneil, Roderick 147
Macolchallum, Gilbert 7
Makerstoun, Borders 80, 157
Manish, W. Isles 174
Mansfield, Earl of 84
Marnoch, Aberdeenshire 56
Mary II, Queen 22
Maryculter, Aberdeenshire 31
Maryton, Angus 140
Maxton, Borders 177
Maxwell, Bishop John 18
Maxwell, Sir John 58
Maxwell, W. D. 18–19
Menzies, Professor 116
Merthyr Cynog, Powys 56
Mertoun, Borders 88
Mid Yell, Shetland 172
Middelburg, Netherlands 36
Midmar, Aberdeenshire 47
Mieras, H. 136
Miller, Edward 13
Millport, Cumbrae 107–8, 114
Mitchell, Sidney 180
Mochrum, Dumfries and Galloway 81
Moidart, Highland 93, 103
Monimail, Fife 165–6
Montrose, Angus 101, 107, 109, 140–1
Monymusk, Aberdeenshire 47, 105
Moody, Dwight 122
Morar, Highland 93
Morer, Thomas 21
Mortlach, Aberdeenshire 144
Morton, Earl of 106
Morvern, Highland 103, 142
Motherwell, S. Lanarkshire 112
Mount Stuart 112
Muck, Highland 9, 61
Muckhart, Perth and Kinross 45

196

INDEX

Murroes, Angus 84, 160
Musselburgh, E. Lothian 102
Mylne, Robert 79, 141

Naarden, Netherlands 32
Nádásdaróc, Hungary 32–3
Nairn, Highland 109
Neale, J. M. 107
Nesting, Shetland 86, 171, 172, 173
Neuchâtel, Switzerland 14, 35
New Abbey, Dumfries and Galloway 97–8
Newburn, Fife 158
Newell, Walter 97
Newlands, Borders 156, 171
Nicholson, Bishop Thomas 93
Nockles, Peter 106–7
North Berwick, E. Lothian 119
North Bute, Argyll and Bute 158
Northmavine, Shetland 75, 178
Nost, John van 163

Oban, Argyll and Bute 50, 71, 87, 112, 142, 161
Old Meldrum, Aberdeenshire 47
Orney, Cornelius 7
Oron-la-Ville, Switzerland 76
Oxnam, Borders 88

Paisley, Renfrewshire 47, 58, 66, 67, 68, 69–70, 94, 96, 112, 120, 121, 123, 125, 127, 182–3
Panmure, Earl of 41
Parker, Archbishop Matthew 34
Paschoud, J. J. 14
Peebles, Borders 102
Penninghame, Dumfries and Galloway 81n
Pepys, Bishop Henry 109
Perth, Articles of 16, 17, 39
Perth, Perth and Kinross 11, 14, 16, 23, 30, 78, 107, 109, 113, 114, 134
Peterhead, Aberdeenshire 101, 105, 140
Phillpotts, Bishop Henry 109
Pitsligo, Aberdeenshire 36, 84
Plockton, Highland 80, 157
Pluscarden Abbey 130
Pollockshaws, Glasgow 120
Polmont, Falkirk 82
Poltalloch, Argyll and Bute 106, 161
Poortugaal, Netherlands 32

Portmoak, Perth and Kinross 169
Portnacrois, Argyll and Bute 104–5
Portnahaven, Islay 63, 161–2
Portpatrick, Dumfries and Galloway 38
Portree, Skye 61, 62
Presholme, Moray 96
Preston, Lord 38
Prestonpans, E. Lothian 38
Primmer, James 118–19
Pugin, A. W. N 99

Quarff, Shetland 63, 71, 86, 137, 158, 172
Queensberry, Duke of 163

Raasay, Highland 61, 62
Rattray, Bishop Thomas 100
Rattray, Perth and Kinross 21
Rayne, Aberdeenshire 47
Redgorton, Perth and Kinross 44–5, 48
Relief Church 23, 26, 50, 51
Rendall, Orkney 55, 149–50
Rennie, Archibald 83
Resolis, Highland 81n
Reymond, Bernard 35
Rhind, David 78
Rhum, Highland 9, 61
Ritchie, William 50–1
Robertson, Henry 48
Robertson, John 127, 183
Rodel, W. Isles 136
Rogart, Highland 73, 86, 167
Rolland, L. A. L. 158
Rosebery, Earl of 104
Ross, Alexander 104, 167
Ross, James 167
Rossdhu, Argyll and Bute 175
Rosskeen, Highland 157
Rotterdam, Netherlands 37
Rouen, France 34
Roxburgh, Borders 153
Rutherglen, S. Lanarkshire 120
Ruthven, Aberdeenshire 144
Ryrie, Alec 5

St Andrews, Fife 11, 13, 16, 29, 38, 105, 109, 127, 181
St Andrews, Orkney 55, 150
St Anneparochie, Netherlands 36
St Boswells, Borders 153
St Imier, Switzerland 35

INDEX

St Martins, Perth and Kinross 157, 169–70
St Monans, Fife 146
St Mungo, Dumfries and Galloway 145
St Paul's Walden, Hertfordshire 42
St Quivox, S. Ayrshire 143, 173
St Sulpice, Switzerland 76
St Vigeans, Angus 125
Saline, Fife 146–7
Saltoun, E. Lothian 20, 21, 22
Sandford, Bishop Daniel 100–1
Sandwick, Orkney 55, 168–9
Sankey, Ira 122
Sanquhar, Dumfries and Galloway 80
Sappemeer, Netherlands 36
Scalloway, Shetland 172
Scarista, W. Isles 86, 156
Schermerhorn, Netherlands 32
Scott, Sir George Gilbert 107
Scott, Sir Giles Gilbert 112
Scottish Church Society 116, 132
Scougal, Henry 21
Secession Church 23, 26
Senn, Otto 135
Shapinsay, Orkney 45
Sharp, Archbishop James 20
Skelmorlie, N. Ayrshire 120
Skinner, Bishop John 101
Slamannan, Falkirk 153
Sleat, Skye 46, 50, 61, 75, 84, 87, 177
Smailholm, Borders 51
Smith, Cromarty 119
Smith, James 166
Snizort, Skye 167–8
Sonvillier, Switzerland 76
Sorn, E. Ayrshire 88, 143
South Knapdale, Argyll and Bute 142
South Queensferry, Edinburgh 38
South Ronaldsay, Orkney 55, 70, 86, 169
South Uist, W. Isles 56, 61, 93, 136, 147
South Yell, Shetland 158
Southend, Argyll and Bute 70, 162
Sowton, Devon 170
Spott, E. Lothian 71, 87
Spottiswoode, Archbishop John 39
Sprott, G. W. 119, 123–4, 163
Spynie, Moray 168
Stanley, Bishop Edward 109
Stevenson, D. W. 181
Stewart, Bishop Robert 6

Stewart, Lady McTaggart 180
Stirling 16, 30, 66, 68, 69, 102
Stobhall, Perth and Kinross 94
Stornoway, W. Isles 49, 50, 75, 87, 174
Story, Principal 116
Stracathro, Angus 141
Strachan, Douglas 183
Stranraer, Dumfries and Galloway 76
Strath, Skye 61
Strathblane, Stirling 153
Strathmiglo, Fife 82, 156
Stromeferry, Highland 123
Stromness, Orkney 55
Stronsay, Orkney 55, 150
Stuart, Prince Charles Edward 100
Sumner, Archbishop J. B. 109
Sydserf, Bishop Thomas 20
Symington, S. Ayrshire 143

Talbot, John 106
Tarves, Aberdeenshire 13, 81
Teignmouth, Lord 46
Telford, Thomas 62
Temple, Midlothian 149
Terregles, Dumfries and Galloway 94
Terrot, Bishop Charles 107, 108
Thomson, William 62, 161, 166, 168, 172
Thornliebank, Glasgow 118
Thorpe Market, Norfolk 42
Thurso, Highland 6, 72
Timogue, Laois 43, 105
Tingwall, Shetland 172–3
Tiree, Argyll and Bute 9, 62
Todd, Margo 7, 30
Tombae, Moray 96
Tomintoul, Moray 96
Tongue, Highland 24, 48, 50, 61, 84, 87, 177
Torosay, Mull 70, 175
Torphichen, W. Lothian 71, 84, 173
Torry, Bishop Patrick 107, 114
Towie, Aberdeenshire 47
Tranent, E. Lothian 51
Traquair, Borders 94, 171
Tulloch, Principal 115, 116
Tullyallan, Perth and Kinross 31, 152
Tunbridge Wells, Kent 106
Tyndale-Bruce, Onesephorus 165
Tynet, Moray 94, 95, 96, 168
Tynron, Dumfries and Galloway 71, 145

INDEX

Uig, Skye 177
Uig, W. Isles 61
Ullapool, Highland 137, 168
United Free Church 26, 27, 121, 131–3, 136
United Presbyterian Church 23, 26, 50, 121, 122
United Secession Church 23
Urquhart, Highland 38, 75, 90, 152, 177

Valleberga, Sweden 36
Villars-le-Grand, Switzerland 76

Wailes, William 161
Walkerburn, Borders 123
Warner, Archdeacon John 42
Wedderburn, Bishop James 18
Weem, Perth and Kinross 21
Weisdale, Shetland 178

Wemyss Bay, Inverclyde 109
Wesley, John 24, 46
Westminster Abbey 20
Westminster Confession 18, 25
Whalsay, Shetland 84, 173
White, W. S. 106
Whitefield, George 24
Whithorn, Dumfries and Galloway 29
Wilberforce, Archdeacon Robert 106
Wilberforce, Bishop Samuel 109
Wilby, Norfolk 36
William III, King 22
Wordsworth, Bishop Charles 107, 113
Wotherspoon, H. J. 119

Yarrow, Borders 80
Yester, E. Lothian 40, 84, 163

Zürich, Switzerland 135
Zwingli, Ulrich 9